HEED THE WARNING

S. KAY MILAM

AmErica House
Baltimore

ISBN: 1-59129-251-4
PUBLISHED BY AMERICA HOUSE BOOK PUBLISHERS
www.publishamerica.com
Baltimore

Printed in the United States of America

*In loving memory of
My father (1906-1985)*

*And for Robyn—
Who always believed.*

Acknowledgements:

With appreciation and heartfelt thanks to all those who helped make this book possible, and especially:

for Sonny and his patience and support,

for Charles Peterson—thanks for the tour & pictures,

for all World War II vets,

for author Marilyn Meredith who shared her knowledge and experience,

for Luther (Luke) at the computer place who helped me find what was lost,

for Diane Brown who provided an opportunity,

for Pastor Ron who accepted my script and unknowingly provided the incentive and—

for those who may read this book. May you always know that "Jesus loves you and will never leave you nor forsake you."

Neither height nor depth, nor anything else in all creation, will be able to separate us from the love of God that is in Christ Jesus our Lord. (Romans 8:39)

Prologue—The Beginning

Gazing out the window at the passing scenery, Shortie Busch willed the train to move faster. As the Northern Pacific snaked through the outskirts of the Coeur d'Alene National Forest, the river below was hidden from view for a few moments by a wall of pine green. Pine trees, tamarack, and fir grew thick along this stretch of the ride, creating dark, shaded passageways. Where tree boughs met, forming black tunnels, all light was cut off for several minutes. Lights were switched on for the passengers' comfort at the same time the train's headlamp cast its brilliant beam against the dark.

Moving into sudden, bright sunlight blinded him momentarily as he drank in the scenic views of the mountain pass. He'd been away from home for a long time and had missed the sights of the Idaho Panhandle. As he tipped his cap back upon his head, a mass of dark curly hair was revealed.

With a combination of dark, naturally curly hair and deep cobalt eyes, he could have turned many a young ladies' head if he chose, but the art of flirtation had never been one of his strong suits. Exhaling with a sigh of contentment, he placed his cap, or "crusher," on the seat beside him. Leaning his head back onto the headrest, he closed his eyes for a moment, taking pleasure in a brief rest before the train pulled into the next stop.

He shifted position restlessly, being uncomfortable crammed into a seat meant for a much smaller person. He wasn't oversized, but didn't fit well into small spaces. His shoulders were wider than the backrest and stuck out on either side of the seat, which caused a kink in the middle of his spine. His legs, bent as close to the seat as possible, cramped because there wasn't room enough to stretch them out, but if he leaned against the window just so, he was reasonably comfortable.

A sense of urgency rose in his mind when the train didn't increase its speed, and when it slowed to a crawl along the steep slope of the mountainside, his anxiety grew to fever pitch. He couldn't be late today. Pulling up the sleeve of his dress uniform, he checked the time. He had to be in Spokane by ten o'clock and being late was not an option. Smiling to himself, he studied his fingernails for a moment, making sure they were clean and neatly trimmed. Taking a small, heart-shaped box from his inside coat pocket, he snapped open the lid to admire twin bands of gold lying on blue satin. He wondered if one adjusted quickly to wearing a wedding band or if it was like wearing a tie—one had to get used to it. Closing the box with a snap, he placed it back in his pocket, where the weight of it pressed against his heart.

The smile on his lips spread to a grin as he marveled at his good fortune. After waiting so long for the right woman to come along, he'd finally found her. At forty-one years of age, Shortie Busch was getting married. He knew most men his age had families with children half grown. But before the war he'd been too busy caring for four younger brothers and six sisters to find a wife, and even though the last couple of years were spent on one army base or the other during the war, the women he came into contact with weren't wife material. He had to admit that shyness and a reluctance to strike up casual conversations with women he didn't know hindered his ability to develop romantic relationships. Hard work, and lots of it, was his only companion until a year ago. He was home on leave shortly after World War II ended, and Evie, his younger sister, was throwing a "welcome home" party for him. One of the guests caught his eye.

The train slowed as it climbed the ascending track. Unconsciously, Shortie pressed his feet into the floor, pressing an imaginary gas pedal. Unless the engineer poured on the coal, he'd be late to his own wedding.

After stopping to board a single passenger, he relaxed. They picked up speed and the swaying motion and click-clack of the wheels soon made him drowsy. Snuggling into the backrest as best he could, he allowed himself a brief catnap. A replay of the events of the past year filtered through his mind as he remembered meeting his bride-to-be.

It had been a hectic year training squad after squad of young men to handle and fire the M-1 semiautomatic rifle. It was his job to teach recruits to fire the M-1 with accuracy, take it apart, put it back together again, and to keep the weapon clean and well-oiled. After firing endless rounds of ammo at mechanical targets and giving lecture after lecture to bored soldiers, he was beginning to show signs of exhaustion. He'd been hard at it for over two years. It was 1946, and with World War II over, the Army's need for sharp shooters was greatly reduced. The CO shook his hand when he handed him his furlough papers.

"Go home for a few weeks, Sergeant. Go fishing or girl watching or whatever it is you do for fun. You've earned the rest and by God you're going on leave and that's an order," he added, interrupting Shortie's objection before it was voiced.

"Yes sir." Master Sergeant Shortie Busch snapped to attention, gave a proper salute, and then hurried out of the Colonel's office. He could hardly contain his excitement as he rushed into the only empty phone booth in the commissary. In his haste he dropped several quarters on the floor, where they promptly rolled out of his reach. Emptying all of his pockets, he found the correct change and inserted it into the coin slot.

"Evie," he yelled as soon as the phone was answered.

"Shortie?" she asked. "Is that you?"

"It sure is, little sister, and guess what?" Without waiting for a reply he rushed on, "I'm coming home. My CO just gave me an extended furlough and I'll be on my way as soon as I can get packed. Expect me in a few days."

"Really?" she screeched. "Oh, I can't believe you're finally coming home. I won't be able to sleep a wink until you're safely here, and wait until Lowell hears about this. He'll want to put on the ritz for your homecoming." Lowell was her husband and the love of her life. "Hurry home, brother, it's been too long." She laughed, "My gosh, if you waited any longer your nephew would be on his way to college. I have a surprise for you, too, but mine can wait. We'll throw you a welcome home party like this town has never seen before. And brother, in the meantime don't take any wooden nickels, okay?"

Ringing off, he rushed to shower, change, and pack to catch the next plane headed north. After a long flight and even longer train ride for a total of sixty-four hours travel time, he finally arrived at the Spokane train depot. Hailing a taxi, he headed to Evie's for a needed shower and rest. She burst out the front door as soon as he stepped from the cab.

"Shortie," she cried. Hurrying as fast as her distended belly would allow, she ran to clasp him in an awkward hug.

"So," he laughed, "is this the surprise you said could wait? Doesn't look to me like you'll be waiting much longer." Folding her in a bear hug, he laughed aloud at her barrel shape. Pregnant with her second child, she absolutely glowed with happiness. Tossing his duffle bag over one shoulder, he kept the other arm around her waist as they walked together to the door. With heads bent close together, brother and sister tried to fill the other in on two years worth of news. When he rolled into bed several hours later, he slept, exhausted, for eighteen hours.

The following night was the welcome home party Evie had promised, and family members he hadn't seen in years were in attendance. By the time all the nieces, nephews, brothers, sisters, aunts, uncles, and assorted shoestring relatives made their appearance, Evie's little house was filled to overflowing. Finding himself outside to catch a breath of air, he played a game of touch football with a couple of his older nephews. A docile game of catch turned rough-and-tumble after he showed them a few defensive moves in hand-to-hand combat. In order to deter the boys' enthusiasm before someone got hurt, namely himself, he went back inside for a drink.

"Wow, those boys have sure grown in two years. I can't believe how tall they've gotten," he marveled to his brother Jack. "They almost got the best of me. I had to come in before they pinned me."

Gulping down a large glass of water, he wandered to the front room where most of the guests were gathered. Going from one group to the other to say hello and catch up on family news, he noticed a pretty blonde perched on the arm of the sofa. She wasn't anyone's sister, a cousin, or anyone he'd seen before. His gaze traveled the length of her body from her shapely legs to her hips, to a tiny waist, to the swell of breasts, and came to rest upon her face. Shoulder length blonde hair, styled in an imitation of Veronica Lake's popular do, fell forward as she turned and faced him with a mocking smile on her lips. She rose, and to his amazement came over and extended her hand. Heat rose up his neck and he felt the throb of embarrassment stain his cheeks a fiery red. Speechless, he took her extended hand and gave it a shake. He'd never felt more like a clumsy clod as he stood there staring, with his tongue glued to the roof of his mouth so tightly his mumbled greeting was garbled.

"Enjoying yourself?" She smiled teasingly with slightly parted lips, revealing perfect teeth. Clasping her hand, he admired the pale pink polish tipping each manicured finger. Tilting her head, she studied him for a moment, allowing his admiring gaze to meet hers eye-to-eye. "My name is Inja Beechman, pronounced Een-yah with a long e, and I'm free tonight if you're not doing anything." Smiling provocatively, she enjoyed his obvious embarrassment. His jaw dropped, shocked at her forwardness. Taking a sip of ice water to moisten his dry mouth, he swallowed wrong and began to cough. Evie came to his rescue. After beating him on the back until the spasm was over, she made all the proper introductions. Within just a few minutes of meeting her, he made a complete idiot of himself, but still managed to get a date for the evening.

For the next month, he spent every waking moment with her and fell hopelessly in love for the first time in his life. He wanted to know everything there was to know about her and asked numerous questions, which she rewarded with vague responses. He constantly pumped Evie for information, but she was reluctant to say much, and Lowell, his brother-in-law, said even less.

"Rand, what is all this interest in Inja?" Evie asked one evening, exasperation evident in her voice. "She's a friend, but not one I'd want for a sister-in-law. You're not in love with her, are you?"

"I'm very much in love with her and I plan on asking her to marry me."

"Oh no," Evie gasped. "You can't be serious; I mean, isn't this rather sudden? You've only been dating for a few weeks and you hardly know her. Don't rush into things," she pleaded. "Have you taken the time to pray about your decision? Are you sure it's God's will?"

"What's the big deal? What could you possibly have against her?" Frowning, he glared with an obstinate set to his jaw that she had seen many times before. "Here you are spouting Christianity and preaching about prayer—wll, your own attitude isn't very Christian. I love her, and I'm going to ask her to marry me, so you'd best get used to the idea."

"I'm sorry, let's not fight." Wrapping her arms around him, she hugged him tightly. Peering into his face, she studied the stubborn set to his jaw then sighed heavily. "You're just mule-headed stubborn enough to marry her whether she's good for you or not. If you're sure, and at your age you should be, then I want to hold the reception here."

"Are you sure?" She nodded her head and hugged him a second time. His anger ebbed as he wrapped his arms around her. The last thing he wanted to do was argue with his little sister. "I'm going to ask her tomorrow night, and I'm hoping she says yes, and if she does, we'll get married within the coming year."

"Okay," Evie answered. "But before you do, would you do me just one favor?"

"Sure, how could I possibly say no?"

"Please pray about this. You used to pray about everything," she reminded him. "I can't count how many times I've seen you on your knees, praying for one of us." She shook her head in thoughtful memory. Taking his hand, she laid her cheek against his palm as she had done when a child and pleaded, "This time, big brother, pray for yourself."

He thought about her request throughout the evening. It was true: he hadn't taken time for prayer since enlisting in the Army and he hadn't opened his Bible in months. He made a mental note to start a prayer life and Bible study time just as soon as he had the chance.

That evening, Lowell and some of his friends gathered for a quick game of baseball. Evie, with Inja's help, settled herself on a blanket to watch the game. Lowell enlisted Shortie to pitch and wanted to bat a few practice balls before the game began. The first ball was a strike and the second low and inside. The third was hit with a crack and streaked deep into left field, right toward Evie. He gaped, open-mouthed, at Inja's one-handed catch. She grabbed the ball and threw it back with lightening speed.

"She used to play on a women's league," Lowell laughed, "so pick up your chin and put it back on your face. She's played baseball for years and has a natural talent. Too bad she doesn't like to play any more, though. I'd like to have her on my team down at the plant."

He shook his head in wonder. Who would have thought a dainty little lady like Inja could throw a fast ball? Leaving the mound, he ran over and whispered in her ear. Her reply was instantaneous and ecstatic.

"Yes," she screamed. Throwing her arms around him, she boldly kissed him full on the lips. He remembered very little about the game or even if his team won.

Afterward, they walked home arm-in-arm. She'd never invited him to her apartment before and on the way explained why.

"There's something I need to tell you before we get there."

"You sound so serious. Whatever could be so awful that it makes your pretty face look so sad? You don't have a husband hidden away somewhere do you?"

"No, silly," she said, punching his arm playfully. "But I do have a little brother. He's four years old and I've been taking care of him since my mother died," she explained. Her words came out in a rush. "I'm not exactly thrilled about mothering my little brother. It's not that I don't like kids; I want a whole houseful someday. I just never dreamed my brother would be one of them. There's no one else," she said with a shrug, "so if you take me, you take him, too." She stopped under a streetlight to catch her breath and peered intently at him. Her lips widened in a smile. He wasn't shocked or angry, just happily surprised.

"It couldn't be more perfect. I've always wanted a son and now I'm not only getting the most beautiful wife in the world, but a little boy at the same time. Let's hurry; I can't wait to meet him. Who takes care of the little fellow when you're out?"

"Oh, a friend of mine," she answered with a vague wave of her fingers.

Her friend turned out to be a next door neighbor with two children of her own. She looked in on Eddie during the day and fed him, but for the most part, the child stayed alone in the apartment while Inja was at work. Shortie was concerned about this arrangement, but didn't want to start an unnecessary argument over the care of a child he'd just met.

Four-year-old Eddie was small for his age, with arms too long for his body and legs too thin. His pixie face was topped with coarse, tawny colored elflocks in constant disarray. His eyes, the same clear blue as Inja's, had a worried look about them. He didn't look at Shortie straight on like most children. His eyes darted this way and then that. Reminded of a trapped animal or a frightened fawn, Shortie's heart was instantly captivated. When the child smiled, revealing a gap between his teeth where he'd recently lost a tooth, Shortie fell in love for the second time in a month. The boy had an endearing quality about him that his baby face only enhanced. Eyes moist, he hugged the child closely, wanting to protect him from a world of war and hate.

Eddie peeked at Shortie through lowered lashes. The man had a kind face, nice eyes, and a big smile. His arms were strong and held him firmly. He looked Eddie right in the eye and spoke to him like he wasn't just a kid.

"Young man, I've asked your sister to marry me. Would you mind very much if we got together to be a family?" he asked.

Eddie didn't know for sure what being married meant, but it sounded nice. He'd like to be a family and Inja seemed happy.

"Yeth," he lisped. Grinning impishly, he hid his head in Shortie's shoulder. Shortie was delighted.

Later that evening, after he'd kissed Inja goodnight for the hundredth time, he returned home, anxious to share the good news with Lowell and Evie. Lowell's reaction was less than enthusiastic, and Evie appeared almost broken-hearted. Her face darkened with concern.

"Are you sure this is what you want? I like Inja, really I do, but never considered her for a sister-in-law. Has she told you much about herself?

"I know everything I need to know. I've met her little brother and I've seen the dump she lives in. It's not her fault if wages aren't enough to provide better housing, but that's all going to change because she won't be working very much longer."

"Do you think she can be satisfied with the attentions of one man, or will she still want all the bees in the hive?" Lowell asked bluntly.

"Lowell." Evie's glance warned her husband to say nothing more. Taking a deep, steadying breath, she turned her attention back to Shortie.

"Inja is a flirt, brother. I've even caught her flirting with Lowell. We're not trying to interfere in your life; we just don't want to see you get hurt."

"For crying out loud, Sis, I'm forty-one years old and have been around the block a time or two. I know Inja is a pretty woman and can't help it if men notice her." Irritated that they weren't as happy for him as he was for himself, he glared at both of them with a familiar stubborn glint in his eye. "Sure, there may be a lot about her I don't know, but isn't marriage a good teacher?" Neither one argued with his logic.

"I know you're certainly old enough, but loneliness is often mistaken for love," Evie persisted. "Please be sure this is right for you before going any further. Pray and ask for God's blessings. If you can't pray alone, then let's pray together right here and now."

"I think I can handle a simple prayer, Sis." Stooping, he kissed her cheek. "Quit playing the little mother. I'm a big boy and can take care of myself. Don't forget who the elder sibling is and who dried your tears when you fell down and skinned a knee. I know what I want, and I want Inja for my wife. Don't you think it's about time this old man got married?"

With that said, he said goodnight and climbed the stairs to the guest bedroom. He was exhausted! Getting engaged was certainly tiring work. As he prepared for bed, he could hardly keep his eyes open, but as soon as he lay down, his eyes refused to close. As he tossed and turned, Evie's reminders about prayer rang in his ears. Getting out of bed, he knelt and began a faltering prayer. In between his stumbling words, the Lord stepped in, giving him the words to say and the wisdom to ask for guidance. Ever since that night, he had experienced a closer walk with the Lord and felt His presence in a very personal way—with one exception. When he asked for God's blessings on his marriage to Inja, a cold finger of doubt would touch his heart. The line of communication between himself and God seemed to close. Was God saying no? He refused to believe Inja was anything more than heaven sent. Hadn't He brought her into his life? Even though Inja wasn't a believer, she would be, given enough time. After they were married, many things would change for the both of them. When niggling doubts continued to rise in his mind, preventing sleep, he squelched them, pushing them back into the farthest recess of his memory. He'd shower her with so much love and attention, she'd never want another man's affection.

The last year had flown by on wings. He returned to base in North Carolina to finish out his obligation to Uncle Sam and made plans for the future. Periodically, he sent money to Inja to help pay the rent or buy new shoes and clothes for Eddie, but most of his earnings were placed in savings. Would there be enough to rent a house, furnish it, get a car, and pay for a wedding? His hard work and patience finally paid off. As soon as he was able, he mustered out of the Army and hurried back to the Idaho Panhandle. In a matter of days, he found a job, rented a house, found some decent second-hand furnishings to furnish the house, and today was getting married. His long-awaited dream was coming true. The only thing missing was the children he dreamed about. He wanted four strapping sons, big enough to wrestle with their old man, and to be good to their mama....

Hearing the conductor's call, he roused from his reverie, stood and stretched stiff muscles. The train pulled into the station with a hiss and squeal of steel against steel. Excitement gripped him as he tugged at his duffel bag, prying it from the tight confines beneath the seat. In a couple of hours, bachelorhood would be a thing of the past and he'd be a family man.

Hurrying away from the station, he hailed a cab. They were getting married in the judge's chambers at the county courthouse, and there was plenty of time, but he wanted to buy Inja some flowers for the wedding. After purchasing a bride's bouquet of tiny white roses festooned with baby's breath and ivory ribbons, he rushed to the courthouse. Taking the stairs two at a time, he arrived with just minutes to spare.

Evie and Lowell stood with them as they made their vows to one another. His voice rang clear and true as he solemnly repeated the traditional words. Eddie stood between them at Shortie's request, as a member of their new family, united by matrimony. He heard himself recite the words he'd heard at the weddings of his brothers and sisters. Repeating the vows, he took the promise to love and honor to heart. He promised to love and cherish Inja for as long as he lived, knowing it would take death to make him break the vows he made to her. The ceremony only took a few minutes, but his promise would last a lifetime. When the judge told him to kiss the bride, he held her tenderly with tears in his eyes.

"Okay," His Honor said, "you have a whole lifetime with her. Let me kiss the bride before I return to court."

Pulling Inja flush against himself, he kissed her longer than was necessary or decent and didn't release her until Evie pulled her away.

"You're a married woman now, young lady, and the only man you're to be kissing is your husband. So come on bride and groom, we've got a little party of our own to celebrate before you leave."

Out of politeness, Shortie shook the judge's hand in parting, and if his grip was a little firmer than necessary, it couldn't be helped. Leaving an envelope on the desk with payment enclosed for his services, he took Inja's arm with one hand and Eddie with the other. He had a family now that he'd just promised to protect, and if protection included keeping the wolves at bay, then so be it!

Coming out of the courthouse into the sunlight of a brilliant fall day, Inja ran to inspect several cars parked along the street. Whirling around, she faced him with a pretty pout on her lips.

"Okay, which one is it?"

"Which is what?" he asked, thoroughly perplexed at her behavior. "I don't know what you're looking for."

"The car," she answered. "Which car is ours? Surely you bought a car with all the money you saved. Is it this one?" She ran to a new model Ford with lots of shiny chrome.

"Inja, I didn't buy a car. I couldn't afford it after making a down payment on the house and I still needed to buy furniture. There's only enough left to buy a few little extras we may need." Gripping her arms, his eyes pleaded for understanding. "I used the money to get us a place, our first home."

"But what about your job?" she asked. Her voice trembled with real disappointment. "Don't you need a car to get to work?"

"I'll walk until we can afford better. For the time being, we'll save every penny until we can buy the house of our dreams. Then we'll fill it with all those children we've talked about."

A stricken expression crossed her face. She fixed him with a frigid stare, and her mouth quirked in annoyance. Eddie stepped close to Shortie's side and took his hand. Both man and boy faced her anger helplessly. Placing a plastic smile on her lips for the benefit of Lowell and Evie, Inja hid her disappointment and made a heroic effort to appear happy.

"Is it a nice house? Will I like it?" She smiled at him hopefully.

"It's the best I could afford. It isn't great, but can be fixed up real cute. Some of our neighbors helped me find a few furnishings and even decorated the kitchen. They're great people and will be good friends to have. You'll like the place and our new friends even more." The look of relief on her face wasn't missed by any of them. "Let's go have some wedding cake and punch," he said, "then make tracks. I've made reservations at Spokane's finest hotel, The Davenport. We'll spend our honeymoon in luxury for the entire weekend."

She was strangely silent on the ride to Evie's, but perked up when guests arrived for the reception. They shared wedding cake, several cups of watery punch, and a hamburger sandwich before opening the pile of gifts from well-meaning family and friends. Inja tore into the gaily wrapped packages with squeals of delight. They received towels, sheets, knick-knacks, dishes, and even a few pots and pans, but no drinking glasses. After each gift was noted in a bride's book, they left for a brief honeymoon.

"Evie," Shortie said in parting, "you give us three years and we'll catch up to you. We're going to start a family right away, aren't we, Inja? By this time next year, we'll be expecting our first, you just wait and see."

"If that's the plan, you have no time to waste because I'm almost two ahead of you already. Now get out of here and start on that family." Evie grinned meaningfully at Inja. He ushered her out the door, anxious for their honeymoon to begin.

They spent an enjoyable weekend at The Davenport Hotel, where they were wined and dined in fine style. He didn't give a second's thought to the property he'd purchased until the cab came to a stop in front of the steps leading from the dirt road to the front porch. Inja had been strangely silent since the train had pulled into town. He tried to picture the place through her eyes and could understand if she was disappointed. The mining town wasn't beautiful but was growing quickly, and their new home was certainly not a palace. Taking her arm, he led her up the twenty-two wooden steps to the front door. Opening the door with a flourish, he swept her up in his arms and carried her over the threshold. She giggled and snuggled into his shoulder.

"We're home." His voice sounded loud in the silence, and he smiled self-consciously. He didn't know whether he should put her down and then kiss her or the other way around.

"So this is the house you bought for us?" She looked around curiously and looked at him expectantly. "Well, are you going to put me down so I can inspect my new home or keep me in suspense?"

"Sorry." Setting her down, he wiped his sweating palms down the sides of his dress pants. He wasn't at all sure of what should be done first, and he couldn't understand why his heart was pounding so loud. He was sure she could hear it, too. "This is it," he said with a sweep of his hands. "I hope you'll be happy here." All of a sudden he was tongue-tied and couldn't think of another thing to say. Stepping back, he waited for her reaction to the modest furnishings.

The smile on her lips seemed glued in place as she looked around. The room was furnished attractively with a sofa and matching overstuffed chair. One of their neighbors had found the set secondhand and allowed him to buy them. A rag rug braided in bright reds, blues, and yellows lay in front of the sofa. It served a dual purpose by covering the faded linoleum and also added a cheery welcome to the room. The windows sparkled from a recent cleaning, and crisp, white café curtains spanned the lower half of the picture window. The neighborhood ladies had been busy.

In the kitchen, a round wooden table took up most of one side. There were four chairs: two matched and two were misfits but could be sanded and stained to match the table. The cupboards didn't have doors, but someone had made pretty red-checked gingham curtains to hang across them. The window over the sink sported a matching set with ruffles all around the hem. Even the window in the backdoor was festooned with a ruffled curtain. Off the kitchen, through a doorway behind the table was a little room with a sloping roof. He was quite proud of the new wringer washing machine complete with tubs for draining and soaking laundry. There was a little round window over the tubs that could be opened allowing a nice refreshing breeze into the room. His Monarch wood stove sat prominently along the far wall. It was warm and a pot of coffee was left to brew on its top.

A good-sized pantry led off the kitchen to the right. The room had a rich aroma of fresh cut pine. He'd already put in new shelves and a potato bin and a second for onions. A niggle of excitement brought his breath in rapid spurts. He couldn't wait to show her the underground cellar out in the backyard.

A six-foot hallway led off the front room to three doors. The first led to the bathroom. The door to the left was their bedroom, and the other was Eddie's. Both rooms were furnished and the windows draped with curtains. They found all their wedding gifts piled on their bed. Evie and Lowell had obviously delivered them from Spokane.

Inja didn't say a word during the entire tour except to occasionally nod her head. At least she still smiled and didn't seem to hate the place. She reached over and took his hand, squeezing it encouragingly. Thinking she was pleased, he grabbed her arm and pulled her out the backdoor to the show off the clotheslines.

"And look at this," he bragged, "it's the greatest find of all." Pulling a door open from ground level, he led her down a narrow flight of steps. Flicking a switch on the wall, he grinned at the sudden infusion of light. "Hard to believe isn't it?" he said in answer to her shocked expression. "I ran electric cable out here so you'll never be in the dark. We'll have a light in the yard, and there's even a light over the outdoor toilet. Look at all these shelves, Inja. There's plenty of room for a two-year supply of canned goods, squash, potatoes, onions, anything you want to store for a length of time. And it's sound, Inja; these are good walls, not dirt. There will be very few spiders, if any." He tapped the wall to prove the truth of his words. Turning to face her, he was surprised at the choked sound in her voice.

"You expect me to crawl into a hole in the ground like some...some mole?" she spit. Charging up the stairs, she stood in the yard and turned first one way and then the other, panic written all over her. For a moment, he was afraid she'd bolt over the side of the mountain and escape back to Spokane.

"This is what we could afford, and if you'd take a minute to really look, you'd see it's a darn sight better than most folks have around here. Sure, it needs a few minor repairs and a coat of paint, but nothing that can't be fixed with a few weekends of work. The roof and foundation are solid and there's plenty of room for our family." As he spotted Eddie running down the hill with his arms spread wide and a wide grin on his face, Shortie's expression softened.

"Look at him, he's already learning to fly—something he could never do in a cramped apartment. He's got a whole mountain to play on and all the fresh air his lungs will hold. It won't take long for that frail appearance to disappear."

"My brother is not frail and I resent the implication that my baby-sitting arrangement was less than ideal. He was taken care of, and it was the best I could come up with at the time." Crossing her arms over her chest, she warned him with a toss of her head not to say anything more.

Shortie was relieved to see Eddie run to join them, giggling with boyish glee. In order to stop an argument before it began, he wrapped an arm around her shoulders and pulled her to his side. "I'm sorry. I didn't mean to upset you." Dropping his arm from her shoulders, he rubbed the back of his neck and shook his head. "I want us to be happy here. Please try to understand." Spreading his hands wide, he tried to make her see his position. "I did the best I could with what money and time was allowed. Give it a chance, Inja. One year, that's all I ask is one year," he pleaded.

"One year," she agreed as she turned to face Eddie with a smile.

"There's a spring on ta' hill, and I've got a whole mountain to play on and my very own bedroom. This is the bestest place." Grinning at Shortie, he buried his head against him bashfully, "Thanks for marryin' me and my this'ter," he lisped.

Grabbing him up, Shortie held him on one arm. "I'm glad, too, boy," he said. Turning to Inja, he walked her to the edge of the yard facing down the mountainside. "It won't be forever, I promise. I'll save every penny and buy you the sort of house you really want. We won't live like kings, but we won't go without either. I will take care of you and Eddie. Please don't be too disappointed; after all, it's got to be better than that two-room mousetrap you lived in before." His serious expression revealed determination and the conviction of his words.

Smiling for the first time, Inja took his free hand and wrapped it around her waist. On tiptoe, she kissed the corner of his mouth teasingly. "Okay, you two have me outnumbered," she sighed. "But remember your promise, because I'll hold you to it. One year is all I'll be able to stand in this God-forsaken country."

"I won't forget. I know how much you want to start a family and so do I. I'm not getting any younger and neither are you, so we can't waste any time." Nuzzling her neck, he kissed a sensitive spot behind her ear just to hear her giggle. "How about starting our family right away? It's legal; after all, we're married and it will soon be Eddie's bedtime."

"There's a lot to be done before bedtime, so let's get busy. The first thing we have to do is unpack and then we'll need to...."

"No, we don't need to unpack tonight," he interrupted. "We have plenty of time. Eddie, how would you feel about a little brother or sister?"

Before the child could answer, Inja's anger erupted with venom. "How can you stand here talking about babies when we've only been married a week? You need to remember that any child we have will not be his brother or sister," she snapped. "He's my brother," she emphasized, "not my son."

"I know, I know," he soothed. "Let's not argue a slip of the tongue." Changing the subject abruptly, he pointed out the homes of their neighbors, the store, and school down on the main road below them. "Tomorrow, I'll introduce you to our neighbors. There's Blackie and Bertie Clegg, Art and Ellen Jones, Tony and Maria—Tony's my partner at work," he added, "and Arden owns the store, and I can't forget Gabriel Stump, alias Gabbie. He's the town patriarch and Blackie's shadow. We'll get an account started at the store so you can buy your kitchen supplies. We'll have a wonderful life together and make many beautiful babies that all look like you. Don't you agree?"

She smiled mysteriously, but didn't respond. And thus began the marriage of Shortie and Inja Busch.

I Corinthians 7:33-34: "But a married man is concerned about the affairs of this world—how he can please his wife—and his interests are divided...."

The Holy Bible—King James Version

Chapter 1

Sitting at the kitchen table, Shortie Busch enjoyed the sun's warm rays streaming through the open door. Stretching lazily, he leaned forward in the chair so his back and shoulders would absorb more of the direct heat. Seven-year-old Eddie, his wife Inja's little brother, sat beside him finishing his supper. The boy grimaced at each bite of cabbage, swallowing painfully. He hid a condescending smile behind his newspaper.

Spreading the paper open on the table, he scanned the headlines until finding one of interest. Settling himself comfortably, he began reading an article on silver prices when a steady jarring of the table disturbed his concentration. Looking up, he noticed the remaining milk in Eddie's glass ripple, as if stirred by the breeze.

The table rocked slightly with an even but steady rhythm. Placing a restraining hand across the swinging, restless legs of Eddie, he was surprised to find them still.

Puzzled, he looked around, trying to pinpoint the source of the subtle, continuous movement. The tenuous tremble increased to a dizzying, rolling motion starting at his toes, sending shock waves through his feet until it reached his stomach and tossed it around. Eddie's head snapped up and his eyes locked on Shortie's, widened in alarm.

The sickening motion intensified as a distant rumble shook the floor. The paper fell from his hands as he rose to his feet, and when the hair on the back of his neck prickled a warning, his muscles tensed, alert to an impending sense of danger.

Freezing for a moment, he tried to locate from what direction the threat came. His chair tipped when an ear-deafening explosion ripped through the house, rocking it to its foundations.

"What the sam hill was that?" he shouted as he leaped from the table to the door. Forgetting about Eddie, he dashed out to find Inja. A storm of falling rock pelted him from above. He covered his head with his arms and sprinted zig-zag, dodging the falling debris. Taking cover at the edge of the porch, he searched for his wife through a deluge of dirt toppling down the mountain. Desperate to locate her, he stepped out into the storm.

"Have we been bombed?" he wondered, but the war was over, he reminded himself. "Why would anyone bother with this good-for-nothing place anyway?"

The answer loomed out of the storm, reminding him of the gold and silver mines peppering the area. Refusing to accept such a thought, he continued his search for Inja. Rounding the corner of the house facing the clotheslines, he caught a glimpse of her crouched on the ground. She was gripping a sheet to her chest like a shield. Her head rose for a moment, revealing blue eyes wide with terror.

When the ground rolled again, her mouth opened in a soundless scream. Everything in front of her was being swallowed by a wide, gaping hole. The clothesline posts teetered back and forth crazily before collapsing in on themselves. Clotheslines and laundry basket sank into the ground, taking Inja with them. Large rocks plummeted off the mountainside, burying all that was left of the yard.

"Inja, where are you?" he shouted into a fresh torrent of earth filling the air.

Forcing himself to be still, he listened hopefully for an answer. Hearing none, he ran into the chaos. Another explosion, seeming to come from the depths of hell, reverberated in his ears as he blindly searched the ground for a sign of her.

Choking on the metallic grit filling his mouth and nose, he yelled again, "Inja, can you hear me?"

His eyes watered, muddying his vision, but not before a speck of fabric caught his attention. Showing through a mound of dirt was a spot of white where Inja had been a moment before. Running recklessly toward the place, he tripped over rocks and mounds of displaced earth. Falling to his knees, he dug frantically.

When his searching fingers brushed against fabric, he grabbed with both hands and pulled as hard as he dared. He toppled over backwards when a corner of the sheet surfaced, revealing Inja's arms and shoulders. Brushing away the debris burying her head, he checked for signs of breathing.

Fearing the worst, his eyes streamed tears of dread. After her mouth and nose were cleared, she finally gasped air into her lungs.

"Thank you, Lord," Shortie whispered. "You didn't take her from me." He continued a steady prayer of thanks as he cradled her inert body in a protective embrace. Picking her up, he ran to the shelter of the porch and gently laid her down. He remembered Eddie alone inside the house.

"Eddie," he called. "Eddie, are you okay?" Not wanting to leave her, he forced himself to check on the boy. Opening the screen door, he found him hiding under the kitchen table clutching a pencil in his hand.

"Eddie," he repeated, "answer me." The boy appeared to be unharmed. Why didn't he respond? "Eddie," Shortie said with a raised voice, "I need fresh water and a clean cloth. I need it now," he ordered. Eddie jumped at the sound of his voice, but remained in place, staring at a wet spot on the floor.

When the house began shaking and the lights flickered, the last bite of red cabbage stuck fast in Eddie's throat. As the tremors became more severe, his heart pounded painfully, cutting into his windpipe. Struggling furiously for air, he fought to keep his roiling stomach from rising into his throat. Running to the bathroom, red cabbage and boiled potatoes spewed from his mouth and nose, soiling the shining perfection of porcelain and chrome. Resting his feverish head against the cool smoothness of the tub, Eddie sobbed incoherently. Giving his mouth a quick rinse, he ran back to the kitchen to find Shortie.

"Wait," he called. "Don't leave me here." As he raced to the open door and the safety of Shortie's side, pain deep in his belly doubled him over. His face twisted in agony as he forced himself to crawl toward the doorway. Then something picked him up and tossed him to the floor, where he curled into a ball with his head tucked to his knees. A thunderous boom followed, so loud it roared inside his head. A trickle of blood dribbled from his nose to his mouth, where the salty taste spread over his tongue. His stomach turned sick and he retched with dry heaves.

"Please," he moaned, "come back, I'm afraid." He tried to stand and found his trembling legs wouldn't support his weight. Feeling strangely disembodied, he grabbed a pencil that had fallen to the floor and held it before him, prepared to defend himself. When the floor rumbled beneath his feet for the second time and the lights flickered and then went out, trickles of moisture splashed down his legs. Sickening waves of terror welled up from his toes, rooting him to the spot. Terrified that the house was falling in and he'd be buried beneath it, he crawled on all fours under the kitchen table. Curling into an even tighter ball, he stared, transfixed, at the open door, unable to move.

Crying softly, he pleaded, "Come back, Shortie." He whimpered like a wounded animal and silently begged for rescue. Vague thoughts about his sister, nipped at the edge of his mind, keeping hysteria at bay.

Moments before the explosion, she had grabbed the wicker basket to retrieve the last of the laundry from the backyard clothesline. He wondered if she would miss him if he died.

He admired Inja and believed she was the prettiest woman in the world. When she smiled and crinkled up the corners of her cornflower eyes, she was beautiful. But Eddie knew two sides to his sister; the one she showed the world and a darker side he knew too well. It didn't matter, because he loved her. She was the closest thing he had to a mother and he didn't want to lose her. Was she okay? Things were better since she'd married two years ago. Shortie made everything right and the nightmares had almost disappeared. Would he pay for being the bad boy she accused him of being by dying alone in this house?

His insides quivered with fear, and he started at the unexpected sound of Shortie's voice. It took a moment for the man's words to register through the paralyzing numbness in his brain. When he spoke for a second time, resting a hand on Eddie's shoulder, relief flooded through him in waves. Crying openly, he flung himself into the man's arms. Rescued from the nightmare, he sobbed out his terror against Shortie's neck.

Shortie shook Eddie roughly by the shoulders. What did he say before dashing back outside? Eddie tried to remember. It had been something about Inja.

She was outside when the explosion occurred and could be hurt. Hobbling on wooden legs to the sink, he filled a pan with water and threw a dishtowel over his shoulder. Fearing for his sister, he moved stiff-legged to the door. Setting the pan of water next to Shortie, he stepped back into the shadows, conscious of the telltale wetness between his legs. He worried it might be noticed. A trail of wet splotches followed him from the kitchen to the back porch, and he felt his cheeks grow hot. He wondered how she would punish him for soiling her floor. In the dimness, he saw her lower body stretched out on the porch, strangely silent and still. Peeking around Shortie's broad back, he saw her legs, but didn't recognize the face. This face was mangled and bloody, like the thing from his nightmares. Chills of dread ran up his spine as he screamed her name over and over again.

Chapter 2

"Eddie," Shortie shouted as he shook the boy by the shoulders. Wild-eyed, Eddie fought to break free from his grasp. Holding the child firmly, he repeated in a softer tone, "Inja is hurt, but she'll be okay if we work together to help her. Do you hear me, boy?"

Releasing Eddie, Shortie acted quickly when Inja began to cough and choke. Pulling her to a seated position, he rammed a finger down her throat, forcing her to gag. Eddie stared, horrified at the blobs of dirt and blood spewing from her mouth and nose. Her body jerked convulsively, her legs and arms flopping like a rag doll's at each gasp for air. Rolling to her side, she spoke his name in a quavering sigh before falling still once more. After Shortie tore the dishtowel in half, the fabric was dropped into the pan of water. Removing the dripping cloth, he squeezed it out over her face. Holding her tightly, he forced an eye open and squeezed water directly over it to clear away any obstruction. The same cleansing was repeated to the other eye. She slapped at him weakly, trying to free herself from his grip.

"Stay still and don't fight me," he commanded. "Try not to move any more than you have to." Relaxing his hold, he peered into her face. With the increased evening darkness and gray murky air, visibility was dim at best. Unable to see clearly enough to judge the extent of her injuries, Shortie turned to Eddie.

"Get my flashlight from under the sink," he ordered, "and hurry." Eddie ran into the dark kitchen without hesitation. Hurrying back, he handed over the light. Shortie fumbled with the switch until a bright ring of light washed Inja in an amber glow.

"Hold it, just like this." He positioned Eddie's hands so the light flooded Inja's face. Trickles of red ran down her cheeks and neck, revealing what had been hidden beneath the layers of dirt.

"Oh, Inja," Shortie gasped. Holding back, he didn't touch her until his hands ceased their trembling. Carefully, he turned her left side directly into the light. Staring in shock, he daubed ineffectually at the flow of blood from her mangled cheek. The cuts and scrapes on her skin were so numerous it was hard to tell which bled worse. As he rinsed the towel, the water in the pan quickly turned from pink to scarlet. Each touch revealed fine cuts and a web of scratches. The worst was a deep gash just under the left eye above the cheekbone. Falling rock had struck her in the head, but razor-edged shale, flying off the mountain like missiles, had sliced her unprotected skin like hamburger.

Shortie's lips moved in continued prayer. At Eddie's sharp intake of breath he put a finger to his lips to silence the boys shocked outcry. He handed the other dripping half of towel to Eddie, and Eddie helped him wash Inja's other side.

"Will it stop? Please make it stop bleeding," Eddie pleaded. Continuing to cleanse the wounds on her face, he looked to Shortie for answers.

"I hope so, boy." Shortie's voice broke, betraying his fear. He wiped tears from his eyes and struggled to maintain his composure. "There's so much blood," he thought. "The more we wash, the more she bleeds. Who would think someone could bleed so much? Oh God, please help me to help her."

She lay still during the cleansing, enduring the wet, painful dabs to her skin. She reached to brush a stray wisp of blonde hair off her forehead that a warm stickiness had pasted to her skin. She peered at her fingertips. The sight of her own blood struck terror in her heart. Shaking off the paralysis of fear, she let her fingertips explore the damage to her face. Screams echoed through the valley as she struggled to sit up.

"Shortie, my face, what's wrong with my face?" Trying to stand, she fell back. Her trembling legs collapsed, buckling beneath her when sharp pain traveled up her left side. Her wounded face remained numb under the probing of her fingers. Covering her eyes with her hands, she rocked forward with her mouth opened wide, wailing and crying pitifully.

As he sobbed, Shortie's lips moved in continuous, silent prayer. She needed medical help he was unable to provide, and there wasn't a chance he could move her without a car. He wasn't even sure if it was safe to move her. For the first time in his life, he felt absolutely helpless. Eddie's tug on his arm got his attention.

"Listen, don't cha' hear 'em? Someone's coming. Ya' gotta answer 'em, so they'll come help," he begged through tear-filled eyes.

Leaving Inja's side, he stepped to the edge of the yard and yelled, "We're here, but Inja's been hurt. Bring help—and quick."

"I'll get Doc Smith," came a muffled reply.

Doc Smith, a retired doctor, still practiced medicine in between golf games and frequent trips to visit his grandkids.

Hurrying back to the porch, he straightened her legs. "It's beginning to sting. Shortie, it hurts so bad," she moaned. "Make it stop." Having nothing else to protect her broken skin, he covered her face with a cool, damp cloth. Her hands clawed at his shirtfront, clinging tightly, as her slight body trembled in his arms. He wanted to carry her inside, but was afraid of doing further damage. Kneeling beside her, he waited impatiently for help to arrive. It wasn't long before voices were heard approaching from the main road.

Recognizing the nasal voice of Benjamin Schultz and the huffing and puffing of the old doctor, he almost broke down with relief. Leaving Eddie with Inja, he hurried to guide them to where she lay.

Doc's white shirt stood out in the dark like a beacon. A middle button strained to break loose from its moorings, pulled tight against his very pronounced middle. Unaccustomed to physical activity, his legs wobbled from the exertion of climbing the steep hill. He panted heavily, and sweat rolled down his face in rivers. Catching his breath, he smoothed the few wisps of white remaining on his otherwise bald pate. Cursing under his breath, he removed his glasses and wiped them dry on his shirttail. Shaking his head, he eyed the steps leading from the dirt road to the Busch property high above. With firm resolve, he tugged the waistband of his pants into place over his sagging gut.

"What's the matter, Doc?" Ben asked. "Is something wrong up there?" He was behind, unable to see around the doctor's broad girth. Doc Smith stood where the mouth of the path they'd followed met with the road. "Come on, move, would ya? I'm losing my footing and starting to slide back down the hill."

"Hold your horses," Doc panted. "Let me catch my breath." Ben rudely jabbed the doctor's backside, forcing him to step ahead.

"There's Shortie. Come on old man, we're almost there." Grabbing Doc Smith's bag in one hand, Ben prodded him ahead with the other.

"Is that you, Ben?" Without waiting for a reply, Shortie hurried down the staircase to seize Doc's arm. Tugging none too gently, he pulled the doctor up the stairs and across the yard to where Inja lay.

Kneeling painfully on arthritic knees, Doc checked Inja's breathing. "She ain't dead, is she?" he questioned in an imperious tone. Glaring daggers, he obviously misunderstood the purpose for the square of cloth. Whisking the towel away, he made a quick, cursory exam. Back in command of himself and the situation, he quickly took control.

Turning to Shortie, he snapped, "Can you lift her?" Without waiting for an answer, he ordered, "Pick her up and get her inside. Light some candles if you have any, and keep that flashlight on. I need to see what I'm doing."

Lifting his wife as gently as possible, Shortie hugged her briefly. Carrying her to the couch as Doc Smith indicated, he handed the flashlight to Ben before racing to the kitchen to find candles. Searching frantically through the cupboards and drawers, he found one candle stub left over from last year's jack-o-lantern. It wouldn't last more than a few minutes. Remembering an old kerosene lamp left in the shed, he ran to find it. The lamp hadn't been used for a number of years, but had plenty of kerosene in its bowl. After he attempted to light the wick, it finally caught and burned. It wasn't a great light, but far better than a single flashlight. Its yellow glow burned brightly, revealing faded wallpaper upon the walls. The tiny front room was well lit, leaving only the corners in shadow.

Hovering near, Shortie wanted to stay close as Doc checked her carefully from head to toe. When Doc was forced to step around him several times while inspecting Inja's injuries, he demanded crossly, "Don't you have something you could be doing? She isn't going to run away, so get out of here so I can see to my patient properly."

Her eyes darted from one to the other of them. Pain etched her features as the doctor's probing fingers continued their examination.

"You're going to be all right, little lady." Patting her hand, Doc smiled broadly. "We'll get these scratches taken care of and stitch up your cheek. Don't worry, you won't feel any more pain, and I promise not to leave scars."

Inja relaxed visibly, giving a slight nod. Closing her eyes, she refused to respond to Shortie's light touch on her shoulder by turning her head to the wall.

"You'll be okay now," Shortie told her. Patting her arm self-consciously, he backed away giving Doc room to work. He regarded her protectively until Doc turned to him and scowled. "Okay, okay, I get the message. I'm not needed right now. I can see she's in good hands." Turning to Ben who'd been waiting patiently for Doc to finish, Shortie motioned to the younger man to join him in the kitchen.

Ben, with his spare build and owlish eyes behind thick horn-rimmed glasses, looked more suited to selling toilet water to little old ladies than to the job he actually held. Trained in explosives during the war, he was the "munitions man" for one of the local mines. If a body needed to blast a tunnel or sink shaft, Ben Schultz was the man for the job. Peering at Shortie with questioning eyes, he stepped closer and whispered, "Close call, huh?"

Without further preliminaries, Shortie demanded, "Was it a bomb?"

"I don't know...I mean, I'm not sure, but I'm fairly certain it wasn't a bomb. Even a small amount of dynamite, strategically placed, would have blown half this mountain away. Whatever the cause, there was only enough force for a few minor rock slides."

Shortie's voice rose angrily. "What do you mean 'minor rock slides'? My wife could have been killed and my home destroyed."

"I didn't mean to imply Inja's injuries were minor," Ben apologized. "I'm only saying that if there had been a bomb, there would be a lot more damage than I've seen."

"Are you absolutely sure?"

"I'd stake my career on it," Ben answered in a serious tone.

"Do you think it was the upper mine doing some blasting on the Q-T when things got out of hand?"

"That's a possibility, but not very likely," Ben explained. "The only time they set off charges is when they're sinking shaft. They always give advance notice with ads in the paper and announcements on the news. The mines weren't involved in this unless by accident. Or...."

"Or what, Ben?" Shortie asked with a crazed look in his eyes. Grabbing the smaller man's shirtfront, he demanded an answer. "My wife was seriously hurt, almost killed." Regarding the doctor as he leaned over Inja, Shortie's expression appeared haggard with worry as he moaned, "It should have been me, not her. She's so little. If only I would have listened...Do you realize she was totally buried? My god, man, she could have suffocated."

Holding Ben's arm in a painful grip, he demanded, "Answer me, Ben, or what? Tell me what you know or I'll...."

"Hold on," Ben yelped. Wrenching his bruised arm free, he rubbed the growing knot under his fingers. "How do we know this was caused by man? Maybe it was an earthquake or some freak act of nature." His voice shook with fear, and, as he became defensive, took on a grating whine. "It's over. I don't believe there was any severe damage, and no one was supposed to be hurt." At Shortie's sharp look, Ben's face blanched.

"What's that supposed to mean, 'no one was supposed to be hurt'?" Shortie studied the younger man critically. He closed a hand around Ben's upper arm, and his grip tightened, cutting off circulation.

"It was a slip of the tongue. You know I ain't so good with words. I only meant no one should have been hurt. If Inja wouldn't have been outside, she wouldn't have been hurt."

At Shortie's look of doubt, Ben pleaded with him to believe what he was saying. "There were only a few minor shake-ups, I swear it. I don't know the cause, but promise to find out."

Satisfied with the answer, he released Ben's arm. Going outside to avoid being overheard, the two men stepped off the porch to inspect the damage. Stepping gingerly over mounds of dirt and rock, they scanned the dark mountainside for a source of the explosion. When Shortie stepped into a pothole that gave way beneath his feet, he jumped back with a holler. "It's gone, it's totally gone."

Ben bolted to Shortie's side where he was circling a small area hunting for something. Ben searched the ground, perplexed, because he didn't know what he was looking for and wouldn't have known what it was even if he found it.

"Don't you get it? Right here, right where we're standing was the doorway to my underground cellar. It's gone, totally caved in. The clotheslines are gone, too?" he said in a tight, strained voice. Picturing Inja by the clotheslines as she'd been before they sunk to the ground, he felt a rising sense of panic. He hadn't noticed if Eddie had come in the house with them. "Eddie, I've got to find Eddie."

Ben stared in puzzlement as Shortie ran across the yard to the house. Staying where he was, he tested the ground around him for soft spots before he dared traipse off into the dark. Feeling the earth give way beneath his feet, he quickly followed after him. Entering the front door, he paced the front room.

"What's the matter, boy?" Doc asked, "you in a hurry for something? Settle down and quit walking in front of my light. Your impatience won't hurry me none, and I'll be done when I'm done."

"How much longer will it be?" Ben pulled a cigarette from his shirt pocket and almost lit it before he remembered where he was. Smoking had never been permitted in Shortie's home.

"What's the rush all of a sudden?" Doc demanded.

"Oh, no big hurry," Ben mumbled. "I just want to get off the mountain before something else happens."

Shortie ran through the kitchen door, in a panic to find Eddie. Pulling up short, he was astonished to find the boy knelt under the kitchen table. With shoulders shaking and tears raining down his face, Eddie peeked out with real despair in his expression. Kneeling, he coaxed the child to him and was so relieved to find him safe that he hugged him with fierce intensity.

Wanting to calm his fears, he held him close and crooned, "Shh now, it's alright. I'm here and nothing is going to hurt you."

Teary-eyed, Eddie gazed into Shortie's face. Removing his clasped hands from his front, he stepped closer. It was instantly apparent what the child had been trying to hide.

Stumbling over his words, Eddie pleaded, "Will ya' tell?" Standing up as straight as he could, he firmed his thin shoulders and wiped his nose with the back of a hand. "Please don't tell. Please don't tell Inja 'cause she'll be 'shamed of me," he begged.

"I promise you, Eddie, I'll never tell a single soul. It's our secret and no one else needs to know." Tears stung Shortie's eyes as he lifted the stricken child in his arms. Taking him to the bathroom, he removed the soiled jeans and washed the tears from his face. As he helped him dress in clean clothing, a lump formed in his throat that wouldn't be swallowed down. When a shriek split the quiet of the little house, it startled them both.

Racing to the front room with Eddie in his arms, the doctor stopped him with an upraised hand. Continuing to speak calmly, he proceeded to explain his diagnosis to Inja. She stared, horrified, at her own reflection in a hand mirror.

"Your injuries look far worse than they really are. Your face is swelling, which doesn't help, and I imagine it hurts like the devil. The bruising around and under your eyes looks far worse than it is. Most of the scratches are superficial and will heal without a trace." Following the direction of her one-eyed gaze to the pan of water he'd used for washing, now dark red with her blood, he added, "All head or facial wounds bleed profusely. Don't let that scare you." The statement was made matter-of-factly and accepted without question. Even though her left eye was swollen shut and her face looked like she'd been through a meat grinder, she accepted every word the doctor said without comment. Turning to Shortie, Doc explained the extent of her injuries and plans for medical care.

"Under other circumstances, I'd recommend a few days hospitalization, but in this situation, the less she's moved, the better. I doubt that mountain behind you is going anywhere, so she's safe enough. You'll need someone to help out for a spell because she'll be off her feet for a while." Pulling the blanket away from her legs, he indicated her left ankle and lower leg, bound in an elastic bandage.

"Bad sprain," he said, regarding the injury with concern. Taking an ointment from his bag, he ordered, "Rub this into that ankle two or three times a day. Use ice packs to reduce the swelling and don't let her walk around unless she has to. She'll get used to using crutches." Handing a jar of white salve to Shortie, he continued, "This salve is for her face. She's to use it frequently, and don't be stingy with it, cake it on thick. Those stitches will be plenty sore by tomorrow and this salve will soothe, soften, and help deaden the pain. It'll help keep those scratches soft, too, and relieve the itch as she heals. And we don't want any scratching," he said in a loud voice. Glancing at Inja meaningfully, he added, "Scratching will irritate the skin, hinder healing and increase the chance of scars, and we don't want that, do we?"

Continuing his instructions, he explained, "The salve is one of Don Meyer's new concoctions. I've prescribed it before and it works like magic. Darn stuff," he grumbled, "cures almost anything. All natural he says. I'll let him know you'll be needing more of the stuff in a few days, and don't let her run out it," he ordered. "Give her these for pain." He thrust a small bottle of pills into Shortie's hand.

"I've prescribed a sedative so she'll sleep for several hours. I'll be back before noon tomorrow to check on her." With a final smile for Inja and a frown for Shortie, he gathered up his things and left as quickly as he'd come.

Lifting Inja carefully, Shortie carried her to bed. Removing her dirt-caked clothing, he replaced them with her favorite nightgown. Elevating her injured leg on pillows, he tucked her in snugly, pulling the blankets to her chin. She followed his every move with her one good eye. Her silence was unnerving and her swollen and mangled features made responsibility weigh heavily upon his shoulders. He blamed himself for every mark upon her skin.

"I'll be back in a moment; I need to check on Eddie." She nodded her head sleepily, beginning to cry again in quiet sobs. Stroking her bare shoulder gently, he reluctantly left the room.

Entering Eddie's bedroom, Shortie sat on the edge of the bed. Patting the child's back comfortingly, he asked, "Where are they?" Eddie pointed under his dresser, keeping his face hidden in the blankets. Gathering the child onto his lap, Shortie rocked him like a baby. As he rocked, he told Eddie a story he'd forgotten until that very moment.

"Fear can do strange things to a man. There was another man that felt afraid, just like you did tonight. A mad bull that foamed at the mouth and had red eyes was chasing him down. The guy started bawling and yelling like crazy and do you know what he did?"

Eddie shook his head. He sat up and stared at Shortie saucer-eyed.

"Well sir, he ran for the nearest fence and rolled underneath it. Then he got himself a big stick and clubbed the bull right between the eyes. Knocked that animal straight to his knees, and I'm here to tell you that bull never chased anyone ever again. The man was my dad and he was afraid too, but stood up to his fear. Do you know what I'm trying to say, boy?"

Eddie gazed at Shortie questioningly with unblinking eyes. He shook his head again.

"It means I'm proud of you Eddie, and I couldn't love you more if you were my own son. You came and helped Inja even though you were afraid." Eddie hugged his neck tightly, expressing feelings he couldn't voice. Folding back the blankets, Shortie told him, "It's time for some shut-eye. I think we've had all the excitement we can handle for one night." Eddie crawled into bed and managed a lopsided grin before his eyes closed in exhausted sleep.

Retrieving the soiled jeans from under the dresser, he hid them in a pile of dirty work clothes. Back in the bedroom he shared with Inja, he found her sleeping soundly. Doc's pain pills worked well. Turning her head carefully, he checked the bandages for signs of seepage. It was important they remain secure without constricting the swollen skin. She moaned softly as he jostled her sleeping body.

Unable to sleep himself, Shortie paced the length of the house restlessly. Nervous energy kept him on edge. His thoughts were awhirl with unanswered questions and he worried for the safety of his family. Escaping the confines of the kitchen, he opened the back door. Peering out into the night, he focused on an unnatural quiet. Where were the night sounds of insects, the occasional dog barking or bird rustling? Stepping off the porch, he stood at the edge of his postage stamp yard, unable to see up or down the draw in the darkness. The quiet, so heavy it blanketed the canyon below, filled his ears with a deafening silence. Shaking his head from a sense of impending doom, he asked himself as he had earlier, "What the sam hill happened, anyway?"

Chapter 3

The following morning dawned with bright sunny skies and not a tell-tale trace of dust in the cool, crisp air. Shortie paced the house, pausing at every sound. As light began to filter through the windows, he went outside to check the fuse box. A few windows in homes below him in the canyon were ablaze with light, so electricity had been restored. Maybe a blown fuse was the reason their lights were still out. Fumbling in the semi-darkness, he replaced all the fuses just to be sure. A faint light shining in the bathroom rewarded his efforts. Coming into the darkened kitchen, he flicked the switch.

Electric light from a single bulb chased the shadows away. Opening the bedroom door cautiously so as not to wake Inja, he checked her condition as he had periodically throughout the night. She remained unchanged. She slept heavily and hadn't moved a muscle. It would probably be hours before she woke. She wasn't an early riser even in the best of circumstances.

There was severe bruising among the various cuts and scrapes, but no evidence of bleeding. Relieved, he smiled to himself. She would heal in time. Adjusting the blanket to cover her shoulders, he stroked a strand of soft blonde hair that lay curled behind her ear and lightly kissed her cheek. Afraid of waking her, he left quietly to peek in on Eddie.

Questions swirled in his head. "What had happened? Was there someone out there who planted the dynamite for some reason or was it an accident? Maybe it was a force of nature, an earthquake or something like Shultz said." He refused to believe the explosion and its aftermath were acts of God.

Entering Eddie's room, he found the child sleeping peacefully with his arms wrapped tightly around a stuffed bear. The child rarely slept with toys anymore and then only in times of great distress. He must have been scared to death. His heart swelled with a humbling sense of pride and gratitude. The kid had the makings of greatness that would become evident one day. Eddie didn't sleep as soundly as his sister, so he adjusted the covers around his sleeping form carefully. The boy would be embarrassed if he knew Shortie had seen him clinging to his teddy bear. He left the room soundlessly.

Sorting through a pile of dirty clothes, he selected several pair of work overalls. Filling a washtub with hot water and a handful of soap flakes, he stuffed the clothing into the tub along with Eddie's jeans. Grabbing his cap off its place on the wall, he pulled on a jacket and went out the backdoor. The backside of the little house faced the hillside and the scene brought him up short.

The tiny backyard was buried under a layer of dirt and rock. From the look of it, an entire section of the mountainside had collapsed into his backyard. Strange though it was, the east and north side of the house showed little difference. The only thing out of the ordinary was a handful of pebbles littering the hard-caked yard in front of him as if some careless child tossed them over the retaining wall and left them for someone to find. The opposite side of the house evidenced an altogether different picture. The wall was split from ground to top in two locations. The log walls, built years before to hold the mountainside in its place, were splintered off. A six-foot section had been pushed forward by the massive weight of the mountain itself. The explosion had obviously shifted the bulk of the mountain on this side. The walls remained secure everywhere else. Walking slowly across the uneven ground, stepping high over mounds of earth and stone, he searched for further signs of damage. Peering over the side of the mountain, he scrutinized the roads running horizontally to the hillside below him.

From the shelf of mountain that was his land, he could see the twenty-two wooden steps leading down to the dirt road that by-passed his property. Most of the surrounding hillsides were dotted with shacks much like his own. Wherever there was a level spot of land, a makeshift house had been slapped together. Dirt roads crisscrossed the opposite mountainside haphazardly. Some led up the draw to the mine, while others led nowhere, their destination forgotten, covered with vegetation and sloughing soil from the hillside above.

During the initial gold rush of the late 1800's, the roads had been leveled out by early miners and settlers. Memories of the people had faded with time, but the roads they'd carved out of the steep mountain slopes gave evidence of their passing. The hillside facing him rose straight up and then rounded at the crest like a haystack. Haystack Peak was nude of undergrowth and had the same coloring as old hay. Huge boulders jutted from one side incongruently, sharp-angled rock that rose straight from the ground as if pushed skyward by some great force. Residents feared the sharp, jagged rock would come tumbling down one day. In the dim, dusky blue of early morning, he couldn't see to the end of the shadowed valley below. Dark shapes of neighboring homes rose in silhouette against a tawny earth background. Second story windowpanes reflected the golden light of sunrise, while many ground-level windows remained dark. Hearing voices, he stepped closer and peered over the edge. Four men approached, speaking in hushed tones.

"Hey," Shortie called softly. "What happened down below? Is everything okay down there?"

Climbing the steep wooden stairway leading from the road to the front porch, the four joined him at a spot overlooking the valley. Blackie Clegg, the big Irishman, led the way, followed by toothless Gabbie. Gab's real name was Gabriel Stump and he hated it. He was nicknamed Gabbie for obvious reasons and the old guy lived up to his name. Art Jones, nicknamed Jonesy, was next, and Leon Mayhew brought up the rear. All were neighbors who lived below in the valley.

Jonesy appeared taller and skinnier than ever. He ran a hand through his sandy-colored hair, leaving it on end. Fear turned his sallow complexion white. His eyes were like two vacant holes.

Speaking in a tremulous whisper, he asked, "Everyone okay here? I could've sworn I heard screaming when that explosion shook us all like rag dolls, but wasn't sure. There was so much commotion going on there for a while and so much noise, I couldn't trust my own ears." Pausing, he raked a shaking hand through his hair again before adding as an afterthought, "Was it Inja? I would'a come runnin', ya gotta' know that, but we was kind of busy for awhile ourselves." Drawing a deep breath, he continued, "We're all okay, but that relic of a shed collapsed. Would have buried James with it except for little Art. He pulled him out of the way."

Tears spilled down his cheeks. Jagged white paths formed in the dust gathered in the lines of his cheeks. Tears dripped from his chin, leaving round, wet circles on his shirt.

Art's trembling fingers and teary voice hadn't gone unnoticed. It was obvious he had "the shakes" and was in desperate need of a drink. Granted, part of his shakiness could be attributed to nerves, but who wasn't scared witless after the night they'd had? Nevertheless, he was a drunk and would be worthless in a pinch. Clapping him on the shoulder Shortie extended sympathy without flowery words. Wiping tears from red-rimmed eyes, Art turned away until his emotions were under control.

Gabbie, face chalk white under the usual residue of dirt and grime, spat once on the ground to clear his throat. Wiping the remaining spittle from his lips and matted beard, he cackled, "It's the end of us all. It's an earthquake I tell ya'. Haven't I been tellin' ya? Haven't I been tryin' to warn ya? Well, haven't I?" Looking to Shortie for confirmation, Gabbie gave a wide, snaggle-toothed grin.

Avoiding Blackie's slap to the side of his head, Gabbie took a step closer to Shortie. Knowing he had a captive audience, he deepened his voice and waved his skinny arms. "It's an earthquake and it'll bury us all. Every last one of...."

"Knock it off, old man," Blackie Clegg warned. "Go back to your bottle."

Taking a silver flask from a deep pocket of his overalls, Gabbie removed the cork with a loud pop. Upending the flask, he drank deeply. Smacking his lips, sheer delight on his wrinkled old face, he tempted Art by waving the flask under his nose before returning it to his pocket. Stepping closer to Shortie, he grinned teasingly. He was safe for the time being.

Wanting to shake up what few brains the old man had, Blackie grabbed him by the neck, but was stopped by a firm grip on his forearm.

"We're all tired after a sleepless night and short on patience," Shortie warned. "And we don't need any more problems from you old man," he added with a glance toward Gabbie.

"Well, was it Inja we heard last night? Looks like your place got the worst of it. Is everything all right up here?" Blackie's deep bass sounded loud in the stillness of early morning.

Pointing to the section of retaining wall that was now a splintered pile of rubble, he described the previous night's experience with vivid clarity. His voice shook with emotion when he described the extent of Inja's injuries and how she had received them.

"Doc doesn't want her to be disturbed and she needs all the rest she can get." Facing them, he gestured toward the road. "Why don't you go see if Arden's open? Maybe he's got the coffeepot on."

"Are you coming?" Blackie asked.

"I really shouldn't. Inja might wake up and I don't want her to find me gone."

"Since when does she ever open her eyes before ten? It's barely past six. We need to plan how we're going to clean up this mess and we need you there." Blackie's tone was unnecessarily sharp, the only indication of a sleepless and traumatic night.

"Okay, okay, Irish." Waving a hand in a placatory gesture, Shortie tried to make him understand. Pointing to the mountain behind them, he said, "What if there's another explosion or whatever it was that happened last night? What if...."

"And what if the wind don't blow?" Blackie exploded. "That mountain has stood where it is over a thousand years and it ain't gonna' pull up stakes and move now. Someone knows what happened last night and they know why." He drilled the point of an index finger into Shortie's chest. "We need to find out who."

"All right, I get the message. Give me a minute to look in on them and then I'll be right with you. Besides, with you out here roaring like a bear in heat, it's doubtful she'll get much rest." Blackie folded his arms over his chest triumphantly.

Momentarily, Shortie returned to go along with them to the store. It wasn't until he rejoined the little group that he noticed their fifth member. Leon Mayhew was a total enigma. Under normal circumstances he was anti-social and rejected their every offer of friendship.

Filing down the steps to the road below, the men walked in silence, each lost in their own worries. About a half block to the north the dirt road led to pavement. Following the paved road to the left led to the store and the Upper Mine. Following to the right led to the city limits of Kellogg. They proceeded left toward the store. The only sound disturbing the silence was the scuffling of boots hitting gravel, which changed to dull thuds upon the pavement. Gabbie's wheezing breaths reminded Shortie of the bellows used by the old blacksmith years ago. The men drew a sense of calm from the beginning promise of a new day.

The fifth among them finally broke the silence. "Does anyone know," Leon asked, "could it have been an earthquake like the old man suggests?"

Gabbie opened his mouth to offer an opinion, but closed it quick at a menacing look from Blackie. "We don't know anything for sure yet," Blackie answered curtly.

"Could it have been dynamite—from up there?" Art nodded his head toward the mine. Keeping his hands in his pockets, Art ducked his head away from Shortie's piercing gaze. Fear gleamed in his eyes like yellow on butter. His eyes darted to the hillsides surrounding them. "I hate this closed-in feeling. It's like we're trapped with no way out," he said to no one in particular.

No one answered him; it was best to ignore such accusations. Not one of them was ready to accuse the mining company who employed ninety percent of the male population. Without the mine's financial support, the entire county would be forced to pack up and leave, and the town would dry up and blow away.

"Morning," Arden called out from the back of the store where he was grinding fresh hamburger for the day. Placing the ground meat in a white enamel tray, he placed it in a refrigerated display case beside two beef roasts, three whole chickens, one roll of bologna, and a large ham. Washing his hands meticulously and donning a clean apron, he made his way to the front where the five men gathered around the wood heater.

Arden, an average-sized man with well-muscled arms and shoulders, moved easily up the narrow aisles. His ever-present white apron hid a beginning paunch, but failed to hide visible signs of physical strength. Most people knew Arden the businessman and believed he was a bit unfriendly, but close personal friends knew Arden was Jewish. World War II was over, but he hadn't recovered from or forgotten the atrocities inflicted on family and friends living overseas. His black hair was cut strictly G.I., and his brown eyes sparkled with good humor.

Extending cold fingertips toward the heat, the five gathered around the little Ben Franklin woodstove. The entire top of the potbellied stove was covered with a huge blue enamelware coffeepot. They watched a cloud of steam rise as the boiling pot spit and spattered coffee all over the stove.

"Get out of the way, let me through," Arden said with a note of disgust as he pushed Gabbie out of the way. Grabbing a potholder off a hook on the wall, he rescued the hot coffee before it boiled away. Holding the pot threateningly, he inquired, "Were you going to wait and see how long it would take for it to boil away or what? Haven't you heard God helps those that help themselves?" He muttered to himself, "And they say a watched pot don't boil."

The men grinned good-naturedly at Arden's scolding. It was one they had all heard before.

Their red-rimmed eyes, tired faces, and worried expressions hadn't gone without notice. Arden opened at five o'clock every morning except Sundays. The phone had been ringing when he opened the doors this morning and had stopped only a few minutes before. Studying them for injuries he might have missed earlier, he silently thanked God there were none.

"Is everything okay with you? Are your families all right? I heard about what happened here on the radio last night. Shortie, you live on that infernal mountain; is everything okay up there?"

"There was a landslide where a retaining wall broke out. Inja was caught in front of it when it broke. Her face was cut pretty bad and...." He couldn't go on.

"Will she be all right?" Arden asked. "We will pray for her recovery." When Arden mentioned praying, Blackie and Art glanced at each other meaningfully. Arden was always spouting stuff like that.

"Ben Schultz brought Doc Smith and he patched her up. The Lord was with her and she'll be okay."

"And what of everyone else here in the valley?" Arden's questioning gaze took in all of them.

"Everyone's okay as far as we know. Except for a few minor damages caused by the shake-up, everything else seems fine," Blackie answered. Art and Gabbie agreed with heads nodding. Leon remained behind—with them, but not a part of them.

Shortie grabbed Gabbie and pushed him to the side as soon as the old man opened his mouth. He glared at him with an injured air and then sauntered to the back of the store. His favorite department in the place was by the cooler where he could ogle the assortment of bottles in the liquor case. Maybe he could borrow a cold beer. His flask was empty and it had been a dry morning.

"Hope you don't mind Arden, but we needed a place to talk and collect our thoughts," explained Shortie. A quick glance at Art was sufficient for the grocer to understand.

"We'll have a cup of coffee and clear our heads," Shortie added for the benefit of Jonesy. No one argued or questioned the suggestion. Art needed time to calm down and collect himself.

"Did you notice anything on your way in from town, anything suspicious? I know it was dark, but something, anything at all?" Shortie's words ended in a whisper as he peered at Arden questioningly.

"The only thing I noticed was the elm tree in the schoolyard. Something knocked her down, and she's lying on her side across the baseball field. I stopped to look things over but all I could see in the dark was a few broken limbs. Elms are hardy; maybe she can be replanted if the roots are sound. But that tree isn't the worst of your problems." Shrugging, the grocer returned to his coffee makings.

Nodding, Shortie pulled up an old apple crate to sit on. Arden opened a cupboard hidden behind the stove and removed five huge cups from its depths. The cups were chipped, cracked, and stained plumb dirt ugly, but held some of the finest coffee in the entire Panhandle. Pouring the steaming brew into each cup, he left room in two of them for milk and sugar.

"Hey Shortie, are you finally going to give up buttermilk and try some of the best brew in town?" Arden joked.

"No, nothing for me." After a moment's thought, "But maybe a bit of that 'hair of the dog that bit ya',' for ole' Art here."

"Got'cha." Grabbing a few bottles off shelves and another large mug, he began mixing one of his famous cure-alls. After the raw egg and Tabasco sauce, Shortie's stomach started a little dance of its own. As a final step, Arden snapped off a celery stalk from the largest bunch on display. Replacing the celery in the vegetable cooler, he positioned it carefully so the missing stalk wouldn't show. Stirring the drink with the celery stalk, he handed it and two aspirin to Jonesy.

"Drink up," he commanded with hands on hips. Shortie couldn't help but laugh at the comical expression on Art's face when the sharp tang of Tabasco and chili powder bit his nose.

A slight tinkling noise from the rear of the store caught their attention. Stiffening, Arden balanced on the balls of his feet, ready to move quickly if he had to. "Old man, get out of my beer cooler before I throw your scurvy hide out the door," he yelled angrily.

Gabbie muttered to himself as he stuffed two quart bottles of beer into the deep side pockets of his overalls, "Man's got ears like a rabbit and eyes in back of his head. Always hearin' and seein' things that aren't there. Who does he think he is, not trustin' a God fearin', ri'spict'able citizen like myself? I'm just borrowin' and will bring it back—maybe tomorrow."

"What's that you're going on about back there, Gabbie? Get your hand caught in the cookie jar again?" Blackie teased with a conspiratorial wink at the others.

As he joined them around the stove, a slight clinking came from one of his pockets. With a knowing smirk, Arden retrieved a bottle from one side pocket, and curling his lip into a sneer, returned it to the cooler.

With another injured look and slow blink of the eyes, Gabbie accepted the mug of coffee prepared for him, sweet and syrupy with lots of sugar and milk. An expression of pure innocence crossed his face as he slurped loudly while contentedly drinking his coffee. Smacking and slurping just to be annoying, he continued until they all fixed him with a threatening glare. It was enough to put an end to the slurps and smacks.

Arden came from the dairy cooler with a pint of pure buttermilk for Shortie.

"I figure there's something wrong with a man who don't drink beer, don't drink coffee, and don't cuss. But when man favors buttermilk over just plain milk, well, it's just not natural," Blackie said with contempt. Making a face, he shivered with distaste.

Grins creased faces as Shortie downed his drink. Wiping his lips with the back of one hand, he licked the remaining drops off the glass rim unselfconsciously. It was cold and thick and just the right thing to take the edge off his hunger. The only thing it lacked was pepper.

Taking the empty glass, Arden returned to the butcher's block.

"Put the cups on the counter when you're through. I've got to get back to work," he ordered.

Dumping the glass into the galvanized sink behind the meat counter, Arden mumbled to himself, "Drinks buttermilk and actually likes liver." Eyeing a fresh beef liver, he quickly wrapped it in paper. There was something about the stuff that made him gag.

Peeking over the meat case, his eyes narrowed, piercing the silent one of the group in an icy glare. "Why is he hanging around?" he wondered. "He doesn't belong with them," he reasoned to himself. "Talk about trouble, you're looking at him." No sooner had the thought crossed his mind when Leon's dark eyes stared penetratingly back at him.

Smiling contemptuously, Leon made a subtle movement with his left hand that went unnoticed by everyone except Arden. His jaw dropped in surprise and warning bells rang in his head. Reeling from shock, his muscles tensed involuntarily. He ached to grab the dark-haired man and beat him senseless. Glancing away quickly, he stepped into the meat freezer to cool off. "The German victory sign," he sighed, "so that's the way of it."

Inside the freezer his breath made vapor clouds. He was shivering violently before he allowed himself to exit. Hefting a quarter side of beef to be cut and wrapped, he glimpsed Leon's profile out of the corner of his eye. Setting the meat on the butcher's block, he studied the man across the room.

Leon sat on a makeshift seat made from a board placed over a barrel and appeared to be enjoying the company of the other four. But there was something about the way he smiled, like a snake ready to strike. When Leon's gaze rested upon Shortie's profile, Arden's blood ran cold. The expression of malice spoke volumes.

As the others talked among themselves, Shortie grew impatient to return home. Not wanting to draw any unnecessary attention, he left by the rear exit.

"Goin' home?" Arden asked.

"I've been gone too long already." He didn't stop to talk, but opened the door anxious to leave.

"Me and the Mrs., we'll be praying for you and your family. Keep your eyes and ears open, though, would you?" Arden asked.

"Yeah, sure," was Shortie's parting comment. Shutting the heavy metal door firmly behind him, he blinked with surprise. Bright sunlight flooded the valley bringing a startled sound to his lips. A quick glance at his watch put his fears to rest.

"Thank heavens," he said to himself. "It's only been an hour." Taking off at a rapid pace, he left the store without a backward glance.

Most people believed Shortie walked faster than most could run, but he broke his own record as he covered the distance from the store to the dirt road leading up the hill to his home. As he sped along, his mind busily calculated the cost and needed manpower to repair any damages he spied. There wasn't a great lot of it, but enough to keep several men busy for more than a few days. Eyeing one of the jagged peaks above him, a shiver ran up his spine. There was more than enough reason for a man to feel plenty nervous about the possibility of a mountain falling on his head.

Chapter 4

Sipping steaming cups of coffee, the four men remaining at the store hadn't noticed Shortie's absence. Gabbie rocked contentedly in a rocking chair, drinking his coffee with tiny little sips, relishing each drop. Puffing away on one of his roll-your-owns, he wasn't anxious to do much of anything.

Blackie thought the scrawny old man was being awfully quiet and became even more suspicious when he didn't butt into the conversation even once. Leaning back in the only chair sturdy enough to support the bulk of his six-foot-four-inch frame, he studied the older man surreptitiously.

The hat on his head was the same one he always wore. Faded and grimy, the baseball cap covered a full head of coal, black hair. Gabbie was proud of his hair. There wasn't a single strand of white or gray hair visible in the whole lot of it. Rarely combed, it hung about his head in straight, unkempt strings when left unfettered by the cap. His lined face was one of those crazy road maps where you couldn't find a starting or an ending, just a myriad of wrinkles scarring his features with time. Black eyes peered from hollow sockets offset by a nut-brown complexion. His entire face sank into a toothless pucker where his lips disappeared, and his chin, if he had one, was buried beneath a thick black beard. It was hard to estimate the old man's age, but he was seventy if he was a day. Scrawny and bow-spined, he gave the appearance of being a helpless old man, but Blackie knew better. The old curmudgeon was as contentious as a she-bear in spring and as sly as a fox.

Eyeing Gabbie over the rim of his coffee cup, Blackie searched the older man's spare frame for telltale signs of a stashed bottle. His ears had heard the unmistakable clink of two bottles bumping against each other. Spying a lump in the old man's left side pocket, he chuckled to himself. Sitting forward with elbows on his knees, he looked around for Shortie.

"Did Shortie sneak out the back door, Arden?"

"He left over thirty minutes ago. While you bums were slurping down all my coffee, Shortie had things to do and wasn't going to waste any more time getting to them," Arden snapped.

"Okay, okay, don't get your apron all in a wad. I can take a hint as well as anybody. Just give me a minute to wake up ole' Art here. Seems the remedy you mixed for him worked so well it put him right out."

Nudging Art's chair with the toe of his boot, Blackie tried to rouse him.

"It's gonna' take more n' a little tap to wake him. He's gonna' have ta' sleep this one off," Gabbie cackled.

"Guess I'll be goin', no one here to talk to anyways." Placing his dirty cup on the floor, Gabbie hauled himself from the chair. Stretching, his chin dropped in a huge yawn. "Yup, no one here abouts ta' talk to," he repeated.

Glancing furtively at Blackie, he hoped to get a rise out of him.

"I'm leaving too, old man, and you're right—there is no one here worth talking to," Blackie responded. His pointed remark didn't fall on deaf ears. Sniffing with feigned affront, Gabbie wiped his nose with a dirty rag dug from a hind pocket. His dark eyes blazed and his mouth opened for a final scathing retort when he was interrupted. They turned simultaneously when the bell above the door jangled.

"I thought I'd find you here," a feminine voice said. Sighing with exasperation, Art's wife Ellen marched in. There was a determined look on her face, and her straight brown hair bounced with each angry step. Shaking Art roughly by the shoulder, she almost knocked him to the floor. Snuffling and snorting, he twisted away from her grasp without waking. Art had been known to sleep through everything from baby's crying to heavy machinery, even when working right next to him.

"He's out for the rest of the day," Blackie said. He studied her reaction guardedly. The last thing he wanted was to end up in the middle of an argument. Ellen's mouth tightened to a grim line, and her narrow shoulders drooped with resignation. It wasn't easy being married to the town drunk.

"I'm sure Bert will be real proud of you for sitting here all day drinking coffee instead of doing something to make sure this never happens again." Her voice was high, on the verge of hysteria. Blackie understood the fear and frustration she felt. After the events of the night before, she needed her husband's shoulder to lean on. She needed to lash out at someone, and he was the only one available.

"Don't get so uptight, Ellen," Blackie interjected. He wanted her to calm down before she said more than she wanted to. She had good reason to be upset, but he wouldn't take a lecture really intended for Art. "Bert's fine and wasn't any the worse for wear when I left the house this morning. In fact, I planned on asking her to look in on Inja this morning. We didn't get more than a little shake-up in comparison to what they went through on the mountain." The expression of anger left Ellen's face immediately and was replaced by concern. The exact response he hoped for.

"Oh my gosh, I've been such a wreck since this happened I haven't given a moment's thought to anyone else. Are they all right?"

"Inja was hurt," Gabbie interrupted. He didn't wait for the big man to continue, but took over the conversation. He vividly described the events of the night before with wide sweeps of his hands and loud pounding on the countertop. Ellen's brown eyes grew round with shock.

"I'd better get Art home in a hurry and then go see if there's anything I can do. Oh my gosh, poor Inja," she sympathized. Placing an arm under Art's armpit, she tried pulling her husband to a standing position. Art was skinny, but twice her height. Sagging under his weight, she almost sank to the floor.

"Let me help," Blackie said as he shouldered Art's weight away from Ellen. A whiff of Art's breath about knocked him off his feet. "No wonder he's not waking up; he's drunker than a brew's fart." Chuckling, he hefted Art over his shoulder and forced himself to choke back laughter. "Quit drinking, huh? Going to turn a new leaf and become a coffee drinker, huh?" he muttered. "The only thing you've changed is the brand of whiskey you're drinking, and whatever it is, it's pure rot-gut." Wrinkling up his nose, he hauled Art out to the waiting pick-up truck that was the Jones's only means of transportation.

Leaning him against the door panel, he played the gentleman by opening the driver's side for Ellen. Holding Art's weight with one arm, he slammed the door closed. Lifting the drunken man over his shoulder, he dumped him unceremoniously onto the seat next to Ellen. She turned the key, and the engine whined and then died.

"Take it easy," he encouraged, "and this old beater will start. Try it again, only this time hold the gas pedal to the floor until the engine takes hold."

Following his advice, the engine caught and sputtered to life. His I-told-you-so look wasn't lost on Ellen.

"And for your information, Mr. Blackie Clegg, my husband has quit drinking. If you smell anything at all, it's that old man you hang around with." Sniffing haughtily, she jammed her foot into the gas pedal. To her surprise, however, the truck didn't speed off with a roar. Instead, the engine raced and the vibration rocked the truck so hard, Blackie was scared unnecessary parts like fly wheels, carburetors, or pistons would come flying off to strike him in the head. Art bounced around inside the cab until he finally fell over. He dropped into Ellen's lap, where his head painfully hit her knee, causing her leg to jerk involuntarily. The clutch popped and the truck took off in a screaming roar of noxious black fumes. Waving his arms around futilely to clear the air, Blackie caught sight of Gabbie pointing and laughing so hard he gasped for breath at every wheeze.

He hooted like an owl, his mouth gaped wide exposing the few black teeth he had. Pointing at Blackie's mottled face, the old man's wheezy guffaws were quickly followed by snorts and gasps. Clearing his throat rudely, he let fly a black gob of phlegm. Chuckling once more, he wiped his mouth with a grimy hand and then turned to slouch off down the road. Eyeing the sickening mass of spittle made Blackie's stomach roll.

"You're a disgusting old man, do you know that?" Blackie yelled.

Grinning slyly, Gabbie responded with a rude gesture. He was rewarded with a comical expression that flashed across the younger man's face. Black eyebrows shot up and became hidden under the shock of blue-black hair that hung over his forehead. Stuffing his hands in his pockets, Gabbie shuffled off, whistling a nameless tune.

Not to be bested, Blackie grinned maliciously. "Hey, old man, what'cha got in your pocket?"

Turning around, Gabbie asked with exaggerated innocence, "What pocket are ya' talkin' 'bout?" Trying hard to appear virtuous, he dug into a hip pocket. "I don't have a blamed thing exceptin' my hankie." Wiping his nose daintily with the filthy scrap of cloth, he blew his nose before returning it to the pocket.

"I didn't mean that pocket," the big man teased. Grabbing up a nice-sized rock, he tossed it with perfect aim at the lump in the old man's left side pocket. His grin broadened in delight as the satisfying sound of tinkling glass sounded in his ears. Gabbie's saintly appearance dissolved immediately. Stunned disbelief etched his features as moisture spread down his legs.

"I meant that one," Blackie taunted.

Holding the soaked pant leg away from his body, he shook his leg like a cat. Glaring daggers, he turned on his heel toward home. Blackie's howls followed him all the way down the hill. Stopping every few steps to shake the wet away, he was appalled to find the moisture spreading across the front of his overalls. Staring at the wet stain across his front and down his legs, he wondered how he'd explain this to anyone that might notice. He knew what it looked like, and furthermore knew most people wouldn't believe the truth. Plotting ways to get even, he entered his own front door.

Still chuckling to himself, Blackie spotted Leon leaving the store by the rear exit. Chucking another stone, he struck Leon in the middle of the back. Pivoting on one foot, Leon faced the big dark-headed Irishman with a forced smile.

"Are you wanting something, or is throwing rocks your only means of getting attention?" Leon's voice dripped with sarcasm.

Blackie never claimed to have patience, and the tone of Leon's voice was enough to light his short fuse. Stepping close to the smaller man, he stood over him threateningly. His light green eyes flashed steel gray with warning, and his ruddy complexion turned a dark shade of red. His gaze raked Leon with contempt, his voice thick with insinuation.

"You've been taking a few walks lately that don't lead to home. You stay away from where you don't belong or I might have to think up a reminder you can't ignore," Blackie warned.

"You been spying on me, Irish?" Leon asked. "It's a free country and a man's got a right to go where he wants." As he faced Blackie eye-to-eye, the flame of bravado died.

In a voice thick with hate, Blackie replied in an unnaturally soft voice, "If you don't stop following the wrong paths, maybe your legs won't work so good, and maybe your face won't be so pretty." Flicking a stray hair off Leon's forehead, Blackie asked, "Any questions?"

"Not at this time," Leon sneered, "but if I ever do, I'll be sure to look you up."

"Good! I think we understand each other perfectly. You stay away from other men's wives and we won't have this little conversation again." Backing away, Blackie spun around and followed Gabbie down the hill.

Leon's courageous front deflated as Blackie's threat echoed in his head. He never planned on nor wanted problems with the big Irishman. He'd wanted a fling, a little fun, but this changed things entirely. Glancing warily to the right and then left, he skulked off on shaky legs.

Chapter 5

Shortie hadn't gotten far from the store when he met up with Tony Martinez. Tony was twenty years Shortie's junior and a good friend. His black hair, dark skin and thick-lashed almond eyes had made more than one woman's heart thump as he gazed soulfully at them. Women couldn't resist his exotic good looks. He was of average height, slender, but with surprisingly broad shoulders and biceps that strained the fabric of his shirts. Turning his sunny smile in Shortie's direction, he clapped him on the shoulder with one hand and clasped the other in greeting.

"I have come to help you, my friend. I would have been here sooner, but Maria wouldn't let me leave. Since she has been pregnant with this child, she is spooked easily," he explained. "But there is much to be done to make your home safe again, and we must also replant the tree in the schoolyard for the children."

"I'm not worried about any tree right now. That's the least of my problems. Thanks for the offer of help, but the only thing I'm going to do right now is get home and see to my family."

"*Si*, Doc told me about Inja. She will be okay, right?"

"Yes, she'll heal, but in the meantime she'll be needing me there to help her." Shaking his head, Shortie rubbed the back of his neck tiredly, clearly at a loss. "I'll need someone to stay with her while I'm at work. Maybe I can get Bert to look in on her."

"You won't need to worry. Everything has been worked out so Inja won't be left alone." Turning to head back down the road, Tony grinned at Shortie, "Since you aren't accepting my offer of help now, maybe you'll join us later? We will be at the school."

Shortie gave a curt nod, and after making arrangements to meet later in the afternoon, he made a hasty farewell. Following the path up the hill to the road running below his house, he felt a familiar ache in his heart.

"A third child," he thought enviously. "No," he decided with a sigh, "I will not give myself an opportunity to dwell on our childless situation. Inja's right, I've been rushing her into starting a family. I need to be more patien.."

Rapid strides brought him home in record time. Catching his breath, he entered through the front door, listening for a moment to the quiet. He didn't want to disturb the stillness, so he tiptoed to the tiny hallway leading to the bathroom and both bedrooms. Peeking into both rooms put his fears to rest. Eddie still slept soundly and Inja purred softly into her pillow. The tension in his body eased and he exhaled with relief.

"Reprieve. She's still sleeping, which I hope is a good sign." Crossing his fingers, he shut her door, being careful to stop the latch from clicking.

He stirred up the last embers of the night fire and added a few sticks of kindling, and a hot fire soon blazed so breakfast could be prepared. He moved comfortably about the kitchen, and the fixings for a meal were quickly assembled. Methodically, bacon, eggs, salt and pepper, bread, butter, and coffee were removed from their places. Realizing that his steps returned repeatedly to the window overlooking the backyard, he took a moment to assess the damage. The underground cellar had swallowed the clothesline posts, and a small hill of rock and debris covered the area where the door had been. His stomach contracted painfully as his mind replayed the scenes of the night before. Feeling nauseous, he gripped the edge of the sink until the sickening sensation passed. Dropping into a chair, he rubbed the back of his neck in a characteristic gesture. Closing his eyes, he took a moment to thank God for His protection and to plead for guidance.

"Father," he prayed, "if ever there was a time when I needed your strength, it is now."

An immediate sense of serenity filled his heart. Feeling refreshed and at peace, hunger pangs replaced the nausea of moments before. Getting to his feet, he started coffee for Inja before cutting a fresh slab of bacon into thick slices. Placing it into a cast iron skillet, he browned the bacon slowly at the lower heat found to the rear of the Monarch woodstove. As the meat fried, sending off a savory aroma that tickled his nostrils, he softly whistled a favorite hymn. Two potatoes were expertly pared and diced for hash browns. They were thrown into a second skillet greased with bacon fat. The little kitchen was soon filled with the enticing odors of fried bacon and potatoes, boiled coffee, and fresh oven toast. He wasn't surprised to see Eddie standing in the doorway, sniffing appreciatively.

"Smells good," he said. Rubbing sleep from his eyes, he stifled a huge yawn. Appearing none the worse for wear after last night's scare, he grinned impishly and hopped into the bathroom on one foot.

Setting the table for two, Shortie checked on his sleeping wife once again. Her position was unchanged, which alarmed him for a moment, but her pulse was strong and regular and her breathing slow and even. She sleepily swatted him away like an annoying fly. He planted a kiss on her forehead before leaving the room.

Eddie sat at the table, waiting patiently for his return. He proudly displayed a freshly scrubbed face and hair combed neatly on both sides. Greeting the boy, Shortie ruffled up his hair, making it stand out in all directions so it matched the hair on the back of his head. Filling a plate with enough eggs and bacon to fill the stomachs of two growing boys, he plopped it down in front of him. The boy dug into the food with relish, being careful not to eat too fast or to gulp his milk.

Filling his own plate to the point of overflowing, Shortie ate with heaping forkfuls. The two ate without speaking, concentrating on filling empty stomachs. Swallowing the last bites of breakfast down with icy cold milk, they both leaned back in their chairs with contentment. An embarrassed expression crossed Eddie's face when a burp escaped his lips.

"Excuse me," he quickly said. Covering his mouth, he glanced at Shortie guiltily.

"In some countries, a burp is a compliment to the cook, and I enjoy my own cooking," Shortie bragged. His deliberate belch of satisfaction was much louder and sent the boy into gales of laughter. Grinning at each other conspiratorially, they froze when the bedroom door squeaked open.

Eddie's chin dropped, staring in disbelief. Shortie thought he'd seen the worst, but was unprepared for the horrible swelling and discoloration around and under Inja's left eye. Her left side had been buried in pillows and blankets and hidden from his earlier inspections. She was bruised and swollen to the point of being unrecognizable. As he struggled to maintain a sense of normalcy, an involuntary pained expression creased his forehead. The look of alarm on his face was all it took to send Inja limping to the bathroom. Unconsciously, Eddie covered his ears with his hands. Shortie's stomach contracted, and his breakfast rose warningly in his throat. Inja's reaction was quick in coming. A high-pitched, earsplitting scream of shock filled every corner of the house. For a split second, all was silent except for the crackle of the fire and the tick of the clock on the wall. Shrill screams filled the house again, sending Eddie to hide under the front porch, before they tapered off into muffled sobs. The short hairs on the back of Shortie's neck tingled.

Entering the bathroom, he found her staring in the mirror. Tears dripped from swollen eyes and dampened the front of her nightgown. Gripping her shoulders firmly but gently, he turned her away from the mirror and helped her into the kitchen to a chair.

"Inja, remember what Doc Smith told you last night? Your face will heal and you'll be just as beautiful as ever. You'll be okay, I promise," he explained in a calm, consoling voice. Placing a cool, damp cloth over her swollen eyes, he talked to her until she sat quietly. Taking a washrag, he carefully wiped away every trace of medication administered the night before. Her skin was stretched painfully over the cheekbones and the lower jaw, and it distorted her face grotesquely. Inspecting Doc Smith's stitches, he was satisfied they hadn't pulled apart.

"Why me?" she whispered. "My face...oh, Shortie," she moaned. Struggling to clear the vision in her right eye, she tried to force the swollen lid to open. "What can I do about my face?" Her hands tightened into fists and she pounded the arms of the chair in helpless anger.

"The first thing you've got to do is quit your crying. It only complicates things. Doc left plenty of medication plus something extra for pain if you need it. You've got to help me to help you recover." Silence weighed heavy between them for a few moments. Shortie felt the weight of guilt. It pressed upon him until he was unable to tolerate the quiet any longer. "Inja, you've got know how much I wish it had been me instead of you." His eyes filled with sympathy. He felt personally responsible for her injuries.

"Maybe I am," he thought accusingly. "How many times has she wanted to move off this mountain? How many times has she begged to leave this place?"

Unexplainable emotion filled his heart as he spread the medicated ointment over his wife's face. Kissing the knee of her left leg, he rewrapped the ankle. Kneeling beside her, he prayed for her to understand how badly he felt.

"I'm so sorry," he said. He gazed sorrowfully into her upturned face. "I'd do anything to change what happened. If I had listened to you, this wouldn't have happened. You asked me to get the clothes off the line, but I refused. It should have been me, not you."

"Leave me alone unless you can fix my face," she ordered. Her bruised and swollen lips made talking difficult. Pushing him away with her uninjured foot, she turned to face the wall with arms folded across her chest in a defiant pose. A pained expression crossed his face, but he couldn't allow her antagonistic behavior to stop him from what he had to do. She was in pain and he wanted nothing more than to take it all away. Daubing more ointment on the tender area beneath her left eye, he spread it gently over the stitches.

"What is that stuff you're torturing me with?" she snapped. Needing to vent her fear and anger, she took it out on him. "It makes my face feel hot and sticky; it's almost better without it."

"This is the medication Doc Smith prescribed, and if you remember correctly, it's meant to speed healing. It may feel warm for a short while, but that will fade. He said if we medicate your face several times a day, you'll heal much faster," he explained, his voice wooden from exhaustion. Searching her expression for a sign of acceptance, he spread the remaining ointment over her cheeks. He felt her one-eyed gaze sear his skin with condemnation. Forcing a smile to curve his lips, he put on a jovial attitude.

"There, the hard part's done. Now, if you'll allow me to carry you to your throne," he invited, "I'll fix madam breakfast." She acquiesced reluctantly, allowing him to carry her to the couch. Smiling and humming to himself, he plumped up pillows to support her head and shoulders. Finding her agreeable to his efforts, he placed two more pillows under her bandaged ankle. Wrapping a quilt around her body, he made her as comfortable as possible. Eddie was instructed to turn the radio to her favorite station.

"Now, what would madam care to eat, and don't tell me you're not hungry. You haven't eaten since yesterday morning."

"I don't care about eating," she pouted, "and quit calling me madam. How am I supposed to eat anything with my mouth almost swollen shut?"

"How about milk toast?" he teased, knowing she hated the stuff. A pillow smacked him in the face. A barely discernible smile crooked one side of her mouth. "Okay, maybe milk toast isn't the best choice. How about eggs and toast?"

Remaining unresponsive, Inja wriggled into the bedding comfortably. She enjoyed the extra attention and didn't plan on recovering any time soon.

Hiding a knowing smile, Shortie placed the pillow behind her head then returned to the kitchen. He prepared her favorite breakfast of scrambled eggs, bacon, and toast.

Eddie helped by digging the turkey platter out of the cupboard and fixing it up as a serving tray. Covering it with a fresh tea towel, he placed a bouquet of wild lilac in the center. Shining the silverware on the seat of his pants, he placed it neatly on a napkin and then presented the tray to Shortie. He waited anxiously for approval.

"That's just what was needed. I was wondering how to serve Inja her breakfast and you've solved the problem. What a great idea and fixed up real pretty, too. Inja will be sure to enjoy these flowers, and I'm sure they are her favorite," he praised. "By the way, where did you find them? I didn't think flowers would be in bloom yet."

"Right out there," Eddie pointed behind the house. Sure enough, the wild lilac bush was in full blossom with huge blooms of purple and white on the same stems.

"Well I'll be," he marveled. They'd lived on the place for two years and this was the first time he'd seen the little bush in flower.

They filled the tray with a plate of food, a glass of milk, and a cup of hot coffee and then served it with great ceremony. Grinning from ear to ear, they stepped back and waited for her reaction.

"How am I supposed to eat this stuff?" she slurred. "It looks nice, but what do you expect me to do with it?"

Crestfallen, Shortie took the tray and Eddie reached to remove the flowers. Inja put a hand on his arm to stop him.

"I love the lilacs; they smell so sweet." Eddie's smile returned and he beamed gratefully at his sister.

"Put that tray back down here and find me a straw. I need my coffee. Maybe if I take real little bites, I could try some of those eggs. I'll need to eat a little something to keep up my strength, you know."

A half-smile lit Shortie's face as he cleaned the kitchen and made beds. Feeling confident for a complete recovery, he was surprised to hear a loud thump. Hurrying to the front room, he found her with arms crossed angrily over her chest. An empty coffee cup lay on the floor.

"I can't read, my eyes are too swollen to see and all that's on the radio is news." Alligator tears of self-pity gathered on her lashes. "I wish we could afford a television set," she hinted plaintively. "How will I keep myself from going insane when I'm left here for hours on end while you're at work and Eddie's at school?" she moaned.

Her question was answered immediately. Shortie had no sooner opened his mouth to respond than a short rap resounded on the screen door. Four woman stood on the porch, all talking excitedly and pointing across the porch to the buried yard. Knocking on the screen door again, they entered without invitation.

Bertie Clegg, Blackie's wife, led the way, carrying a huge cake tin. "I hope you like coffeecake," she commented to Shortie as she breezed by. Her frizzy hair stood out from her head like a red Brillo pad. Her hair matched her ginger skin perfectly. Built like a wrestler, she moved heavily on moccasin-clad feet. Her well-muscled arms showed biceps with real definition when she flexed or moved her arms just so. There was little about Bert that could be called gracefully feminine except her soft heart and taste in shoes. She loved beaded moccasins and patent leather pumps with bows. She loved most people, had a soft spot for all children, and was always the first to offer assistance to anyone in need. Shortie was very fond of her because she was the first to come visit the day they moved in. She had welcomed them with a casserole in one hand and home-baked rolls in the other. Ellen Jones, Art's wife, followed Bertie into the kitchen.

"Art's not feeling well today. A real case of nerves after last night," she confided, "but all the guys are meeting a bit later. You'd better go and keep them out of trouble. And while you're at it, see if you can get my lazy husband out of bed." Commandeering the coffeepot, she made a fresh pot and set out plates and forks for serving the cake.

Bert stuffed the firebox full and motioned that he'd better chop more wood. The last to enter was Maria, Tony's wife, and Holly Mayhew, Leon's wife. Maria, looking very pregnant, was wearing a dainty pink maternity smock that offset her long black hair and brown skin. Her almond eyes, framed by a fringe of heavy lashes, were her best asset. She was a beautiful woman in every sense of the word.

Holly looked out of place sitting in Shortie's front room but gave every indication of having been there before. Full-figured with a tendency toward fat, she wore bright-colored dresses that were too short and too tight. She was a peroxide blonde, and her heavily lacquered hair was always worn swept up into a fancy French roll with huge spit curls glued to either side of her face. Her lipstick was too red, her mascara too thick, and her perfume usually too strong. He didn't care for her loud voice or unladylike jokes, but was glad she came with the others. Inja was quite fond of her.

Gratefulness filled his heart as the women gathered around his wife. Sitting on kitchen chairs or cushions, they settled themselves for a long afternoon. They would fill Inja's need to be fussed over and pampered.

Trying to break in on their conversation, he tried to get their attention. They turned deaf ears to his inquiries. Figuring he had no other alternative, he pulled Bert out of her chair and into the kitchen. Taking a deep breath, he prepared himself for the inevitable. Bert's huge arms wrapped around him as she greeted him with a bear hug.

"You'd better get a move on," she boomed. "Blackie's already filled me in, and you're supposed to meet him at the school." In a softer voice, she added, "And don't worry about anything here. Inja's in good hands."

Spying Eddie as he tried to sneak out the back door, she stepped in front of him to bar his exit. Snatching him by the scruff of the neck, she held him in a bone-jarring hug. He had no choice but to submit to being smothered into her ample bosom. Holding him out by his shirt collar, she handed Eddie to Shortie. The child, totally humiliated by Bert's exuberant greeting, flushed three shades of scarlet at being held aloft like a chicken on display.

"Take the boy with you. There's no reason why he should hang around a bunch of women all day. Let him go and work with the men. I'm sure there's something a little tadpole like him could do."

"Can I? I mean, could I really go and help?" Eddie asked hopefully.

Bert escorted the two out the door and winked at Eddie as she turned back inside. "Chocolate cake for dessert and fried chicken for supper," she promised. "I expect that will fill the stomachs of two hungry men, don't you?"

Eddie nodded, firmed his chin, and jutted out his chest. He stretched his step to match Shortie's, and they walked down the hill hand in hand.

Chapter 6

Bert rejoined the women in the tiny living room. A thick layer of dust lay over everything. Her fingertips detected the gritty feel of ground rock on the coffee table, and the little oval throw rug in front of the couch was dingy with muddy footprints. The window ledges were filled with the same brownish-gray soil that filled the nearby yard. Studying Inja from across the room, she figured it would be several days, maybe even weeks, before she would be capable of doing a thorough housecleaning. Her tender heart twisted with sympathy when tears gathered in Inja's one good eye.

"Stop that crying. You'll only make yourself feel worse," she sniffled. Plumping the pillows under the younger woman's head, she fussed unnecessarily. "Poor little thing, all beat up and almost blind. I don't want you to worry about a thing except getting yourself well. I'm going to see to things around here personally." Turning to face them all, she nailed them with a fleeting glare from her squinty eye.

"We'll all help get this place cleaned up, won't we, girls?" Even if they disagreed, not one of them dared object. When Bertie looked at one down her long, straight nose with her squinty left eye flashing green ice—beware. The women all liked Bertie—in fact were indebted to her—but were admittedly scared to death of her Irish temper. She wasn't like any other woman they'd ever known. She was stronger than most men, barrel-bodied with tattoos across both biceps. She also sported a tattoo across her left breast that she had secretly shown to Inja and Ellen once. She spoke her mind and didn't appear to fear anyone. Bert and her husband Blackie were well suited. She complemented his rugged good looks.

"Where did you meet your husband?" Ellen had asked once in conversation.

"I met Blackie in an underground wrestling arena in old Seattle," she'd boasted. "I married him because he was the only man big enough to pin me. I guess you could say he won me fair and square." Bert laughed at the shocked reaction of her listener.

Pulling up a chair, she planted herself beside Inja. Accepting a cup of coffee, she sipped daintily while balancing a cake plate on her knees.

"Who's going to stay and help take care of her while Shortie's at work?" Ellen, always the most practical, liked having things planned out in advance. She hated anything that hinted of spur-of-the-moment.

"I'm going to be right here," Bert spoke up. "No one will come through that door unless they get an invite from me. She'll need her rest, and I plan on being around until she's all healed up and as good as new."

Eyebrows raised in surprise. Holly, looking insulted, placed her empty coffee cup on the kitchen table and left in a huff. The only one disappointed was Inja.

"You're such a good person," Ellen said as she hugged Bert's broad shoulders. "If you're here keeping an eye on things, we won't have to worry about Shortie or Eddie either. I know you'll take good care of them."

Inja didn't comment. She wasn't exactly pleased that Bertie Clegg had volunteered to be her nurse. Closing her eyes, she resigned herself to a long, boring recovery.

Over the next few days a steady stream of well-wishers came to visit at the Busch home. News of their misfortune spread quickly throughout the valley, and presiding over everything was Bertie Clegg. She saw to Inja's every need, but also limited her callers and the time allowed for visitation. She issued orders freely to everyone, including Shortie. Women of the community did their share by preparing meals, which they brought with them on their daily visits. Soon the kitchen and tiny pantry was filled with casseroles, roasts, cakes, cookies, pies, and fresh baked bread. Arden, from the store, generously delivered a huge ham dinner complete with all the trimmings.

While Shortie and Eddie filled their stomachs with a rich variety of food, Inja was filled with an outpouring of neighborly love and all the gossip she could stand. Shortie's heart was filled to overflowing, and he was overcome with God's goodness. His thankfulness was voiced through prayer, humming, or whistling favorite hymns. Inja thought his whistling was especially annoying and would cover her ears with pillows when it began. Through it all, Bert sat back with a self-satisfied smile. Under the heavy mask of salve on Inja's face, her skin was healing. The only flaw on her pretty face would be a tiny scar under her left eye.

The next few days were filled with activity, keeping Shortie and the other men busy. He never worried about Inja. Bert appeared on their doorstep every morning promptly at five o'clock, and as he went out the door to go to work, she came in. She cared for Inja, cleaned the house, prepared meals, did the laundry, and watched over Eddie. While Bert played nursemaid, Shortie's time was freed up to complete the repairs that required immediate attention.

The elm tree in the schoolyard had been replanted and seemed to be thriving after its uprooting. Confident they could fix almost anything, the men tackled the next job on their list. Retaining walls that fell, split, or were weakened with stress cracks had to be replaced. Homes built closest to the mountains, or in Shortie's case on the mountain, needed the walls to hold back sloughing rock and debris during spring run-offs. They also provided protection against snowslides in winter. The walls, built from massive rock or logs trucked in from up the river, usually worked well. They couldn't, however, hold back several tons of rock and dirt spilling down the mountain at a high rate of speed. There were four major breakouts, a direct result of the unexpected explosion. They were lucky. All the work would be completed with just a few days hard work. The worst area was to the side of Shortie's home.

"I'll need to rebuild that entire wall," Shortie explained to Blackie. Art, Tony, and Gabbie joined them on the main road as they stood with fingers pointed to the hillside by Shortie's place. They looked above them to the rock wall that ran parallel to the mountainside. Shortie drew an imaginary line along the wall from a stress point to a heap of debris to the left of the house. Splintered timber shafts pointed skyward from the log wall that had split in half.

"Your place certainly got the worst of it. Aren't you afraid of another cave-in or landslide?"

"Nope," Shortie replied with a shake of his head. "That stuff's pretty solid. I braced it securely with the butt of an old stump. This rocky soil dries fast with these nice warm days and it set up hard, almost like cement. It'll hold 'til I can get to it. And if you're worried about Bert, they're both fine. Even though it doesn't look like it from here, the breakout isn't behind the house."

Heads turned to the little house that appeared minuscule beside a mountain of dirt. The little place stood out incongruously not only because of size, but because the mountain had spit out a portion of its bulk into his tiny yard. The scene above their heads emanated a sense of menace. Involuntary shivers ran up their backs as they returned to work.

"You're not planning on doing all that alone are you?" Blackie faced

Shortie with legs spread wide and hands at his hips. His coloring went three shades darker as he glared with eyes steel gray. He didn't like rejection in any form. "We," he swept his hands over the entire group, "are going to help rebuild that wall. It's too much for one man to do alone." Heads nodded in support of the big man's words with one exception. Gabbie liked being involved until anything that hinted of work was mentioned.

"The repairs at my place will be completed by yours truly," Shortie said, jabbing a thumb at himself. "Inja needs rest, not a bunch of guys tracking in and out of the house making noise." Blackie spit out the side of his mouth.

"We ain't going for a social call," he growled indignantly. His eyes narrowed and his nostrils flared as he stared coldly into Shortie's face.

Shortie didn't flinch or look away from Blackie's threatening façade. "I appreciate your concern, but please try to respect mine." His blue eyes turned suddenly icy.

"Okay, okay." Tony came forward with forced joviality. "You both win! You're both proud and hardheaded. Now can we all shake and be friends?" His handsome face split into a grin as he clapped both Blackie and Shortie on the back. "Now remember, children," he teased, "if we can't say something nice, we don't say anything at all." He tilted his head back, squinted at them both and strutted around like a rooster, imitating Blackie's threatening pose. His comical antics relieved the tension, and sheepish smiles soon replaced anger.

Shortie was the first to apologize. His calloused hands spread in a placatory gesture. "I appreciate your concern, but...I won't, I mean I can't take any chances up there."

"I empathize with you and understand your concerns, but you can't shovel a mountainside back by yourself," Blackie stated with an emphatic flourish. "We'll help whether you like it or not."

"I can use all the extra dirt to fill the cellar in. If I keep at it, I can have it finished in just a few days." Shortie's chin jutted out in a familiar gesture that spoke for itself. His decision was final, but so was Blackie's. German stubborn met with Irish determination in a "no-win" match of will. Finally, Shortie turned away with a derisive snort. Grabbing his shovel, he put action to his words.

Shaking his head in disgusted admiration, Blackie whispered loudly to Art, "Don't he take the cake for a hard-headed, stubborn old mule?"

Art didn't want to appear disloyal, so remained silent. Taking up his shovel, he followed after Shortie to do his share, but not without occasional nervous glances up the mountain.

Leon stood to the rear of the little group that surrounded Shortie. When the big Irishman and the drunk began speaking in hushed tones, he stepped forward with a disinterested look on his face. Moving cautiously toward the two, he kept his ears open to hear what he could hear.

Catching a flash of movement from behind him, Blackie turned to face Leon with a mocking grin. His right hand clenched into a fist and his eyes turned smoky.

"You want something?" he asked. The smaller man backed off with cool indifference.

"What was that all about?" Shortie asked Tony.

"Who's to say? Maybe it's the weather, or maybe our big friend doesn't like snakes," Tony answered with a shrug of his shoulders. It was clear he wasn't the only one who didn't care for Mayhew. He wondered what Leon had done to offend Blackie. The big guy was usually easy to get along with, but became downright testy any time Mayhew was around.

The men met again in the early morning dawn of the following day. Ellen served fresh coffee to all except Shortie. He was handed a tall glass of fresh, frosty buttermilk sprinkled liberally with black pepper. He drank it down in three gulps and relished every drop. Thanking Ellen profusely for the treat, he handed the empty glass back to her and with a nod to the others, hurried off to work.

Art, nursing another hangover, worked alone. Every time his shovel hit the ground or scraped against rock, his head pounded all the louder, swelling inside his scull until he thought his brains would burst out his ears. The others recognized the signs and left him alone in his misery with the exception of Blackie. He couldn't resist such an open opportunity.

"Feeling under the weather," he boomed as he gave Art a bone-jarring slap on the back in passing. Art held his head and leaned on his shovel handle with eyes closed. His face blanched and for a moment, Blackie thought he was going to pass out.

Flashing an apologetic grin to Ellen, he removed his own shovel from the bed of his truck. "Poor kid," he murmured to Shortie. "If I came home drunk all the time, Bert would lay me out." Rubbing a lump on the back of his head, he remembered the difference of opinion that had put it there. Bert had gotten her point across in no uncertain terms. "No doubt about it," he added, "she'd lay me out but good." Shortie nodded in agreement. He'd seen Bert angry once, and "thank the stars above," once had been enough.

Work had never been Gabbie's idea of fun, and he disappeared if anyone dared suggest he do any. The very idea of work reminded him of backaches, chest pains, corns, gallstones, or any disease he could lay claim to so he would be excused from participating in activities that raised a sweat. He liked being part of the planning and would discuss it for hours, but that was as far as he would go. "I'll take care of it tomorra," was a favorite expression. He rose early on the morning the work crew met at Art Jones with purpose in mind. While still dark, he ambled down to Art's place so he'd be there before Blackie arrived. Revenge was such an ugly word, downright unchristian and practiced only by heathens and atheists. He wouldn't plot revenge against anyone, but there was nothing wrong with an old man teaching a younger one respect for his elders.

It wasn't full light when he reached Art's. Shortie, recognizing the unmistakable shuffle, wasn't surprised to see him. The old man always showed up when he was least needed.

"What brings you out so early?"

"I come to help." Switching a mouthful of tobacco from one cheek to the other, Gabbie spit out of the corner of his mouth. Wiping his lips and beard with the cuff of a ragged sleeve, he stared intently at the younger man, waiting for an argument. Picking up a shovel and throwing it into a wheelbarrow, he glanced expectantly at Shortie. Shortie shrugged his shoulders, figuring it didn't pay to argue with a man when his mind was set.

"Are you sure what you're getting yourself into? This won't be any picnic," Shortie warned. Pointing to several dark heaps lying next to the retaining wall running alongside the base of the hillside, he explained, "Every one of those humps is several hundred pounds of dirt and rock. All of it has to be shoveled back behind the wall and then tamped down tight. It's hard work, backbreaking work, work that may be more than you can handle." His tone softened when Gabbie's features flushed with insult. "It's not that I don't appreciate the offer, but maybe you'd best supervise instead."

Gabbie shrugged off Shortie's suggestion. Lots of volunteer help had shown for the day's work. Taking positions near the breakout, they lifted their shovels to begin. Gabbie took up the handle of his own wheelbarrow and flashed a toothless grin at Shortie, and then trundled over to the work area. Coming up behind one of the men, he inquired, "Do ya think thar's enough dirt to fill in that hole or should another load be brought in?"

"What's the matter, old man, are you blind? There's plenty and more than enough to fill two holes that size," the man answered, grunting as he hefted a shovelful over the wall. The dirt landed squarely to begin filling a jagged hollow on the opposite side. Grinning broadly, and not in the least bit put off at the man's sharp tone, Gabbie persisted.

"See that big fella' over yonder?" he asked with finger pointing to the broad back of Blackie Clegg. "If'n ya need ta' get rid of one of them piles, just wheel it over to him. He ain't got near enough." The man nodded, and Gabbie proceeded merrily to his next victim. An hour passed as news spread that the big fella' working next to the split in the wall needed additional fill-dirt to close a deep gap behind the wooden barrier. With the first leg of his plan set into motion, Gabbie took a quick swig from his flask. Chuckling to himself, he hid the wheelbarrow behind some bushes. He might need it later.

Wandering over to where Blackie worked, he made his way up behind the man on silent feet. Even though the chill of early morning hadn't lifted, sweat soaked through the front and back of the man's flannel shirt. Working in a perfect rhythm, the shovel blade showered the ground with sparks as it scraped against stone. With the next breath the shovel tip sliced through the hard, rocky soil; buried clear to the handle. On the exhale, a shovel load of dirt went flying over the wall to land precisely along the deepest gap in the wall. Blackie worked at fever pitch and hated interruptions. He pivoted slightly at the waist, ready to toss the next shovelful over the wall.

"What'cha doin'?" bellowed Gabbie.

Blackie was startled at the interruption, and his timing was thrown off. The shovelful of dirt meant to be tossed over the wall missed its mark. It flew from the shovel with the momentum of his swing, and the entire contents landed in a heap at Gabbie's feet. Angry at the unwarranted interruption, Blackie barked, "What does it look like I'm doin', having tea and crumpets with the queen?"

Gabbie regarded the hill of dirt at his feet solemnly and shook his head. He gazed at Blackie with silent accusation.

Totally unnerved, Blackie swelled up like an angry hornet. Stepping over the mound of dirt separating them, he stood over the old man imposingly.

"You crazy old coot, what are ya' doing around here? If you came down here just to get on my nerves, well, it worked, and I suggest you scram before I really get sore," he emphasized with a finger pointed up the hill.

Gabbie faced Blackie's threatening glare without blinking an eye. With a thoughtful expression, he kicked at the mound of dirt at his feet and spoke aloud to himself.

"Can't throw nothin' uphill cause it always come a'slidin' back down.

Yes sir, won't do nothin' but come right back at 'cha." Without acknowledging Blackie's presence, he walked away, continuing his one-sided monologue. "No siree, I seen a man doin' what he was a'doin'. Took 'im half a day to realize he was throwin' th' same dirt over and over agin. He just ain't got respect fer his elders, and I only come to help."

Complaining to himself, Blackie returned to work with a vengeance. He plied more force to his shovel than intended, and when he hefted a huge shovelful, he threw it high up on the hillside in one powerful toss. His mouth dropped to his knees in astonishment when the whole load tumbled back down. Seeming to defy gravity, it fell as a lump, heaped at his feet, and buried the tips of his shoes. For the next ten minutes he shoveled more dirt than five men and cursed every shovelful with a colorful vocabulary not meant for sensitive ears. No matter how far he tossed each load of dirt, he missed his mark every time. It came back down the hillside to shower him with fine gray dust.

Cursing Gabbie, old men, and the dirt around him, Blackie threw down his shovel and broke the handle.

As the morning progressed, mounds of dirt grew smaller as the gaps around the barriers filled. Blackie needed a break to cool off. He left his post momentarily to search for a replacement shovel. Gabbie had waited for just such an opportunity. Shortie stared, openmouthed, when he spotted the old man running along the retaining wall to some brush just above it. Thinking he was in a hurry to relieve himself, he was shocked to see Gabbie pull a wheelbarrow out from behind a bush. He then hurried over to help a man fill it with dirt. The younger man wheeled the loaded barrow over and dumped it on what was left of Blackie's dirt mound. Scratching his head in disbelief, Shortie returned to the handle of his own shovel.

"Who would believe it?" he wondered aloud. "Who would believe Gabbie could move faster than a crawl? For that matter, who would believe he could lift a shovel, let alone use one?"

When Blackie returned to finish a small amount of shoveling, the hill he'd been working on appeared larger than it had before, but he was so mad, he wasn't certain. Wanting to get the job finished, he tackled the remainder with a frenzy. Out of the corner of his eye, he spied two men coming his way. Each pushed a heavily loaded wheelbarrow. His chin dropped to his chest when they nonchalantly dumped it on the growing mountain of earth next to him. Smiling good-naturedly, they gave a parting wave, loaded their tools into the back of a pickup and drove off. So mad he was speechless, he stared after them in astonishment. When a third man approached with a full wheelbarrow, the air was split with cursing.

"What's wrong? What's the problem here?" Shortie panted, out of breath after sprinting across the yard. The unsuspecting man, petrified before the temper of the big Irishman, dropped the handles of the wheelbarrow. It tipped over and spilled its contents next to the pile of dirt and rock that had been ground level, but was now waist high.

"Now calm down, Irish. Don't let that temper of yours get carried away with itself." Shortie did his best to calm Blackie down and make amends to the offended stranger.

"I was only doing what the old man told me to do," the man explained.

"What old man?" asked Shortie.

"Well, you ought to know, you were talking to him earlier this morning. He seemed to be a helpful old fella' and was real concerned that this section of wall be filled in and tamped down. Two of my buddies and I filled a couple of smaller holes in the upper wall over an hour ago. Since then, we've dug half the mountain away on the opposite side and wheeled it over here just as fast as we could go. Funny thing though, seems we'd no more than start shoveling down the hillside than somebody would throw it right back at us. Took us quite a while to load the extra dirt you wanted and get it wheeled over here." The man removed his cap and scratched at a bald spot on the back of his head. "Didn't we wheel in enough?" he asked.

"Do you mean you've been throwin' dirt down the mountain as I've been throwin' it up?" Blackie's face turned the color of pickled beets and his eyes shot fire.

"Well, yeah, we did what we were asked to do. You don't have to get so steamed about it." The smaller man looked from Shortie to Blackie with a puzzled frown.

Shortie held in laughter until he couldn't any longer. It exploded from his chest, mouth and nose with snorts and loud guffaws. Pointing at Blackie, he tipped back on his heels and laughed until his belly hurt.

"The joke's on you, Irish. Gabbie pulled a good one this time, and you didn't even see it coming. No wonder he hid a wheelbarrow behind those bushes," Shortie said with a pointing finger. "He brought back everything you threw over the wall and then some. It's no wonder your hill kept growing instead of shrinking. Every time your back was turned the old man dumped another load and then walked away to a safe distance to watch the fun."

"This ain't one bit funny, and if I get my hands on that old man's scrawny neck, I'll...." Blackie blustered. "No wonder my shoulders are as sore as two toothaches; I've tossed almost a ton of dirt and rock over that wall and here it still sits," he said with a disgusted wave of his hands. Vowing to do serious damage to the old man's head the next time he saw him, Blackie began shoveling again with an expression black with thunderclouds. He was mollified slightly when Shortie and the stranger quickly loaded a second wheelbarrow. As they wheeled it closer to the wall to dump it over, their shoulders shook with unrestrained mirth. Their snickers turned silent when Blackie glared at them both with a look that plainly said, "keep your mouth shut."

As Shortie and the stranger plied their shovels to the task at hand, they exchanged hidden grins. Blackie still stomped and sputtered around, vowing vengeance against old men in general. Strangely enough, Gabbie wasn't anywhere to be found.

Chapter 7

With the help of many volunteers, the retaining walls were quickly restored to their original position. Shortie took special care that each breakout was reinforced with pylaster bracings. Every wall was tested by purposely starting rockslides that swept down the bare hillsides with explosive force. He wasn't satisfied until each wall was high and sturdy enough to hold back even the smallest pebble from flying over the top. When several walls had to be reinforced a second time, many volunteers disappeared. This didn't bother the remaining work force. They could finish the remaining handwork without others getting in the way.

Eddie was allowed to bring Blackie and Shortie's lunch, all prepared in abundance by Bert's generous hand. Blackie ate the huge amount of food with an occasional complaint about the skimpy portions. He was a large man and had an appetite that more than equaled his size. He frequently begged leftovers from another man's lunch if his hunger wasn't assuaged by the gargantuan lunch Bert prepared. Shortie, unaccustomed to rich foods served in such variety, was reluctant to share his bounty, but did. Lunch took on a whole new meaning and was certainly more appetizing than a slab of baloney slapped between two slices of buttered bread to be eaten with one Walla Walla sweet onion. He loved onions, and Bert always included a peeled, sliced onion all carefully wrapped in wax paper.

He was sharing his lunch with Eddie one afternoon when the boy wrinkled up his nose and quickly scooted away. The sharp aroma of onion filled the air, bringing an instant reaction from Eddie.

Holding his nose and with eyes streaming, Eddie demanded, "Why do you eat onions? They stink!"

Blackie, Art, and Tony all sat upwind from the offending onion odor and listened attentively for Shortie's response. They also wondered why he ate raw onions when there were so many other good tasting foods to choose from. Some guys might enjoy an occasional apple or orange in their lunch, but he always ate an onion and seemed to enjoy every bite.

"Well, it's like this, son," he answered, "onions are good for what ails you. They help keep a person healthy and protect them from catching colds. They even kill germs." Smiling conspiratorially, he added with his head bent close to Eddie's as if sharing an important secret, "Ever wonder why flies and mosquitoes leave me alone?"

Eddie had never noticed this phenomenon and Shortie knew it, but he asked the question anyway.

"No—why?"

"Good bug repellant," Shortie said emphatically. "No self-respecting bug will get within twenty feet of a man when he's ate a good onion." Taking another huge bite, he leaned back comfortably against the log wall and offered some to Eddie.

Eddie smiled incredulously and gestured disgustedly. "No way."

Shortie's listening audience had accepted his explanation without doubt. Not one of them could remember a time when the man had ever had a cold. With the same thought in mind, the men nodded in silent agreement that onions made good insect repellant. His onion breath sure repelled those that worked closest to him for a long while after lunch.

On the third Monday following the explosion, newspaper headlines screamed, "MINE DENIES INVOLVEMENT WITH BLAST." Several articles were printed in local and city papers from the mines in the local area. Mine executives denied knowledge of the blast, and not one of them planned to use explosives in the near future.

Men employed at the Upper Mine and at the Lucky Spur Mine were questioned closely by superiors. They all related a similar story. Afternoon shift was at lunch, and underground miners were enjoying a last cup of coffee before punching in when the lights went out. No one had been too excited about the sudden darkness because electrical outages were a common problem underground. Lighting a few lanterns relieved the dark and provided enough light for the men to continue working. Packing up their lunch boxes, men prepared to return to work when the ground began to shake, jarring support beams and filling lower shafts with thick dust. Men were evacuated from both mines until damage assessments were completed. No one had been hurt, and the only harm found was to some wiring that supplied necessary electricity underground. Sections of wire were tangled, knotted like a ball of yarn after a playful kitten had discarded it. Even electrical engineers couldn't explain how or why the cables feeding electricity into the breaker boxes tangled as they did. New cabling and connections were quickly installed, and work resumed as usual.

Shortie, as well as other community residents, puzzled over the miners' comments. If the mines weren't blasting or sinking shaft, then the only plausible explanation would be an earthquake. But not everyone living up the draw had been effected by the shake-up. If that weren't puzzling enough, seismologists out of Salt Lake City, Utah, Los Angeles, California, and even Spokane, their closest big city, released similar statements to newspapers and radio news. They agreed with each other. There wasn't a tremor, movement of the earth, or anything else unusual on the evening in question. In fact, one seismologist intimated the entire story was a hoax dreamed up by the business community in the hope of increased revenue from curious out-of-town shoppers.

If sensitive seismographs and the specialists that worked with them could find nothing, then what had caused it? The pain in the small of Shortie's back was a nagging reminder of the endless hours of shoveling a mountain back into place.

Chapter 8

Back to work at the dairy after taking a few days off to repair the break-out near his home, Shortie mulled over every scrap of information he had about the explosion. As he loaded empty milk cans onto a handcart for transport to the train, he worried the problem over. How could he protect his family if he didn't know what had happened in the first place? Mechanically, he finished loading the cart. Back inside the plant, he donned rubber boots, gloves and an apron before entering the next room. Stepping onto the concrete floor of the "sanitizing room," he loaded dirty milk bottles onto racks which he slid into a giant washer. Flipping a switch, he watched momentarily as scalding water filled the tub and sloshed around the racks of bottles. As a precautionary measure, he stopped the machine and readjusted a few bottles, and then waited to be sure the cycle was running smoothly. Once in awhile, if a bottle was slightly out of alignment, the tub jammed and wouldn't turn. He wasn't in the mood to clean up the mess this caused. Before exiting the sanitizing room, he poured lye into the final wash before the rinse cycle began. After the lye solution had been added, he removed his protective apron, gloves, and boots. It was time to move the handcart to the depot; the Burlington Northern milk run was due in at any time.

Pulling the handcart to the train for loading and unloading was a major part of his duties at White's Dairy and Processing Plant. It didn't matter what shift was working; fresh milk had to be delivered from the train to the dairy for processing. When winter brought ice and snow, the job became a ponderous task. The wheels sometimes froze to the ground, and when this occurred, a sledgehammer or heavy pickaxe was required to clear it away. It was backbreaking work, and he was grateful spring weather remained warm, making the job easy.

Clean, empty milk cans were loaded on the train twice during a shift. They would be returned full of fresh milk gathered from neighboring dairies along the route between Cedars and River Town. Emptying the cans, he poured the fresh milk through screens, ridding it of dead mice or whatever might be floating in it. He'd found a drowned kitten once, which sickened him to the point that he'd sworn off milk for a couple of months. The next step in the process was to remove the screens from the vats and set the cream strainers in place. The strainers were lengths of cheesecloth stretched on a frame that rested on top of the milk. As the cream rose, it collected on the cheesecloth where it was easily removed to be processed for whip cream, ice cream, or whatever.

Removing a screen from the vat, he was relieved to find it clear of any floating critters. Hosing the screen off to cleanse it of accumulated milk curd, he scrubbed it clean with a special solvent that cleaned and deterred the growth of bacteria. He'd just set the strainer in place when the door opened to the processing room. Tony motioned it was time for their noon break.

Grabbing their lunch buckets from off the shelf, they stepped outside into cooler and fresher air. Sitting at the outdoor table the company had for employees, they both breathed in deeply, removing the cloying scent of sour milk from their lungs.

Tony opened his lunch box and smiled broadly. Inside, he found a lopsided heart cut from red paper that one of his children had placed there. Taking the scrap of paper, he proudly pinned it to the front of his overalls. Grinning at Shortie, he bit into his sandwich. Between mouthfuls, he asked, "Your wife, she is better?"

"She's healing quickly and is doing very well," Shortie nodded. "Doc says we can remove the bandage from her ankle in a few days. Bert's taken good care of Inja and little Eddie."

"The cuts on her face—they are healing, too?" he inquired.

"The swelling is gone and so are most of the bruises. There's one or two that are fading slowly, but only around the eyes." Shortie took a bite of his own sandwich and chewed for a moment before continuing. "That salve of Don's must be pretty good stuff," he said animatedly. "She's healing faster than Doc thought she would. He doesn't think she'll have any scarring. You know," he bragged, "that Doc Smith is alright. He might be cantankerous, but he's treated my Inja right."

The worried frown on his face contradicted his air of unconcern.

Tony nodded, more concerned for him than for her. "You must stop worrying, my friend," Tony advised. "We may never know why—and maybe we aren't meant to. You'd best be thankful Inja will be all right." Flashing one of those smiles that lit his handsome, young face with good cheer, he turned his attention back to his sandwich. Swallowing the last bite, he drank a soda thirstily. Growing unusually silent, his gaze was drawn to the upper draw where early afternoon shadows hid the valley sheltered between mountain peaks.

"Will Inja want you to move away from the valley?"

"She might want to, but we won't because we can't afford it," Shortie answered flatly.

At the end of shift, Shortie and Tony walked to the corner of Division and Main to wait for Blackie. He worked at one of the local mines and would pick them up on his way home. Normally, they rode to work with Jonesy, but he was on afternoon shift this month. They laughed and pointed as Jonesy went speeding by, late for work again.

In just a short time, Blackie's truck appeared. He paused just long enough for Shortie and Tony to get seated and then took off for home. The three were thoughtfully silent throughout the short ride, so Blackie's uncharacteristic silence went unnoticed.

Tony waved to them as he walked the few steps to his front door. Maria, his wife, was in her fourth month of pregnancy. She waited for him on the porch with one dark-eyed child slung on a hip and the other standing at her side. Both little girls resembled their mother and would be beautiful young women someday. Maria had dark, expressive eyes set in a face of exquisite beauty. Her waist-length black hair only emphasized her exotic looks.

Shortie watched the Martinez family with a pang of envy as Tony drew them into a bear hug. Sighing heavily, he gathered up his lunch bucket and jacket to begin the ascent to his own front door. He hoped Eddie would be waiting for him. Blackie stopped his departure with a hand on his shoulder.

"Do you have a minute?" he asked. "I need to talk to you. Didn't you tell me Ben Schultz was the one who brought Doc Smith that night?"

"Yeah, why do you ask?"

"Why do you think Ben was out on the mountain instead of at home with his own family? Most people were too shocked to do much of anything, so why was he snooping around? Did he say anything?"

"Why the twenty questions?" Shortie fumed, irritated at the delay. "I've gone over this at least fifty times and I've told you what happened. Doc was taking care of Inja and Ben was outside with me. I was trying to find what caused the explosion. That's when I found my cellar caved in."

"Did Ben say anything or do anything, about the cellar, I mean?"

"No, why should he?" Shortie answered. He grew impatient with all the questions. "Get to the point; what are you hinting at?"

"Don't you think it odd that the central area of damage was only around your place? Sure, two other cellars caved in that night, but both of them were unused and in a straight line down from your place."

"I'm not drawing any conclusions, Irish," Shortie accused. "You haven't told me anything I don't already know. Now, I'm tired and want to get home, so get to the point, if you have one."

Blackie looked his friend straight in the eye. Uncertainty darkened his expression as he chewed his lower lip. He decided to tell what he knew. "Ben Shultz quit his job last week, and a couple of days ago he packed up his family and moved out in the middle of the night. It was obvious he didn't want anyone to see them leaving. He was scared speechless; I know because I saw him myself. He couldn't wait to get away from here." Shortie's incredulous expression showed shock and disbelief.

"Are you implying Ben knew more than what he told us? Did he say something that made you suspicious?" Shortie's eyes narrowed as he scrutinized his friend's features. A flash of momentary anger swept fatigue from his body at the idea of someone having information they refused to share, but the weight of helplessness brought it crashing back down. There was something or someone that posed a threat to him and his family, and he didn't know who, what, or why.

"He was in too big a hurry to answer any questions and kept insisting there was nothing to worry about."

"Well, I can't worry about what I don't know. We'll just have to watch and wait."

Both men got out of the truck. Spex, Blackie's mixed breed dog, came running to meet him, almost bowling the man off his feet in his enthusiastic welcome. Holding Blackie's hand between massive jaws, the animal refused to release him until his ears were stroked and his head patted.

"He never leaves so much as a tooth mark," Blackie chuckled. "We go through this everyday. I'm darn glad he's a friend, though; have you noticed those teeth? He could tear my arm right off if he took a notion to," he exclaimed with a note of pride.

Shortie patted the dog's head in farewell, then turned to climb the mountain path. "Thanks for the information," he called over his shoulder with a wave.

Following Shortie's retreating figure, Blackie shook his head, mumbling to himself. "As if he doesn't have trouble enough—and now there's Mayhew. Too bad one of those rocks didn't knock some sense into her." Feeling guilty for harboring angry thoughts against another man's wife, he glanced once more to the mountaintop and then sped into the house.

Chapter 9

Eddie was waiting for Shortie, and as soon as he spied him coming up the road, he ran to meet him with skinny arms waving. Grabbing Shortie around the middle, he hugged him excitedly. His little face beamed, "welcome home."

"She's up," Eddie shouted. Hopping first on one foot and then on the other, he made a complete circle around Shortie before he slowed long enough to catch his breath.

"Is she really?" Shortie asked with awe in his voice. He glanced toward the house as if expecting Inja to come running out at any moment. All of a sudden fatigue vanished and the dark mood that had plagued him the last few days became elated. A sense of excitement flooded through him. Grabbing up the boy, he piggybacked him the rest of the way home. Expecting Bert to be waiting, he was surprised to find Inja alone. Putting Eddie down, he entered the house on the run.

"Inja," he panted, slightly out of breath from his race up the steps. She turned from the sink where she was peeling potatoes and smiled with a familiar teasing glint in her eyes. He'd never seen anything more beautiful than his wife with a towel tied around her middle, a potato in one hand and a paring knife in the other. Giggling girlishly, she dropped the potato in the sink and pirouetted in front of him.

"How do I look?" she asked. His admiring glance told her all she needed to know. There were still a few bruises, and the stitched cheek remained red and sore to the touch, but most of her face had healed completely. She was definitely better, better than she'd ever been in her life.

"Doc's miracle salve," she raved. "If it weren't for him, I'd probably look like something out of Halloween." Retrieving a hand mirror from the table, she examined her reflection for about the thousandth time. "When Doc Smith removed the bandage, I was afraid to see the damages, but he says there won't be any. What do you think?" She peered expectantly at him over the rim of the mirror.

"You look like a million to me," Shortie answered. Pulling her to him in a loving embrace, his voice broke as he murmured into her hair, "I've been so worried. You have no idea how relieved I am to see you up and around and healed so perfectly. I'm thankful, truly thankful, but you have to know I'd love you anyway. I married the you inside here," he said pointing to her heart, "not just your pretty face."

Stiffening, she pushed him away, her mood turning suddenly peevish. "You would, wouldn't you?" she huffed. "Well, I wouldn't love me, and pretty soon you wouldn't either." Throwing the knife into the sink, she dropped into a chair and crossed her arms defensively over her chest. Glaring, she silently dared him to say anything more.

"You've probably done too much today," he said, trying to placate her sudden mood change. "You rest while I finish preparing dinner." Pouring a cup of coffee, he handed it to her as a peace offering.

Accepting the olive branch he extended, she rewarded him with an apologetic smile. He was forgiven, and whistled happily while preparing the meal.

Inja followed her husband's movements with an inscrutable expression upon her face. Eddie had observed the exchange between the two adults through the screen door, and the expression on his sister's face gave him an uncomfortable sense of unease.

Down the hill at the home of Blackie and Bertie Clegg, the evening meal was also being prepared. Bertie bustled about setting the table, slicing fresh bread, and serving up a beef casserole.

"How's the patient doing?" Blackie asked as he washed at the kitchen sink.

"Weak as a kitten until...." Her voice trailed off and a pucker wrinkled her forehead.

"Until what?" her husband demanded.

Biting her lower lip nervously, she reluctantly answered her husband's probings.

"There she was swaddled in blankets and bolstered by pillows when she spied Doc a-huffing and a-puffing up the hill to see her."

"What's so odd about that?" Blackie pressed. "He's been to see her every day for the past two weeks. Woman, you had me scared there for a minute." As an afterthought he added, "I didn't think a fat man could move as fast as he does. He's pretty spry for a man of his age and size."

"It wasn't Doc's visit that was odd," Bert corrected. "It was who came with him. Guess who it was!"

Sighing with exasperation, he snapped, "How do I know if you don't tell me? Get on with it, woman, who was with Doc? It better not have been Mayhew," he glowered. "That wolf needs to be taken for a ride and taught a lesson he won't soon forget." Bert didn't need to say more, her expression confirmed his suspicions.

"It was Leon all right," she added with a nod of head, "and of course Holly wasn't with him. He didn't say much, just kept smiling at Inja, like they shared a secret or something. After Doc and Mayhew left, she gets out of bed and demands to take a bath. A bath of all things! She made herself up, did her hair for the first time in over a week, and then sent me packing without so much as a thank you."

Blackie cursed under his breath. A fleeting look of menace darkened his face before he spoke.

"Should I say something to Shortie about this or will you have a talk with Inja?"

"No, not yet. We won't say anything to anybody. All we know for sure is Mayhew came to see Inja in full view of Doc Smith and myself. Shortie has enough problems without adding unnecessary suspicion. She's doing okay, so I wouldn't be there much longer anyway, and hopefully things will return to normal real soon."

He nodded in agreement. On the surface, he appeared totally unconcerned, but she knew the tension was building. She hoped the tongue-lashing she'd given Inja would be enough to stop her foolish flirtation, no matter how harmless she claimed it was. She almost felt sorry for Leon because if Blackie ever got hold of him, the man wouldn't have a chance of defending himself.

Chapter 10

Standing upright to rest his aching back, Shortie stretched with arms raised to the sky. He'd been hard at work since first light and had already moved several wheelbarrow loads of dirt to fill the uneven ground where the cellar had been. The cellar would be sorely missed. It had housed their winter store of canned jams, jellies, fruit, and vegetables.

"We were lucky," he said to himself. He didn't like thinking about all the "what ifs" that plagued him. What if Inja had been in the cellar? What if Eddie had been playing in the loose dirt that covered the cellar's roof? His mind refused to dwell on the tragic result of such questions.

Shaking his head to clear the frightening picture of Inja and Eddie buried under several ton of rock, he returned to work. It had been about a month since the explosion, and this was the last job to be completed. He shuddered at the memory of Inja buried by fallen dirt and rock. She still refused to step foot into the backyard and would remain at a safe distance on the porch. The entire affair remained a mystery, and a reasonable explanation remained elusive. Shoveling fill dirt into a remaining hole, he sighed with great relief. Except for leveling the ground and raking the soil, the job was done.

Removing an oversized handkerchief from the hind pocket of his Big Mac overalls, he wiped away the rivers of sweat running down his face. Standing back to assess his work, he thanked the Father for protecting Inja once again. Her injuries could have been much worse. Gathering his tools together, he placed them in the wheelbarrow. A sudden flash of a bluebird's wing drew his attention down the draw.

Blue smoke, which normally permeated the air, was dissipating as sunlight burned through the haze. It had been thicker earlier in the morning and burned in his nose and throat. Smoke from the smelter hung like thick, blue fog over the valley, leaving a metallic taste in his mouth. From his vantage point on the mountain, he had a clear view of the valley below. On the opposite side of the canyon was Haystack Peak. Rising from the valley floor, it didn't peak at the top like most of the surrounding mountaintops, but was rounded and dome shaped. Very little foliage adorned its sides, and the earth covering it was the color of an old, dry haystack. Smelter smoke killed off anything hinting of green. Turning to study the mountain he stood upon, he took in the sparse scrub brush and stunted trees that dared to take root. The poor trees clung tenaciously to a shallow scattering of leaded soil, which barely supported patches of weeds and grass.

At the head of the draw was Jackass Peak. It grew a few trees, but most were scraggly and sick looking, not the lush, green pines found flooding the mountainsides just a short distance out of River Town. Hills surrounding the valley rose in jagged peaks with little growth on their steep slopes. It was no wonder rockslides frequently occurred, especially when the soil became saturated during spring rains. Rousing from his reverie, he gazed with satisfaction at the leveled ground. Mentally, he plotted out the garden. Inja would enjoy a few fresh vegetables and maybe a flower or two. The new clothesline posts, painted a brilliant white, shone brightly in the sun. Life was finally getting back to normal. His stomach rumbled loudly, reminding him it was long past breakfast, and pancakes with syrup were waiting. Inja always made his favorite breakfast on Saturdays. Taking up the handles of the wheelbarrow, he hurried to the house. After putting his tools in the storage shed, he hurried to the outdoor standpipe to wash the sweat and dust away. He was as hungry as three bears and could eat them toenails and all.

Inja watched her husband from the kitchen window. For an unguarded moment, her eyes admired him from across the distance. When he released his overall straps, allowing them to trail down his back, and removed his shirt, the view was impressive.

Splashing the icy water over his head and chest, he wiped away the excess from his chest with his shirt. Shaking his head vigorously, water droplets flew to form tiny rainbows in the brilliant, morning sunlight. His hair, normally confined under a cap, sprang out in glistening, dark curls. Inja jealously drank in the sight of him. Other women admired him from a distance, but she could look at her leisure.

Turning toward the house, Shortie caught her admiring gaze. Flexing his muscles and posing, he winked knowingly at her. A rare moment of playfulness came over him as he struck first one pose and then another. Inja's glare of mock anger weakened, and a smile tipped the corner of her mouth. They both laughed aloud as his antics became more animated.

Wiping her streaming eyes with a corner of the curtain, she motioned that breakfast was ready. With a final suggestive smile, she turned from the window, still chuckling. Her demeanor turned sour as she spied the frown on her little brother's face.

"Eddie, stop wasting time and eat your breakfast. You'll sit there until your bowl is empty," she threatened.

Cooking a big breakfast hadn't been high on her agenda, and besides, the kitchen was already too warm. It didn't make sense to heat up the woodstove just to prepare pancakes when oatmeal was more nourishing, quicker and easier. For a moment she wished Bertie was still doing all the cooking and other household chores. She admitted to no one but herself that meals tasted better when prepared by Bert's expert hand.

She knew Shortie looked forward to Saturday morning pancakes, so thick slices of fresh bread slathered in butter and left to brown in the oven was substituted. Oven toast went well with oatmeal, and he loved fresh bread. Pouring a third cup of coffee, she sat down at the table to wish over all the items in their newest mail-order catalog.

Eddie frowned with distaste at the bowl of cold, lumpy oatmeal. She'd really outdone herself this time. As a norm, her cooked cereal was clumpy with a light crust on the bottom. It was palatable if enough brown sugar or syrup was added to sweeten it. But this stuff, ugh, couldn't be made edible no matter what he added. It had the texture of dry flour paste. As his taste buds shriveled in rebellion, he stuffed another spoonful into his mouth. Trying to swallow quickly and not chew, the scorched cereal lodged in his throat, causing him to cough. A drink of water dislodged the food, and he swallowed, trying to identify the taste as it went down his throat. Yes, it was definitely burnt paste with an occasional oat flake thrown in for texture. He spied Shortie coming toward the house and shoveled another spoonful of his sister's poison into his mouth.

Hanging his cap behind the door, Shortie inhaled deeply. Noticing the bare stovetop, he asked disappointedly, "No pancakes with syrup? No bacon?"

"I didn't feel well this morning," Inja pouted, touching her left temple. "There's oatmeal in the warmer and oven toast," she added temptingly.

"Do you have another headache? Are you okay?" Shortie asked with concern. Since the accident, she'd had frequent headaches and he worried about possible injuries the doctor couldn't detect. The headaches always went away, however, and her doctor claimed there weren't any problems.

Eddie gagged, drawing his attention.

"Don't take such big bites," Shortie said as he patted Eddie's back. Eddie's expression of contempt was misinterpreted by Shortie, but clearly understood by Inja.

Trying to appear unconcerned, she stole furtive glances at Shortie as he filled a bowl with the remaining cereal.

Spooning out the burned oatmeal, he dropped it back into the pan. The toast, now cold and dry, crumbled when he bit into it. Poking the shriveled bread with a fork, he wondered it if was really bread or a piece of hardtack purchased at Army surplus. Frowning, his expression mirrored Eddie's as he seated himself next to the child. Inja's eyes followed him so he tried to make light of the situation.

"Oatmeal is good," he said as if to reassure himself. Eyeing the mixture of milk and cereal dubiously, he spooned sugar generously over the top. "It will fill the hole in our stomachs, right, Eddie?" he asked with forced heartiness. Ruffling the boy's hair, he bravely speared a large lump from his bowl and jammed it into his mouth. When charcoal hit his taste buds, the reaction was instantaneous. Eddie grinned with delight as Shortie choked just as he had earlier. The noxious concoction lodged in his throat, where it rapidly swelled to the size of a hen's egg. Jumping out of his chair, Shortie grabbed the bowls from the table and ran to the sink. He spit out what he could and swallowed the rest with mouthfuls of water.

Eddie stared with wide-eyed amusement. He'd been forced to eat half a bowl and was glad he wouldn't have to eat any more. Grinning, he averted his face away from his sister.

"Inja," Shortie said condescendingly, "don't cook oatmeal for me. I've taught you to make pancakes, so stick with what you know. They're easy to prepare and we like them, don't we Eddie?" he asked, including the child in the conversation.

Taking the remainder of a loaf of bread, he sliced it into three huge slabs. Stoking up the fire, he placed the bread on a rack in the oven to brown. Removing two mugs from the cupboard, he filled them halfway with canned milk, sugar, and unsweetened cocoa. Stirring rapidly, he added boiling water. A steaming cup of cocoa was placed in front of Eddie. While sipping his own, he waited for the bread to brown. The toast, spread with melted butter, was best when dipped in the hot chocolate. It was a rare treat! Eddie and Shortie sipped with identical expressions of sheer bliss.

Inja watched the two eat and drink as if half starved. She shook her head in disgust. The remains of her breakfast setup like cement in the pan and the bread burned to black crisps.

"Want a cup?" Shortie offered. Wanting to recover the earlier mood of fun, he grinned at her boyishly, winking one eye, openly flirting with his wife in front of the boy.

Returning has gaze with a halfhearted smile, she turned the moment to her advantage.

"I'm sorry my cooking is so terrible," she said pointedly. She was insulted and wanted him to know it. Dropping her eyes to hide the anger, she gestured toward the stove. "I just can't get used to cooking on wood heat. Will you forgive me?"

"There's nothing to forgive," he answered in a soft voice. Returning his wife's steady gaze with eyes full of adoration, Shortie remembered Eddie's presence. It was his turn to drop his eyes and force himself to calmly finish his cocoa. Checking his emotions, he fought the impulse to demonstrate his love in a more physical way. Eddie looked from one adult to the other, clearly puzzled at the sudden tension in the room.

Inja knew how much he adored her and pressed her advantage. "How much money do we have?" she asked sweetly.

Her question brought him back to earth with a jolt. She knew their financial status as well as he did. What ulterior motive spurred the question? Unwilling to dampen her good humor, Shortie responded in a controlled voice, "There's our nest egg in the bank and a few dollars in my pocket for the week's groceries. Why do you ask?"

Excitedly, she spread the catalog open on the table and turned to a marked page. "Look at this lovely pitcher and glass set. Leon got Holly one and they're just perfect for serving cold drinks."

"When were you at their house?" Shortie asked in a tight voice.

"Quite awhile ago; in fact, it was before the night of the explosion," she answered casually. Waving the catalog under his nose, she coaxed, "Look at them, they're on sale and we need a glass set, you've said so yourself. They don't cost very much."

Shortie's brows snapped together in tight furrows. His eyes grew hard and staring. Ignoring the warning, she waved a hand in a disgusted gesture toward the cupboards. "I hate the set we have, all chipped and mismatched. I want something new that's pretty and hasn't been handed down from your sister or bought secondhand."

Her eyes pleaded with him, but he didn't hear a single word. "Was Mayhew here in my house?" He dreaded the answer he knew was coming.

"He came here once with Holly," Inja explained. Her voice rose in defensive anger. "Would you quit worrying about them and answer me? These glasses only cost a few dollars and I know we can afford them." Placing her hands on her hips in defiance, she glared, daring him to deny it.

"Do we have to go over this again, Inja?" he asked tiredly.

"I guess we do," she snapped. "Why do you insist on hoarding every spare dime?" Spreading her arms out, she added, "With just a few dollars I could make this place look more like a home instead of a miner's shack."

"And what's wrong with our home?" Shortie asked defensively. Before Inja could answer his question, he answered for her. With a great sigh of exasperation, he explained, "I know this old shack isn't much, but we can afford it and save some money, too." Looking around as if seeing the place for the first time, he continued with a wistful tone in his voice, "Someday, we'll have a house with cupboard doors, real carpet on the floor instead of cracked linoleum, and furniture so new it squeaks. Now just isn't the time. I've saved every nickel I can scratch together and placed it in our savings. Soon we'll have enough for a down payment on a new house. We'll have enough in six months to a year," he promised. "Soon we'll have a bigger place and we can start planning for a child of our own, just like you promised."

Her tight expression was unyielding. "I'm tired of waiting, Shortie," she wailed. "I hate this place. It's ugly. If you won't give me any money to fix it up, then...."

"Then what?" he shouted, losing patience. "How can I give you money I don't have?" He turned his pockets inside out to emphasize his point.

Inja regarded him with bitter resentment. As far as she was concerned, the situation was hopeless and he could go to the devil. Storming to the bedroom, she ended the argument on a bitter note when the door locked behind her.

His shoulders drooped as if a great weight was placed upon them. Stacking the breakfast dishes, he worried over Inja's angry words. It wasn't that he didn't want to give her everything she wanted, but there was never money enough to go around. He was anxious for them to have a child, too, but it never seemed to be the right time. He didn't understand her anger or fear of motherhood. All women wanted children, he reasoned, and Inja would come around when they had a nicer place and a few extra dollars in their pockets. Giving the floor a quick swipe with the broom, he went out to vent his anger at the chopping block.

Collecting his axe from the old outhouse turned into storage shed, he made his way to the woodpile. Eddie shadowed his every step. Shortie knew the boy would avoid the house until his sister was in a better mood. Inja was easy to get along with as long as she got her own way.

Pulling a chunk of dry white pine from the pile, he chopped it into kindling with sure, rapid strokes. The heavier lengths of fir and tamarack stacked at the opposite end of the pile were cut into larger pieces for slow burning and sustained heat. Leaving the boy to fill the kindling bucket with the freshly cut pine, Shortie moved down the pile to select a heavy round of fir.

Stretched out on top of the woodpile was their cat, Old Joe. As he basked in the sun, his black hair gleamed like buffed flint. He yawned as Shortie neared, revealing fangs too large and sharp for a common housecat. Joe, part bobcat and part domestic cat, had become a part of their family two years before. The cat, then a tiny fuzzball, had wandered into the house through an open door. He'd stalked into the kitchen with an air of propriety and immediately claimed the warm space behind the woodstove as his own. At first, they'd fed the scrawny kitten table scraps, but he soon proved his worth by hunting his own dinner that he frequently tried to share. Shortie buried the carcasses of birds, mice, moles, gophers, and a few unidentifieds before Inja found them. The cat's overall bulk and massive size evidenced his hunting prowess. They hadn't expected the little ball of fluff would grow to have a yowl loud enough to split your ears or claws long enough to shred bark from trees. He was a good pet, however, and earned his keep.

Scratching the animal's ears absentmindedly, he regretted his heated words. Angry with himself for not understanding Inja's position, he vowed to make things right with her as soon as possible. It wasn't easy to live in this valley, and living on a mountain, scared to come out of your own house for fear the mountain will fall on you, only made it worse. As he glanced quickly to the mountaintop, a shiver of trepidation traveled the length of his spine. Shaking off the feeling, he continued splitting the day's supply of firewood.

With every swing of the axe, he pictured Leon sitting in his front room, grinning malevolently. He never doubted the integrity of his wife and wanted her innocence to remain untarnished. Mayhew was a different story.

"You just can't trust a man like Leon Mayhew," he remarked to the cat.

Blinking his great, yellow eyes, the cat purred in understanding, sounding like a DC-9 prepared for lift-off.

"Who ya' talkin' to?" asked Eddie as he approached from behind. Caught talking to himself, Shortie mumbled something unintelligible as he stacked a massive armload of split wood on one arm.

Eddie trailed behind him to the house, carrying the filled kindling bucket with two hands. Dropping it into place by the stove, he looked expectantly at Shortie

"Go on and play," Shortie told him. "It's too nice to hang around here all day."

He figured it was a relief for the boy to get away for awhile. The child's nightly tossing and turning had wakened him on several occasions, bringing him to the boy's room on the run. Wanting to reassure and comfort him, he'd find Eddie's arms wrapped tightly around his teddy bear and his body curled into a stiff, tight ball. When had Eddie started sleeping with the bear again? Was he also startled awake at the slightest sound? It was hard to imagine what terrors haunted his dreams.

Chapter 11

In the bedroom, Inja preened in front of the mirror, turning this way and that, inspecting the fit of her new Sunday dress. It was a castoff of Holly's, but looked new. She deliberated whether to raise the hemline. A picture of the church matrons and their disapproving scowls came to mind, so she hastily discarded the idea. The dress looked great on her even if a little too long. Smoothing the silky fabric over her hips, she admired the curve of her figure. Her stomach was flat and her breasts firm.

She knew her husband wanted a baby and he wasn't aware of her firm resolve to avoid pregnancy at all cost. Sticking a pillow under the waist of her dress, she envisioned herself with a rounded, pregnant body. Shaking her head at the unattractive line of her distended belly, she removed the bulge from under her skirt. There would be no babies as far as she was concerned. She refused to have sagging breasts and a lardy stomach. A picture of Ellen Jones's trim figure came to mind. Ellen, mother of five, remained slim, and her flat stomach was to be envied. Pushing the mocking figure of Ellen to the back of her mind, Inja scrutinized her reflection in the mirror once more.

Leaning close, she examined her face. That special salve Doc gave her really had worked a miracle. In fact, the cuts and abrasions on her cheeks and around her eyes had healed flawlessly. Even a few age lines that had appeared around her mouth over the past year were gone. It was as if she'd developed new skin. Regretfully, she fingered a slight scar under her left eye. Hardly noticeable, it marred the perfection of her face. The tiny mark, still a bright pink, reminded her of that night. She still had nightmares of being buried alive and would awaken suddenly, screaming and out of breath with her heart pounding in her throat. Reliving the moment when her mouth and nose filled with dirt, cutting off her air, she fought a momentary sense of panic. But then, Shortie always soothed and calmed her fears. She smiled to herself; tender thoughts of him filled her mind. He was a good man and loved both her and Eddie. She loved him fiercely at times, but yearned for something more—something she couldn't identify and remained just out of her reach.

Her parents had lived in poverty all of their lives. When Father drank himself to death after Mother died from pneumonia, she'd been left to care for three-year-old Eddie. She made a solemn promise to herself never to be poor or to live as her parents had. Reluctantly, she took on the responsibility of raising her little brother until marrying Shortie two years before. He'd been so handsome in his uniform, she'd broken her own vow and fell head-over-heels in love. It wasn't until after their marriage that she realized how poor he was. Realistically, she knew it wouldn't be this bad forever because he had too much drive and ambition to remain at the bottom. But she also knew there would never be the wealth she dreamed of. Well, she had dreams too, and not one of them included living in a shack on a mountaintop without any of the nicer things money could buy. A flush of anger sparked in her eye at the memory of Shortie's refusal to buy the pitcher and glass set. Noticing the angry frown lines set in her face, she consciously relaxed her facial muscles.

"At the age of thirty-six, every frown leaves a wrinkle," she reminded herself by quoting something her mother had said.

Removing the dress, she donned a pair of slacks and a sweater. In a couple of days it would be Sunday and she would accompany Shortie and Eddie to church for the first time in over five weeks.

Smiling at her own reflection, she anticipated the attention she was sure to receive. She loved the way she looked, and if that was being conceited, then what of it! Giving herself a parting smile in the mirror, she removed the dress and hung it in the back of the closet.

During the past few weeks, she'd refused to set foot out of the house. Vanity had kept her housebound, but she no longer had an excuse to stay confined. She'd milked as much time out of her convalescence as she could, and it was time to get on with life.

The mountain peak stood in shadow, signaling late afternoon, by the time Shortie finished preparing the garden plot. He'd already planted three rows of peas, two rows of corn, and two hills of squash. He didn't expect much from the rocky soil but hoped it would produce enough to offset their loss of canned goods. Stakes marked each row, with the vegetable name written neatly on each one. The garden plot was small but the best he could do with such confined space. Rows nearest the house were left unplanted. He figured Inja would want to put in a few marigolds or pansies.

Hanging the hoe and rake in the old outhouse, he watched Eddie climb the hill. Grasping and pulling at the underbrush, the boy made his way up a seldom-used pathway.

"If he isn't a sight," Shortie chuckled to himself.

Eddie's hair stood out in spiked bristles, with the exception of a single lock plastered to his forehead. Rivulets of sweat ran down a dirty face, leaving muddy streaks on his cheeks. One knee of his britches was ripped out, and it looked like a hind pocket hung loose enough to flap back and forth in the wind.

"I made it," he told Shortie as soon as he topped the hill and stood on level ground. Grinning, showing a gap where he'd recently lost a tooth, Eddie wiped grimy hands on the seat of his pants. Shortie took the child's hand in his own, and they climbed the wooden steps together.

"Do you think she's still mad?" Shortie eyed the boy questioningly.

"Yup." Eddie's terse reply was painfully honest.

"I suppose you're right," Shortie responded. "Do you think there's anything I can do to make it better?"

"Yup. Ya' gotta' buy her somethin' so she won't be sad." Eddie blue eyes lifted to Shortie's in a steady gaze. "She only wants somethin' pretty."

"I know," Shortie agreed. An uncomfortable feeling settled on his mind as he thought over the child's solution to an adult problem. "Eddie, you're pretty smart for being just a kid. You see things other people don't."

"Yup." He nodded wisely.

Before opening the front door, Shortie brushed off the boy's rear and attempted to smooth down his hair. Eddie returned the favor by dusting garden soil off Shortie's knees. Grinning at each other like conspirators, they cautiously entered the house. Inja's smiling presence in the kitchen was a shock to them both. Hesitating uncertainly in the doorway, they weren't sure what they should do.

Greeting them with an inviting smile, she was anxious to make up for her tantrum. Giving the potatoes a final turn, she came forward and wrapped her arms around Shortie's neck. Resting her head against his chest, she gave a great sigh of contentment.

"I'm sorry," she said contritely. Her lips curved into a sweet smile and she snuggled close, inviting his embrace. Knowing she was forgiven, she pulled away, wrinkling her nose against the sweaty smell of him.

"You need to wash the stink off if you plan to eat at my table." Tossing a clean towel and washcloth to him, she pointed to the bathroom.

"I guess she means us, Eddie," Shortie said with a happy smile. "You need more than a washing, you need a bath," he told Eddie. "Is there time?" he asked with a quick glance toward Inja. At her affirming nod, he ushered the boy into the bathroom. Less than thirty minutes later, they seated themselves at the table. Their cheeks shone like apples and their damp hair was slicked down with water. Both wore clean clothes and looked more like Sunday morning than Friday night.

"Don't you both look handsome," Inja praised. Eddie beamed under her praise. He rushed to pull her chair out. Shortie poured her coffee and played waiter, kissing her hand chivalrously as he served her plate. Giggling at the unexpected gesture, she admired her husband with eyes full of promise.

Joining hands, they formed a family circle. Shortie dropped his head to pray over the meal. Inja sat with unbowed head, wishing he'd hurry so they could eat before everything grew cold.

After dinner while Inja cleaned the kitchen, Shortie brought in more firewood and stoked the stove against the coming evening chill. Eddie, dressed in cotton pajamas, lay down on the floor in front of the radio. Lying on his stomach, he worked a puzzle while he waited. Inja and Shortie sat close together on the couch holding hands.

"Okay Eddie, turn on the radio," Inja prompted. For the next two hours, they listened to Hank Williams, Ernest Tubb, Minnie Pearl, and Eddie's personal favorite, Britt Reid. Via the wonders of modern radio, "The Grand Old Opry" and "The Green Hornet" were brought into their living room every Saturday night. They hadn't listened for the last few weeks and had missed their family evenings. Snuggling against Shortie, Inja wished aloud.

"If we had a television, we could actually see Hank. Can you imagine what it would be like? It'd be almost as good as meeting him face-to-face," she said dreamily.

He didn't answer right away. The exploits of the Green Hornet had his full attention, but her comment yanked him back to the common place with a jolt. Televisions were expensive and they couldn't possibly afford one, but somehow a traitorous idea wouldn't let him go. Could a person make payments? Pushing the thought from his mind, he reaffirmed his resolve to leave their savings untouched until there was enough for a down payment on a house.

"The antenna wouldn't bring in good reception this far up the mountain," he said with a note of finality.

"What are you talking about?" Inja asked, confused by the statement.

"The antenna," Shortie explained. "The television receives through an antenna and wouldn't pull in enough radio waves for decent reception. I doubt one would work here on the mountain."

"Oh, but they do," she blurted without thinking. "Holly told me their television has better reception than most people in the valley."

"I'm sure Holly and Leon are the experts when it comes to television reception," Shortie muttered peevishly under his breath. Inja glanced sharply at him, and her expression turned sour. Not wanting to spoil the mood, he ignored the mention of Leon and choked back further caustic comments. She relaxed at once and smiled secretively. Usually it made him wonder what she was thinking, but this time, he knew she was hoping for an RCA television set.

When the programs were over, Shortie turned off the radio and carried Eddie to bed. He always fell asleep before his favorite program was over. Tucking him in, he placed the teddy bear within easy reach.

The living room was empty when he returned, and he stumbled over a throw rug in the semi-dark. Inja was in the bathroom, preparing for bed. Sighing, he opened up the sofa to remake the bed he'd slept in for the past few weeks. Not wanting to jostle or disturb Inja's rest during her convalescence, he'd been sleeping on the couch. She hadn't objected to the sleeping arrangement and seemed to prefer it. Spreading another blanket over his makeshift bed, he heard the bathroom door open.

Turning to say good night, the words stuck in his throat. She stood by the bedroom door wearing a gown of rose colored satin. Shimmery fabric clung to her every curve, shadowing her feminine parts provocatively. Her hips, outlined enticingly by the filmy gown, curved down to her shapely legs. Keeping his back to her, he refused to let her see the need etched on his face.

"You'd better go to bed, Inja," he croaked.

"What are you doing out here?" she asked in a low, sultry voice.

"What does it look like; I'm making my bed," he answered.

"Not tonight," she whispered huskily.

Turning to face her, he looked at her questioningly, unsure of her meaning.

"Not tonight," she repeated. Her perfume tickled his nose invitingly as she took his hand and led him into the bedroom.

Chapter 12

Shortie woke early on Sunday morning, and stretching lazily, was reluctant to get out of a warm bed. Knowing he'd wake Inja with restless tossing and turning, he rose and dressed quickly. Opening the bedroom door quietly, he gazed with open adoration at her sleeping form. Her hair lay in a golden mass around her head. She had one arm bent over her head and her face tipped toward the window. He marveled that such a beautiful woman was his wife. Wanting to do something special for her, he remembered Eddie's comment about Inja wanting pretty things. Guilt helped him make a decision he hoped he wouldn't learn to regret.

When they first moved to the valley, she'd wanted to move into one of the more expensive homes along the main road, but he'd already bought this place. The price was right and it was the best he do at the time. This house was cheaper, a little bigger, and had a whole mountain for a backyard. If he'd only known then what he knew now. Responsibility for his family's safety rested heavily on his shoulders. He had failed them and didn't like the feeling. Redirecting such negative thoughts, he headed for the kitchen to start a fire. Pancakes, bacon, fried eggs and hashbrowns sounded like a great way to start the day.

The fire was totally out without so much as a single spark. He opened the grates to release cold ashes into the ashbox. Stuffing a small bit of wadded paper into the firebox, he laid kindling atop and soon had a hot fire burning. Opening the oven door of the old Monarch range, the kitchen warmed quickly. The smell of bacon frying woke Eddie. Jumping out of bed, he tiptoed to the kitchen to see who was cooking. If it was Inja, he really wasn't hungry anyway. Seeing Shortie sifting flour and stirring pancake batter, his mouth began to water and his stomach growled. Rushing to the bathroom to dress and wash, he was back to the kitchen in a flash.

Inja's nose quivered as the aroma of hot coffee and bacon tantalized her to wakefulness. Donning her bathrobe and slippers, she joined Shortie and Eddie. The house was already comfortably warm and filled with breakfast smells. Shortie pulled a chair up close to the stove for her and placed a cup of coffee in her hands. Resting her feet on the oven door to roast her toes, she sipped coffee while her men cooked. Shortie whistled softly under his breath as he flipped pancakes and browned the hashbrowns. Eddie hummed the theme song to his favorite radio program. It was going to be a perfect day.

Later, Shortie paced the kitchen restlessly. Breakfast dishes had been done over an hour ago and Inja had been in the bathroom primping the entire time. He shaved and spruced up for church in the kitchen and made Eddie do the same. Inspecting the boy for the fifth time, he made him sit in a chair until time to leave. He'd actually gotten the boy's hair to lay down. It was neatly combed, and he was determined it would remain that way.

"Inja," he called through the bathroom door, "if we don't leave soon, we'll be late for church."

"I'll be ready in a minute." He could tell by the vague tone of her voice that a minute would lapse into at least ten.

Glancing at his watch impatiently, he paced the kitchen until she opened the door. She wore a light blue, full-skirted shirtwaist that swung about her knees as she walked.

"Do I look okay?" she asked with a final pat to her hair.

He whistled and cleared his throat several times before answering. "You look great. It makes me feel like a million just standing next to you."

Satisfied, she handed her sweater to him. Helping her into the garment, he caught a whiff of her perfume. If he ever had to sleep on the sofa again, it would be too soon.

Shortie took church seriously and listened attentively to the sermon. The topic was on the stewardship of God's blessings and importance of tithing. When the offering plate went around, he put in his usual ten percent.

Inja fumed as the five-dollar bill was casually thrown into the offering. Moving away from Shortie's side, she glimpsed a familiar face out of the corner of her eye. Turning around, she gave a startled gasp of surprise. Holly and Leon were seated directly behind them. Shortie, curious as to what caught her attention, turned also. His smile vanished when Leon's arrogant smirk looked back at him. Crossing his arms over his chest, he sat with a stony expression throughout the remainder of the service.

After church, Art and Ellen offered them a ride home, but they declined the offer. The idea of sitting together in tight quarters wasn't appealing. Besides, Shortie needed time to walk off his anger.

"You invited those people to our church just to spite me, didn't you?" he accused.

"I most certainly did not, and just in case you hadn't noticed, I was more surprised than you." She vehemently denied his accusation, and he grudgingly admitted he'd jumped to conclusions.

"I'm sorry for getting so upset, but there's something about him that sets me on edge." He took her hand, and they walked in silence for a short distance.

"Truce?" she asked.

"Truce," he agreed readily. He certainly didn't want a silly argument to come between them. Breathing a sigh of relief, he pointed at Eddie. "I wish some of his energy would rub off on me." The child scampered ahead of them, needing to run and move about after the subdued atmosphere of church. He ran ahead of them, then rushed back, finding it difficult to walk their slower pace.

"Can we play checkers later?" he asked. At Shortie's nod, he skipped along happily for a few steps, trying to hurry Shortie's pace. They wouldn't be pushed, so he ran ahead again. "It isn't a race, but my feet feel like running," he yelled. Glancing back at them, he grinned, then sped off over the rise of the hill. He was the first one home.

By the time Shortie and Inja arrived at their doorstep, angry thoughts were forgotten. Taking her hand, he led her around the side of the house to show her the garden.

"What do you think? We could plant a shade tree if you want." He looked at her with hopeful eyes.

"No trees," she said emphatically. "This place is shaded enough. What I really want is red roses. Let's plant a couple of rose bushes." At that moment, she could have asked for the moon on a stick and he'd have gotten it for her.

"Roses it is." He nodded in agreement. Hugging him enthusiastically, Inja ran into the house to change out of her Sunday dress. All afternoon she pored over magazines, trying to decide what color flowers went well with red and what she wanted to plant in her garden.

After eating an early dinner, Shortie played three games of checkers with Eddie while Inja read aloud from an adventure series they enjoyed. By early evening they were ready for another voice besides their own and tuned in the radio to hear the local news. The only item of interest was the birth of twins to a local family. He responded to the announcement with excitement.

"Did you hear? Some lucky family had twin girls last night. Can you imagine what fun twins would be?"

"I can't imagine and I don't think it would be fun. It's expensive trying to keep one child clothed and fed without caring for two. I feel sorry for the mother. She won't have a moment's peace to herself until they're old enough to start school." She shook her head as if the idea of twins was the most foolish idea she'd ever heard.

Grabbing her hands, he gazed solemnly into her face. "Inja, we aren't getting any younger, and I want at least one child of my own. Won't you ever want any children? Do you ever wonder what it would be like?"

"I know what it's like, remember?" she said with a thin smile. "I was there when Eddie was born. Besides, if we have a baby, what's to become of Eddie?"

"You know I love the boy as my own son," he reminded her. "Eddie will make a wonderful older brother to any children we may have. He wants me to adopt him and make our relationship official, if you'd only allow it. I have enough love in my heart for you and Eddie with plenty left for our children. Don't you?"

Jerking her arm away and gesturing angrily, she refused to discuss the matter further. Mistaking her meaning, he pushed forward.

"Inja, you know I love you and would never do anything or allow anything to harm you. Women have babies every day and some more than one. Why are you so dead set against it?"

"I never said I didn't want a baby. I just don't believe we should bring children into the world that we can't support." Rising to her feet, she strode to the kitchen in a huff. Giving a snort of derision, she crossed her arms tightly in front of her chest and leaned casually against the sink. Shortie tailed behind her, wanting an answer to his questions. They squared off in the kitchen, each as stubborn as the other. "Let's face it," she told him defiantly, "you don't bring in enough money to feed another mouth at our table."

His face flamed scarlet. He hadn't intended for this conversation to turn to mud-slinging. Fixing her with a level stare, he asked, "Is it just my child you refuse to consider? You're not a young girl anymore, Inja, and it's high time we had children of our own before it's too late for either of us." At this, she covered her face with her hands and wailed broken-heartedly.

"I love you, Shortie, you know that." Extending her hands imploringly, she pleaded, "Give me more time. I'm afraid there will be complications, you know, like Mama when she had Eddie."

"Go see a doctor. A thorough physical and exam should put your fears to rest, and a good doctor can detect problems and take steps to remedy them.

You'll feel differently when you have the assurance of a healthy pregnancy," he suggested.

"Why should we be in such a hurry to have children, anyway?" she asked with eyes brimming unshed tears. "You know this subject upsets me terribly," she sniveled. "I remember when Eddie was born and...." Her voice tapered off into another bout of sniffling.

Placing his arms around her, Shortie felt his anger vanish. Heaving a great sigh of disappointment, he patted her back until the crying subsided. Wrapping his hand in the softness of her hair, he breathed the scent of her.

"Inja, it's okay, we won't talk about this now," he whispered brokenly. She wrenched herself roughly from his embrace, mocking his words in a sing-song voice.

"Inja, I'm so sorry, please forgive me," she said acidly. "You sound like a broken record. I'm sick to death of discussing this baby thing. Is that why you married me, to make babies?"

Reeling with astonishment, he stared open-mouthed at her flushed face and unyielding stance. What triggered such animosity? Forcing himself to smile, he dropped his eyes and tried to ignore the venom in her words.

"You don't mean what you're saying. We'll discuss this again when you've calmed down and are in control of yourself." Slapping his hands away, she smiled maliciously.

"Oh, don't I? I have news for you," she sneered. "I don't want a baby, not now or at any time in the future, do you get that?" Shooting him a final glare of defiance, she stomped out of the kitchen to the bedroom. The door slammed behind her with such force the bathroom window rattled in its frame.

Shortie's shoulders drooped, and his stomach contracted into a tight little ball. Struggling for control, mixed emotions shook him to the core. He tried to call out to her, but his voice failed him. "Sweet Jesus, what do I do now?" he whispered fervently.

Eddie hid in the bathroom at the first sound of arguing. Crouching behind the bathroom door, he almost screamed when the window came crashing down. He had watched his sister carefully during the entire encounter and knew she hadn't shed a single tear. He'd seen that scary look on her face before. Shuddering, he stepped from his hiding place to draw closer to Shortie. Something bad was going to happen, and he hoped it didn't involve him.

Chapter 13

After a restless night tossing and turning, Shortie finally fell into a fitful sleep. Waking late, he skipped breakfast in order to catch his ride to work. In semi-darkness, he hurried down the hill without taking his usual caution. Catching his foot on a twig, he was sent sprawling. As he rose to his feet, a sharp pain shot up his right leg. Limping, he arrived in time to spot the taillights of Jonesy's pickup speeding down the hill. Cursing himself for sleeping late, he walked the rest of the way to work. It was the first and only time he was ever late for anything.

When he entered the dairy, blood streaked his trouser leg, and he limped badly. The skin was torn right up the shinbone, and it bled worse than it hurt. At the sight of blood, Tony ran for the first aid kit.

"What happened to you?" he asked.

"I fell," he mumbled.

"How did you fall? This looks bad! Did you slip on something? If I didn't know better, I'd say you fell off a mountain," he chuckled.

"I did." At Tony's incredulous look, Shortie bellowed, "I was late for work and tripped as I was coming down the hill. Does that satisfy your curiosity?" Sitting with arms akimbo, he sat like a stone statue with jaw set stubbornly. Glaring daggers, he dared Tony to ask any more questions.

Wisely, Tony said nothing, but he couldn't keep his lips from twitching. It was hard to believe that his stoic friend had fallen in the first place. If it were himself, or Jonesy, or even Blackie, it wouldn't be so funny. After all, they were ordinary guys who often did dumb things. But Shortie wasn't the ordinary-type guy.

Reaching into the medicine box, Tony pulled out the Mercurochrome and began to shake the bottle, mixing the contents. Shortie eyed the red mixture with a certain amount of consternation. Breaking his silence, he gestured toward the bottle.

"Is this really necessary?"

"It kills germs and keeps infection away," Tony answered with a disarming smile. His medical advice was based on a recent advertisement he'd seen in the drug store window.

"Hand me that medicine kit. I can bandage my own leg," Shortie growled. He didn't trust the glint in Tony's eye.

An angelic grin creased the younger man's face as he held the tin box out of his reach.

"First the medicine, then the bandage," he explained as if talking to one of his own children.

Shortie made a grab for the box. When he lunged for it, he fell slightly off balance, and when he righted himself, Tony smeared the red liquid over the torn, raw skin. His eyes opened wide in shock. Jumping to his feet, he fanned the fire on his leg with his hat.

"What the sam hill!" he exclaimed. Hopping up and down, he cursed Tony and his mother at the top of his lungs. His yelling soon brought the attention of other employees, and within minutes, the entire crew was crammed into the locker room watching the spectacle with great delight. Tony waited patiently for Shortie to calm down, and when he had, Tony slapped a gauze bandage across the open wound.

"Isn't that better?" he asked with mock innocence.

Veins stood out in livid ridges on Shortie's neck. Unable to speak an intelligible word, he stalked out of the room with as much dignity as he could muster. Intending to load the handcart for delivery to the depot, he gave the handle a hard yank. His jaw dropped in disbelief. The handle came off in his hand. The bolt holding it had snapped in two. Storming off to the supply shed for another bolt and a wrench, he mumbled angrily to himself. His expression, as black as a coal miner's lung, warned co-workers to stay away until he had cooled off.

As the morning wore on, his temper cooled and hunger displaced his anger. When the noon whistle blew, he beat Tony to locker room. Grabbing his lunch bucket off the shelf, he followed Tony to the picnic table. After eating his customary bologna sandwich, onion, and Tony's apple, his mood lightened and he was smiling once again.

Tony bought himself a soda and one for Shortie as a token peace offering. Taking a deep drink of his cola, he handed Shortie a root beer.

His eyes lit up when he spied the drink. Root beer to Shortie was another man's beer or whiskey. Upending the bottle, he drained half its contents in one gulp. Wiping his mouth, he leaned back with a contented sigh.

"Thanks," he said, indicating the bottle. Taking another swallow, he burped on the acid bubbles.

"Does your leg hurt?" Tony inquired after catching the slight smile tilting the older man's lips.

"It's fine," Shortie replied curtly. He wasn't ready to return to his usual good humor. The morning's humiliation rankled in his mind, and he still smarted from Inja's angry words of the night before. Guzzling the last of his soda, he gestured vaguely to his friend. "Time for work." He trudged back to the processing room with shoulders bowed.

The afternoon was spent loading and unloading freight, a backbreaking job. He didn't mind the chore because it allowed his thoughts to roam. Wrestling over Inja's heated words, he wondered if he was wrong to want a child of his own. Maybe she was right and he didn't make enough to pay for the needs of a tiny infant. But Jonesy's paycheck was the same as his own, and they supported five children. Lowell, his brother-in-law, supported two children, and surely his paycheck wasn't a lot more than his own. He wondered if other couples fought over the same things they did. Sometimes married life was terribly lonely and unfulfilling. Sudden inspiration hit him like a bolt out of the blue. Of course, it all seemed so obvious. All the couples he knew had nice things decorating their homes. Inja would be much more receptive to the idea of motherhood if she had some of the nice things other women had. What was it Eddie had said? "She only wants pretty things." If spending a few dollars would make her feel happy and more secure, then she'd want to start a family, he reasoned.

Making a quick decision, he brightened perceptively. Withdrawing a few dollars from their savings to buy a few doodads would be worth the loss if it made her happy. Besides, if he picked up a few extra weekend jobs over the summer, he could easily replace the money. Taking the last milk can off the train, he smiled for the first time that day. Tossing the 145-pound container effortlessly onto the handtruck, he thought, "Boy, will she ever be surprised."

After work, Tony eyed Shortie speculatively as they walked Hill Street to catch their ride home. He'd heard him whistling long before their shift was over and knew it was a sure sign that whatever had troubled him earlier had come to a satisfactory resolution. The whistling didn't bother him, but the Cheshire cat grin did. Shortie was smiling brightly, teeth gleaming white against his swarthy skin. Tony's curiosity got the better of him.

"Is everything okay with you?" he probed.

"Everything is perfect," Shortie answered heartily. His blue eyes twinkled merrily, and his expression bore no hint of malice toward his young friend.

Coming to the corner where they waited for Blackie, Shortie left Tony there on the pretense that he had errands to run. He didn't want to reveal his secret to anyone. Waving, he called back, "Don't wait for me. I'll catch a ride later or walk."

"We can wait," Tony answered. "Blackie won't mind. Hey, do you want me to come with you?"

Shaking his head, he waved farewell. His plans required no company. Hastening his steps, he turned a corner to escape Tony's puzzled gaze.

Rushing into the furniture exchange, he raced over to a startled salesman and blurted out his request before he could change his mind.

"Where are your television sets?" he inquired, panting heavily from his sprint down Main Street.

"You're standing in front of them, sir," replied the salesman dryly. "Would you like to see our latest model?"

"Yes, sir." Eyeing each vacant screen, he felt out of his element. He knew nothing about TVs and didn't know the right questions to ask. He rubbed the back of his neck in a nervous gesture.

"This is the best model on the market," bragged the salesman as he extended his arms theatrically, indicating a console TV. Beaming like a proud parent, he rattled off the features of the set as if reading from a memorized script. Kneeling to point out the vertical and horizontal controls, hidden behind a sliding door, he regarded Shortie with a lofty expression.

"This particular set is a fine piece of furniture and requires a sizable down payment." Looking down his nose at Shortie's stained work clothes and heavy, worn boots, he waved toward one marked "used." "Maybe we should look at another?" he asked pointedly.

"How much?" Shortie pointed to the large console. He didn't like the attitude of the salesman and refused to be intimidated. Jangling the change in his pocket nervously, he waited for the salesman to tell him the bad news. When told the amount, he smiled triumphantly into the sneering face of the clerk.

"I'll be right back," he told him, "I have an errand to run, but I'll be back to buy this set. Have it loaded and ready to go by the time I return." Turning on his heel, he sped out the door and up the street to the bank.

Stepping to the teller's window, she looked at him questioningly. "Are you making another deposit, Shortie?"

He had banked at this branch long enough that everyone called him by name. They were aware that he saved every spare penny, socking it away into a growing account. Her thin eyebrows raised in surprise when Shortie announced he was making a withdrawal.

A sudden anxiety stabbed him in the stomach as he signed the slip. He withdrew an amount that had taken him almost a year to save. After counting each bill carefully, he folded it into a wad and stuffed it into his pocket. Rushing to the door, he literally ran into Pastor Adams.

"Hello, Pastor, sorry to bump into you this way. See you in church," he said as he took off without a backward glance.

"It was good to see you, too, and how's Inja getting along?" Righting his hat back on his head, Pastor Adams found his inquiries lost on Shortie's retreating figure.

As he passed the corner drug store on his return to the furniture store, a glint of crystal caught his attention. Pausing to admire the window display, his eyes were dazzled by the sparkle of sunlight off cut-glass. There in the window was a pitcher and glass set that made the one in the catalog look cheap. The pitcher was wide bottomed and narrowed at the lip with a graceful downward furl. There was sixteen glasses in two sizes arranged attractively around the pitcher. The smaller ones were wide mouthed with squat bottoms and the taller were suspended on graceful stems, so slender he'd seen thicker blades of grass. A sign next to them boldly declared, "On Sale-50% OFF." Without a moment's hesitation, he marched into the store and bought the glass set without asking the price. The salesgirl was pleased to box and wrap them. Stuffing the package under his arm, he was out of the store and on his way in less than five minutes.

The salesman at the furniture store hadn't expected him to return and was taken aback when he raced up to the counter and threw down enough money to pay for the set in full.

"Did you get it loaded on a delivery van?" he asked, slightly out of breath from his hurry.

The demeanor of the clerk changed the instant green hit the countertop. All of a sudden he was Shortie's best friend, fawning over him embarrassingly.

"We were just getting it ready for transport, sir," he said with a pretentious smile. Preparing a sales slip and breathing the remains of a tuna sandwich into Shortie's face, he asked in an unctuous voice, "Is there anything else I can show you today? A nice, comfy overstuffed chair perhaps?"

"I don't need a chair." Shortie's nose wrinkled up in distaste. He hated dealing with towners like the shallow, pasty-faced man before him. "What I want," he said with an edge of impatience in his voice, "is to see that TV loaded on a delivery truck before it becomes outdated."

Fearing the loss of a paying customer, the clerk scurried to the back of the store and shouted ineffective orders at the deliverymen. Unhurriedly, two men came from the loading docks, and ignoring the clerk, inquired of Shortie.

"Which one is it?" asked the larger of the two.

"That big console on the end." He pointed it out to them.

"This here's a good one," volunteered the smaller man. "I bought one of these a month ago. I've been real happy with it. They're easy to fix, too; you can almost do it yourself."

Very satisfied with his purchases, Shortie followed the two out to the truck. He helped them tarp the television and a fancy dinette set.

"Can you give me a lift?"

"Hop in," the driver told him. "Maybe you can lend a hand when we unload this," he said, pulling a tarp off an upright piano.

Shortie's eyes gleamed when he spied the ivory keys. He itched to sit down and play a chord or two but knew they needed to be on their way. The piano would require the muscle of all three of them to unload.

Purple-hued shadows filled the valley when the delivery truck headed up the hill. They were exhausted after delivering the piano. The woman receiving it had wanted it moved from one wall to the other until deciding it looked best where they'd placed it the first time. Turning off the pavement road, the truck sped up the steep dirt road to Shortie's house.

"Any time you want a job, give us a call," the driver told him. "It isn't often we work with a guy that has enough muscle for the work we do."

"I think I'll stay at the dairy. It's less pay, but a whole lot easier on an old man's back." Shortie rubbed a tender spot along the base of his spine. He was thankful there had been only one piano moved six times instead of six pianos moved once. He signaled them to stop in front of the stairs leading to the little house above them.

"Isn't there any other way up there?" groaned the smaller man.

"It's the only way, and they don't get better in the dark of night," Shortie answered.

Getting out of the truck, the three grabbed the heavy console to lift it off the truck. Eddie heard the men's voices and ran from the kitchen to greet them. Throwing open the door, he gaped open-mouthed as the TV set was lugged up the stairs and into the front room. After a moment's rest, the deliverymen made the necessary connections, put up the antenna, and completed all the adjustments before Inja was allowed into the room. Noticing their temporary help's pretty wife, they smiled knowingly at each other.

"If anything goes wrong, tell that little wife of yours to give us a call and we'll come fix it at no charge," they said as they went out the door. Eddie closed the door firmly after them. After making sure the two men were on their way down the road, his exuberance returned. He was so excited to see Inja's response, he ran into the kitchen, then to the front room, yelling at her not to peek.

Shortie blindfolded Inja before leading her into the front room. He carefully unboxed the glass set and placed them on top of the TV. Golden light from the lamp reflected off the finely chiseled glass, casting a prism effect on the wall behind them. He whisked the blindfold off with a flourish.

"Oh my gosh," she squealed. Jumping to her feet, she ran to the set and turned it on. "Is it really ours?" she asked as she turned first one knob and then another. Smoothing a hand over the oak finish reverently, she rushed to Shortie and hugged him tightly about the neck. Giving him a quick peck on the cheek, she gazed at the TV with ecstasy. Spying the reflection on the wall, she picked up one of the slender stemmed glasses and flicked it with a finger to hear a musical bell-like peal. "Real crystal," she breathed. "Thank you, this means so much to me."

"Can we eat in front of the TV?" Eddie asked. Shortie almost shook his head when he glimpsed the same hopeful expression mirrored on his wife's face.

"Just this once—it will only be for tonight, I promise," she pleaded.

He liked having meals seated around the table where they could share conversation and look each other in the face, but this time he was outnumbered. Nodding in agreement, he enjoyed how much happiness this simple gift brought to his wife. Even Eddie's little face beamed with excitement.

"Wait till the kids at school hear about this," he said importantly. "They'll all want to come here for dinner."

"Let's not get carried away, and remember, we eat dinner here in the front room only this one night. We won't make a habit of it," Shortie admonished.

Inja hurriedly filled plates with food and set them on the battle-scarred coffee table. Shortie filled two of the long-stemmed glasses with milk and handed one to Inja as if it were the best champagne money could buy. Gazing into each other's eyes, they touched glasses together in silent tribute.

The delicate stemware looked incongruent alongside the stained and chipped melmac plates, but they didn't care. She thought the rich shine of the oak finish on the console made the room appear less shabby. Inja used the glasses often and bragged about them to all her friends. She was proud of them and of him for buying them for her. She never told him the glass set wasn't for lemonade, but was meant for mixing and serving cocktails.

Chapter 14

As May slid into June, peace reigned temporarily at the little house on the hill. The television's arrival had restored a sense of unity to their marriage. Fits of temper ended, and Inja's angry words were soon forgotten. Early summer brought more daylight and longer days, which meant an increased workload at the dairy. Shortie had little spare time as it was, and what time he had was put to better use than to worry over their marital spats.

Inja's days were spent glued to the images on the television screen. Too often, Shortie returned home from work to face a hastily prepared meal. The standard became sandwiches or canned soup, and it was on rare occasion the family sat together for the evening meal. Even though he hated the square screen dominating her life, he held his tongue. She seemed happy and frequently mentioned how nice it would be to have a little girl to do things with. When he returned home, she ran to greet him with a kiss and a hug. Other than the incessant intrusion of the TV, things were going well.

His day had been long and he was so tired, he was almost asleep on his feet by the time he arrived home on Friday. Trudging up the steps, he was nearly knocked off his feet when she burst out the door.

"What's the matter?" he asked. His heart pounded with alarm while his feet did some quick maneuvering to maintain balance. Grabbing her by the upper arms, he unintentionally shook her. "Is it Eddie? Has something happened to the boy? Answer me!"

"What's the matter with you?" Backing up a step, she glared at him with anger. Rubbing her arms where he'd gripped a little too hard, she pierced him with a condemning stare. "I was anxious for you to get home, that's all," she pouted.

"I'm sorry, but you startled me. You'd better watch those exits; you came close to knocking us both down the stairs." He steadied her until both their balances were regained. "Is everything all right?" he repeated.

"Yes, everything is fine and Eddie is fine," she answered curtly. As she decided to forgive him, her face lit up with excitement. "Haven't you heard?"

Taken aback at the quicksilver change in mood and at the question, he stared at her dumbly.

"Quit looking so surprised and come in the house," she ordered. "It's been on the news all day. Oh, this is so exciting," she trilled. Tugging on his free arm, she pulled him up the remaining steps.

"What's been on the news? How could I hear about anything? I've been at work since five this morning," he reminded her.

"Shh, listen," she said with a finger to her lips. Pushing him closer to the television, she stood to the side and waited for his reaction.

Glancing tiredly at the screen, he was reminded of his hunger by an empty, sounding growl from his stomach. He'd worked over thirteen hours and was more concerned with filling his stomach and getting some rest than staring at a news commentator. However, his chin dropped and his lunch bucket hit the floor when he realized what and who was on the screen.

"What in the name of...isn't that....?" He pointed at the images and then looked at her, speechless. Shock registered in his expression. He gazed at her questioningly, and she only nodded her head, confirming his unspoken question. The picture showed the entrance to the Lucky Spur Mine, and standing in front was a newsman busily questioning an employee. Five important-looking men dressed in three-piece suits surrounded them. The suits, obviously from out of town, wore frowns on their faces, and their arms were folded across their chests. They weren't happy. Shortie paid little attention to the suits or the one they questioned, but kept his eyes glued to a big man who stood off to the side. There was a grim-faced Blackie with arms akimbo as he watched the proceedings from a distance.

"What can you tell us about the missing crates of dynamite?" asked the newsman.

"I really can't say much," the man answered with a nervous quaver in his voice. Glancing quickly at the unsmiling faces around him, the man firmed his voice and spoke directly to the camera. "All I know is, I was told to bring a box of explosives to number seven shaft. We were ready to set the charges to break through a rear wall to open a new tunnel. We have to keep track of every stick of dynamite removed from inventory, you know, and I'm always real careful to keep an accurate count," he said with another look toward the suits. Receiving no response, he cleared his throat and continued. "As I was sayin', we have to count each box and make sure it adds the same as the last tally taken and if it don't, somebody's in real hot water.

"Go on," the newsman urged.

"Like I already told ya, I started adding, and things didn't total up to what was marked on the tally sheet. The sheet showed fourteen boxes, but there was only eleven. I checked and rechecked and then had the supply man do the same. Sure enough, there was no getting' around it; there were three boxes missin'. It sure is suspicious that the last one to remove anything from inventory was our explosive's man, Ben Schultz. Word has it he's an expert with the stuff and knows how to place it and where it'll do the most good. He quit the day an explosion shook the upper valley."

"Now wait just a minute, you can't accuse a man without evidence. You'd best be real sure of your facts before you say anything more," warned a familiar, gravelly voice. Turning away from the camera's eye, Blackie shouldered his way out of the gathering crowd. The newsman tried to pull him back but couldn't. Facing the camera and the microphone, he glared contemptuously at them all. The newsman, dwarfed by Blackie's overall size, released his grip on the big man's coat sleeve and backed off. He stalked away from them without a backward look. The last glimpse the audience had was of his shoulders as they filled the screen as he stalked away.

Stunned, Shortie stared at the TV, unable to believe what he'd just heard. With vivid clarity, questions about Ben Schultz flooded his mind. Ben had been a friend and it was hard to believe he'd do anything to harm anyone. Or maybe he hadn't been such a good friend after all. Doubt clouded his thinking. He squeezed his eyes shut tightly to clear the picture of Schultz as he'd left Shortie's porch the night of the explosion. The man hadn't been just scared; he was petrified and in an awful hurry to get off the mountain. Why hadn't he seen it before? Rubbing the back of his neck, he said aloud, "What the sam hill?"

"Quit talking to yourself," Inja broke in on his thoughts. "Do you think they'll find him?"

"Find who?"

"Ben Schultz," she said as if speaking to someone slow-witted. "Who else? I think it's fairly certain they'll be looking for him," she said with certainty.

"Who would be looking for Ben? Do you mean the police?" He couldn't believe what he'd just heard. The idea that Ben deliberately tried to hurt them and then came to their rescue was absolutely ludicrous.

"There are laws against stealing explosives, aren't there?" Her question dripped with icy sarcasm. She stood before him in a defiant posture with hands on hips. Clearly, she was prepared to do battle to prove her point.

"There are severe penalties for having explosives in one's possession," he agreed. "But I just can't believe he had anything to do with it. He was our friend," he reminded, "and he came to help us, to help you, Inja."

"He needed a good alibi, and what could be better than posing as 'Good Samaritan' to the very ones he tried to harm. Wake up, Shortie; the man's friendship was a sham."

"Why would he do such a thing? What would he gain from such a nefarious act?"

"I don't know and I don't care," she said with a careless shrug of her shoulders. Sniffing self-righteously, she touched a tiny scar on her left cheek, the only remaining trace of her injuries. "Yes," she said in a bitter, detached voice, "I hope he rots in prison for what he did." A look of hate blazed in her eyes and heated her cheeks to fire red. The woman standing before him bore no resemblance to the sweet girl he married.

An ominous shiver ran up his spine as he stared at this stranger. He didn't know what shocked him more: the unfamiliar expression or the threatening tone in her voice.

"We don't know the entire story, Inja," he gently reminded her. "I'm too tired and too hungry to worry about this right now. Maybe I'll think more clearly with a full stomach and after a good night's rest," he hinted.

"It's in the warming oven." She waved vaguely toward the kitchen. Her attention was riveted on the screen as another miner was interviewed. Totally absorbed in the unfolding story, she finished eating a sandwich as she watched.

Opening the porcelain door of the warming oven, Shortie was pleased to find a hot beef sandwich beside a mound of mashed potatoes, and a saucepan of beef gravy, still warm. Pouring the gravy over the contents on his plate, he ate alone at the kitchen table. He wasn't surprised when someone pounded insistently at his front door. Rumors had to be flying from house to house after the newscast. He expected Blackie to be on his doorstep with his Irish temper ablaze.

Stepping into the front room, he snapped off the TV before opening the door. "Make some coffee; we've got company and it might be a very long night."

Irritated, Inja touched the dial to turn the TV back on, but had second thoughts. His mood was suddenly disagreeable, and no purpose would be served with an argument. Holding back the complaint that flew to her lips, she meekly went to the kitchen to make coffee. She hurried, spilling dark crystals all over the counter. A storm was brewing and she didn't want to miss a single word of it.

Hurrying, Shortie opened the door before Blackie knocked it down with his fist. Bert tailed behind him, looking unusually pale under the cinnamon sprinkling of freckles across her broad face. They both sailed past Inja, disregarding her presence entirely.

"Well, come on in," Shortie invited unnecessarily. Both of them headed to the kitchen, where Bert helped herself to cups, cream and sugar. She set a plate of oatmeal cookies, still warm from the oven, on the table.

"We didn't mean to interrupt your dinner," Blackie said, noticing the half-eaten meal, "but things have happened you need to know." The big man fidgeted nervously and paced the room like a caged cat.

"Let the man finish eating," Bert ordered. "I hope you like elk roast. Inja told me you hadn't had one for a month of Sundays, so I brought leftovers from yesterday's dinner."

"Woman, no one cares about pot roast when far more important things are brewing," Blackie bellowed in exasperation.

Inja stood in the kitchen doorway listening to the conversation. She felt her face flush as Blackie's cold, dark eyes shrewdly assessed her. Squirming, she felt like a bug under a microscope.

Shortie didn't understand her obvious discomfort. Blackie looked at everyone that way. Now knowing which way the wind blew, he decided to feign ignorance and watch and learn.

"As a matter of fact, I have enjoyed each and every bite, and if you don't mind," he paused to sit down and take up his fork, "I'll finish eating while you clue me in." Spearing a chunk of meat, he regarded his visitors with raised brows. He wondered how long it would take to get the entire story out of them. He'd never known Blackie to be in a hurry to tell a story if dragging it out would add suspense.

Pulling out a chair and turning it backwards, Blackie straddled the seat and rested his arms on the backrest to collect his thoughts. He exhaled loudly as if he'd been holding his breath for too long. Rubbing his palms on denim-clad thighs, he glanced nervously at Shortie. There was every indication that he was reluctant to tell what he knew. Raking a hand through his hair, he glanced questioningly at Bert. At her nod of encouragement, he told a story that was hard to believe.

"You watched the news tonight?" he asked.

"I saw enough of it to know that some sticks of dynamite are missing and it's suspicioned that Ben Schultz took them."

"There's more to it than that. Did you see the suits when they interviewed Shaugnahan?"

"Is he the guy who found the stuff missing?" Inja interrupted. Blackie regarded her with a cold stare. She sensed his disapproval and indicated she wouldn't interrupt again.

Since their arrival, the Cleggs' attitude toward Inja left Shortie totally baffled. What could she possible have done to offend them? Trying to be as encouraging as possible, he broke the uncomfortable silence.

"Well, is Shaugnahan the one that discovered it or not? Don't stop now, tell me what happened!" he demanded.

"I was coming off shift when a black limousine pulled up to the mine. Can you imagine that? A limousine in Kellogg, Idaho," he marveled. "Anyway, the suits marched into the super's office, and a few minutes later he comes out and locks the door so no one can come in. Twenty minutes later he comes running out and yells at Shaugnahan to recount all the stuff in inventory." Leaning over the table, he dropped an unanticipated bomb. "Sometime yesterday morning, Ben Schultz turned himself in. He admitted he was the one who stole the explosives, but denies setting off the charges. The FBI is holding him somewhere in Spokane. The suits are here to conduct a thorough investigation into what happened and claim they won't rest until all guilty parties have been arrested. Now, if Ben didn't set them off, who did? Who would want to blow half this mountain away and take you with it?"

Shortie's fork dropped from his fingers and clattered loudly onto the floor. His throat was suddenly tight and dry. Leaning forward, he drew close enough to count the tiny hairs growing in his nostrils. His blue eyes bore into Blackie's, demanding answers.

"Isn't that a bit of an exaggeration? Most of this mountain remains intact, and any evidence of damage is long gone."

"It isn't all gone, not by a long shot," Inja said angrily. Rubbing the tiny scar under her eye, she raked his face with condemning eyes, a reminder of the injuries she'd suffered.

He remained silent, picked up his fork, dusted it off, and took another bite of food. It tasted like sawdust.

The Cleggs kept their eyes glued on Shortie. They ignored Inja's outburst. Blackie, not a patient man to begin with, paced the small kitchen with quick steps. Growing more impatient by the minute, he watched the fork travel from plate to mouth until he couldn't stand the silence any longer. Exasperated beyond belief, he shouted with arms waving in the air, "What's the matter with you? How can you continue to sit there, calmly eating, when there's a maniac walking around out there with enough dynamite to blow us off the map?"

He returned his friend's glare impassively. "The only maniac I see is here in my kitchen," he said in a quiet voice. "What purpose is served if I act on emotional guesswork instead of facts? Besides, a man needs to eat in order to think rationally." Shrugging his shoulders, feigning indifference, he motioned for the big man to sit down. "Calm down. Let's not lose our heads."

"Emotional," Blackie retorted with fire in his eyes. "Man, you have plenty to get emotional about if you'd just take your head out of the sand."

Shortie heard Inja's sharp intake of breath. She clenched her sweater together at the throat and turned to the stove. Without thinking, she grasped the metal handle of the coffeepot and burned the palm of her hand. As she dropped it back onto the hot stove, the full pot splattered her with boiling coffee.

Hurrying to the bathroom, Shortie returned with a tin of bag balm. Taking up a gob on two fingers, he spread it generously over her palm and forearm. "Use a potholder next time; that's what they're for," he ordered. "You're getting all worked up over nothing." Snapping the lid back on the ointment, he studied Blackie warily. "Explain your last statement if you please."

"Tell him, old man, tell him the rest," Bertie urged. "Tell him what you told me. That's why we came up here," she pleaded. Tears glittered in her eyes, surprising them all. Bertie never cried, and certainly not in front of anyone. Not wanting to upset her further, Shortie placed a protective arm around her shoulders. Pulling a chair out from the table for her, Blackie awkwardly helped her to it. He'd only known his wife to cry twice before during all their married years. The first was when they got married, and the second when she was told they'd never have kids. He looked helplessly at Shortie; crying females were out of his expertise.

"Look what you've done," Inja said venomously. Moving quickly to Bert's side, she patted the older women's back. Remaining at Bert's side, she shot daggers of contempt at both men.

Bert drew a shaky breath and smiled for the first time. Wiping an errant tear from her cheek, she stayed Inja's sharp tongue with a finger to her lips.

"Tell him the rest," she commanded her husband, "or I will."

"I'm sorry about that comment about your head bein' in the sand. I was just spouting off the way I do when I get riled," he apologized. "But to get back to the heart of the matter, Ben said some other things, too, things that made the feds real suspicious about some of the people living around here."

"Suspicious?" Shortie asked incredulously. "Suspicious about who and what for?"

"Ben said someone around here knows where the dynamite is. He said the explosion last April wasn't big enough to account for much. They think someone up here has the rest of it and is going to use it to blast into one of the mines empty shafts to steal ore."

Shortie's eyebrows shot up in amazement. Disbelief etched his features as he gazed dumbly back at Blackie. "Did 'they' mention any names?" he asked. He didn't want to know who "they" were and guessed beforehand what the answer would be.

Blackie's dark features were suddenly pale. Gulping loudly, his mouth opened and then closed again, as if unsure of what to say. As he gathered himself together, his black eyes stared unwavering into Shortie's blue ones. "It seems someone put a bug in their ear laying suspicion on you. Your name was brought up more than once. They figure your place received minimal damage, just enough to make it look good. They think you had more in that cellar than just a few jars of jam and a sack of potatoes. They'll be coming round tomorrow and snooping around like a pack of half-starved dogs. Everybody will be questioned and...." Raking his hand through his hair once again, he dropped his gaze to the floor. "Shortie, I know you're innocent, and this town knows it, too, but they're looking for someone to pin this on, and they don't care who. What should we do?"

Rising to his feet on shaky legs, Shortie placed a hand on the back of his neck. "What the sam...." he started to say, but his throat was suddenly too parched for words and his lips drier than dust. Shaking his head, he forced himself to make sense out of his dazed thoughts. His shoulders sagged, fatigue assaulted every muscle, and for a moment, anger drove away common sense. The walls of the kitchen pressed close, squeezing the air from his lungs. Taking a deep breath, he forced himself to think rationally before doing something he would be sorry for later.

"I guess we'll answer their questions and try to cooperate. Only a guilty man would do otherwise," he replied. "But have I offended someone so bad they would retaliate in this way? Lord, help me, I've never had an enemy before, and help them, because now they've made an enemy of me," he muttered under his breath. Bitter sadness filled his heart.

Bert's eyes filled with tears, threatening to overflow with sympathy. Shortie's face was suddenly drawn and haggard, and the laugh lines around his mouth and eyes turned down in sorrow. Red images danced across the backside of her eyes as rage began to build at the unfairness of it all. Patting his hand, she empathized, "We're all under suspicion, not just you."

Inja, with hand over her mouth, stood motionless beside Bert. Shocked beyond belief, she couldn't understand who would want to spread such lies about such a gentle and caring man. Turning stricken eyes upon him, her heart filled with compassion. Moving to his side, she took his hand, holding it, giving moral support.

Bert watched the loving wife gestures with disdain. At that moment, she almost hated the younger woman. Afraid the intensity of her emotions would show in her eyes, she dropped her gaze and picked at an errant piece of lint on her skirt.

"We'll stick together, all of us," Blackie vowed. Helping his wife to her feet, he placed one hand on Shortie's shoulder. "Someone is taking great pains to cause you grief. The only solution is to find out who it is and shut him up before this thing goes any further. It's rumored a town meeting is gonna be held at Arden's first thing in the morning. We don't need more trouble than what we've got. Will you join me in making sure things remain peaceful?"

Walking them to the door, Shortie nodded and agreed to meet them at the store when it first opened. Turning on the outdoor light, he saw his friends down the steps and then turned back into the house with a disheartened sigh. Some days it just didn't pay to get out of bed. Leaning his head against the door, he turned to the source from where strength is drawn.

Dear Lord, whatever can go wrong has indeed gone wrong. Give me wisdom and the strength to do your leading.

After locking the front door, he went straight to bed. He didn't say goodnight to Inja or wait for her to turn off the house lights. Within minutes, he slept soundly. He didn't dream or remember going to bed. He didn't remember sleeping or waking, but with the dawn came complete restoration of vigor.

Chapter 15

Shutting the bedroom door without a parting glance at Inja's sleeping form, Shortie waited until he was seated in the kitchen to put on his heavy boots. He didn't know how long he'd been awake, but he was alert and ready to accept whatever challenge the day would bring.

Expertly, he started a fire in the cookstove to ward off the morning's chill. As he waited for the kindling to catch, he sat before the stove trying to ignore the persistent voice nagging at him. His head ached, and the voice became more insistent.

Hear me. I am the Great Shepherd. All those that call upon the name of the Lord will be saved.

Great, now I'm hearing voices, what next? How can He help me out of the jam I'm in anyway? But wasn't He supposed to be in control of everything? Why did God allow this to happen to me? Maybe He doesn't really care. I didn't ask for trouble and I certainly didn't go looking for it. I had nothing to do with the explosion and can't understand why I'm being accused unless God is getting back at me for something. Lord, if You're there, please be with me today.

Warmth filled his body, and for a time he didn't feel cold or see the dark kitchen. The sensation lasted but a moment, and then the dark of the room and cool morning air penetrated his thoughts. Thinking he was still half-asleep and dreaming, he rose to his feet and flicked on the overhead light.

As his eyes adjusted to the sudden brilliance, he looked about the room as if expecting someone to step from the shadows. Shaking off the feeling, he threw a few handfuls of oats into salted water and set a pan on the stove to boil. As he waited, one question snaked through his mind, leaving icy imprints on his brain. Who hated him so much and why go to such lengths to accuse him? His head pounded harder. Thinking the headache was from hunger, he ate the oatmeal straight from the pan in eight precise spoonfuls.

Hunger satisfied, he filled the woodbox, fed a few scraps to Old Joe, and banked the fire to keep the kitchen warm. Grabbing his jacket, he hurried to meet Blackie. Deep in his own thoughts, he didn't notice a small shadow following him up the hill.

Tinges of pink and orange streaked across the horizon by the time he reached the main road. He was surprised to see several neighbors making their way to the store in the dim early morning sunlight. Gabbie, bleary-eyed, plodded slowly up the hill. He looked like something any self-respecting cat would leave behind.

"It's a fool's errand," he announced as he fell into step. "Only a durned fool would be out of bed this early on a Sat'a'day mornin'." Shortie didn't reply, which was response enough for Gabbie.

Spying Blackie with Bert at his side, he waded through the growing crowd to join them. Several people clasped his arm and shook his hand as he passed by. He was more than a little surprised to find some neighbors with entire families in tow. When Arden opened the doors, the aroma of fresh, hot coffee wafted out, lifting noses to sniff the breeze like bird dogs on the hunt.

"Coffee," murmured Bert. "I sure hope it's hot. My eyes don't work until pried apart with a cup and the hotter the better." Her remark was echoed throughout the crowd and the thirsty throng pushed them inside.

Stepping onto the cement porch, Arden held the enameled coffeepot high. "Ten cents buys a hot mug of coffee and one doughnut. If you're interested, step inside, if not, then stay off my porch and don't block the door," he hollered. Gabbie sneaked in the back door and came up behind him. Grinning, he held out a bent coin in a grubby hand.

"What's this?" Arden asked. Peering at the silver piece suspiciously, he examined it until satisfied it was legal tender and not a nut off a loose bolt he'd swiped from somewhere. "Just remember, old man, a dime buys one cup of coffee and a doughnut, not four cups and five doughnuts."

Gabbie's greed opened the floodgates. The coffeepot emptied and the platter of doughnuts disappeared. Arden, being a good host, refilled the pot and replenished the platter. As the crowd continued to grow, spilling out into the street and then across to a vacant lot, his net profit grew and more than doubled with every ding of the cash drawer.

Shortie was amazed at the numbers, and more were driving in from hidden gulches outside of town and along the river. It wasn't long before hushed murmurs became loud, angry voices. How could it be otherwise with such a large body of people? From the porch, he recognized miners, loggers, and towners that under other circumstances never spoke to one another.

"Coffee! Here's fresh, brewed coffee," Arden barked. Pushing doughnuts into angry faces, he tried to soothe tempers before a brawl started on his doorstep. Blackie, Bert, and Shortie mingled throughout the crowd, acting as peacekeepers when necessary.

"This is the power of television at its best," Blackie commented. "You'd never see so many gathered in one place if it hadn't been broadcast on the local news. I'll bet there's not more than five or ten of them really interested in what happens here today, but they're bored and want to see some action. If something don't happen soon, they'll start something on their own," he said with a disgusted snort.

"Yeah, I s'pose you're right." Shortie's vague response could barely be heard. His attention wasn't on the conversation, but on three young toughs spoiling for a fight. "Don't start something I have to finish," he whispered to one.

His warning was enough for the three to move to a better location to end their disagreement.

He was so intent on keeping an eye out for trouble that he didn't notice the change in the crowd until a sudden hush stilled their voices. A long, black limousine pulled alongside their outer perimeter and parked in the middle of the road. The crowd parted like the Red Sea when the doors opened and the occupants stepped onto the pavement.

"Well, I'll be d—," Blackie muttered. Releasing his hold on one hot-tempered young man, he pushed the kid away, forgotten. His eyes locked on the group standing by the limo.

Stepping forward, the two shouldered their way to the front of the crowd. Bert followed Blackie with his grim expression mirrored in her own.

Five men exited the car and nervously faced the crowd. Not one person spoke, but stared at them, measuring their mettle to decide if they were worth speaking to. It wasn't until a second vehicle approached that the group dared move or attempt to address the crowd.

Removing a pair of dark glasses, one of the suits stepped boldly forward. He wasn't afraid and moved toward them confidently. Surveying the crowd with keen, sky-blue eyes, he studied each face. Feet shuffled nervously as the threatening façade posed by the throng was defused. He was almost as tall as Blackie, but not nearly as heavy. His blonde, wavy hair set off a tanned, handsome face. It was easily ascertained that this man commanded others and respect was his due. Completely at ease, he didn't back away, but shook the hands of men close to him.

"My name is Frank Howard. I'm an investigator hired by the local mine to figure out what happened here last April. These brave souls are my associates." He indicated the five huddled by the limo with a wave. "We don't want trouble and we aren't here to cause any. I'm sure we can expect the citizens of your fair community to give us your full cooperation." His smooth voice didn't ask for permission, but expected it. Smiling brightly in a show of friendliness, he stepped into the crowd. A full head taller than most men, he grabbed stray hands to shake as he made his way into the store. He warmly greeted all he passed.

A shrewd eye couldn't miss the nervous sweat that glistened on his forehead. In a sudden show of admiration, Shortie shook his hand and led him inside. He introduced Arden as proprietor and host, and Gabbie as a fixture in the community.

Instead of shaking the proffered hand, Arden filled it with a mug of hot coffee. His dark eyes assessed the man, sizing him up. If they were looking for a Judas, then they had come to the wrong part of town.

The five left standing by the limo threw anxious glances at each other as a mass of people moved in too close for comfort. One man, dressed in a brown striped suit, smiled continuously through clenched teeth. It gave him a spastic appearance, and a couple of young guys began to hoot and jeer at him. Another, dressed in gray, kept one hand clenched on the door handle, just in case. The third and tallest of them wore a black suit which rendered the unfortunate wearer a resemblance to an undertaker. He was hated at first sight. Sweat poured profusely down his face, and he never smiled or looked anyone in the eye. The fourth wore a nondescript dark blue suit. His open jacket revealed a silver badge gleaming in the bright morning sun. The fifth, and last, was the Lucky Spur foreman, John Maxwell.

John elbowed one of the suits and laughed loudly when the man jumped at being goosed in the ribs. "Relax," he told him. He laughed and motioned toward the crowd. "They're not here to ruffle your tie or mess up your suit. All they want is a look at this fancy car. Isn't that right, boys?" he asked as he swung the car doors open wide. It was all the invitation necessary. The car was immediately filled to capacity and a bottle of Scotch was found and passed around. Left to the mercy of the crowd, the limo was on its own.

Several miners yelled, "Save some of that fancy hooch for us. We want a taste of what our hard work pays for." Stepping closer to the loaded car, men, women, and children alike admired the sleek lines of the automobile. Color flooded the pale face of the nearest official when he realized they weren't going to be beaten to a pulp by an angry mob. The suits headed for the safety of the store. Federal officers mingled through the crowd, keeping their eyes peeled for trouble.

Inside, Frank Howard took a tentative drink of his coffee and scorched his mouth on the scalding brew. Gabbie noticed his unintended wince and snickered rudely.

"Hot, ain't it?" he asked. Taking a huge swallow of his own, he smacked his lips. Arrogantly, he placed a roll-your-own between his lips, lit it, and then turned his back in an open show of contempt.

Unwilling to show his frustration, Frank raised his voice to address all those within hearing.

"Does anyone know where we might find a man known by the name of Shorty?" His face flushed a brilliant scarlet when every head snapped in his direction and eyes turned cold, vacant stares. Voices stilled, leaving the store in silence. Appearing out of nowhere, a couple of federal marshals and the four suits joined him in the center of the tiny, open space next to the counter. Howard stood with arms folded across his chest and feet wide apart. He gave the impression that if trouble started, he would end it.

When Shortie's name was mentioned, his heart somersaulted into his throat. He wasn't a coward, but didn't relish facing jail time for a crime he didn't commit. From behind him, a gravelly voice broke the silence.

"They call me Shortie, and what of it?" Blackie snarled. The big Irishman faced Howard eye-to-eye, daring him to make a wrong move. Stepping in closer, he repeated, "I'm Shortie. What do you want with me?"

"And he's a bald faced liar," Art Jones volunteered. Wrapping an arm around Howard's shoulder, he leaned heavily on the taller man. Weaving from an all-night drunk, he breathed cheap whiskey into his face. "I'm Short, and getting shorter all the time." His voice tapered off to a whisper when he sagged at the knees. Staggering dizzily, he beamed drunkenly at the crowd. "I need a drink," he ordered with an arm upraised. Falling to the floor, he lay sprawled at their feet, totally blitzed. A grin of contentment creased his features as he rolled onto his side.

Federal officers regarded the scene with cold speculation while the suits gawked in disbelief. A slight smile tilted Howard's lips as he surveyed the fallen Art. He cleared his throat to hide a good-natured chuckle.

"That's my man," Ellen exclaimed as she bent over Art, "always the center of attention."

"And you are....?" asked the nearest officer as he placed a restraining hand on her arm. It wasn't until several angry men stepped close that he realized his mistake. Ellen stared at the errant hand until he dropped it to his side and stepped backward.

"Keep your hands to yourself," she said with hauteur. "And in answer to your question, I'm Mrs. Shortie."

"You are not Shortie's wife, because I am and I can prove it," Inja bellowed as she stepped from the throng. Mouths dropped as she approached the officers with fire in her eyes and icy fury on her face. She'd never looked more beautiful. She faced them, ready to do battle if necessary.

"Now just a min...." Shortie tried to say, but someone pushed him back and a hand clamped over his mouth.

"Señors," Tony said with a theatric bow. "Forgive me for not coming to greet you sooner. I believe I am the one you seek. My nickname is Shortie." He winked at the appreciative crowd and grinned.

Angrily, Shortie pushed Tony aside. Stepping in front of Inja, his fist clamped onto one officer's wrist when he took hold of her arm. "Take your filthy hands off my wife," he thundered. The officer didn't argue as the bones in his wrist were squeezed to the breaking point. "I'm Shortie Busch, and any talking you need to do, you do with me," he said in a steely voice. An officer stepped to each side of him, but before they could lay hands on him, a small wildcat appeared in their midst.

Arms, hands, feet, and teeth attacked from all sides. Yelling like a banshee, Eddie kicked, bit, and slugged all that came near. Calming slightly to catch his breath, he stood before the group panting. He was David facing his Goliath! "I'm Shortie Busch, and he's my dad," he exclaimed with a shaky finger pointed at Shortie.

In the stunned silence, Blackie was heard saying for the second time, "Well, I'll be d—."

Chapter 16

The unfolding drama was the most excitement many had witnessed in a good long while. Onlookers leaned in closer, encircling the little group in their midst. They were eager for more, and eyes glittered maliciously, hoping to see a good fight. Shortie placed a hand on Eddie's shoulder, overcome at such a show of support from family and friends. Holding the child protectively to his side, he addressed waiting officials.

"I'm Shortie Busch and these people," he waved a hand over the mass of people, "are concerned family and friends with a misguided sense of loyalty. They mean no harm. I'm here to answer any questions you have, but leave my family out of it. They know less about what happened last April than I do."

Eddie regarded the stern faces of the officious looking group and decided he definitely did not like them. "He's not afraid of you," he boldly declared, and surprised at his own show of bravado, shrunk tightly against Shortie's legs. Embarrassed and close to tears, he turned his face away.

"Out of the mouths of babes," Bert quoted. Wedging herself between the officials and the crowd of spectators, she nudged one of the suits none too gently against the counter with an exaggerated swing of her capacious hips. At the roaring approval of those nearby, she grinned broadly and clasped her hands above her head. She sobered immediately at the sight of Shortie's stony expression.

"This is absolutely ludicrous," an officer muttered. Facing the onlookers squarely, he warned, "Don't force us to take actions we never intended on. All we want is to ask a few questions, and if you have nothing to hide, you have nothing to fear." Turning to Shortie, he spoke quietly. "Will you answer a few questions here, away from your audience, or do we need to go elsewhere?" His tone was intentionally gruff. Softening, he waved at the mass of people with a disgusted gesture, "Can we at least get away from your chaperones?"

Shortie's cheeks warmed with embarrassment at the obvious affront.

"If this charade is your idea of a joke, I'm not amused; in fact, I'm losing patience with the whole lot of you." The officer turned away and wandered to the rear of the store, giving Shortie time to decide what he wanted to do. Shortie followed after him, and the two were soon engaged in private conversation.

"What can you tell me about that night in April? I want to know everything you did that day, including who you spoke to, what time you got up, when you went to work, and when you got home. Don't leave anything out because I'll be checking your story."

"I gave a statement to the authorities shortly after it all happened. What more could I possible add?"

"Don't know," said the officer with a shrug, "but humor me and go over it again. By the time we're through, I want to know everything there is to know about you including when you use the crapper. Now, I've got all day, so start talking."

"If you say so, but I'm afraid my life story is pretty boring. Do you want me to start at the beginning or pick up somewhere around mid-April? And by the way, it's every morning at about five o'clock, as regular as clockwork."

"What? You tryin' to be smart or somethin'?"

"I'm only trying to cooperate, officer. You wanted to know when I use the privy so...."

"Oh, I get it." The officer looked at Shortie for a long time before he allowed himself to drop the pretense. "I guess I came on a little strong, but I don't want any applesauce. Don't take offense. Answer a few more questions and then you're free to go. I have to tell you, you're a prime suspect, but so is half the town."

"I'll tell you all I know. And go ahead and check out my story because I have nothing to hide." When the tension between them broke, they talked for a long time in hushed tones with heads close together. The attitude of the crowd relaxed when the two laughed at some private joke. They stepped out the back to escape prying eyes.

The man in the black suit turned his attention to Eddie. His undertaker's appearance changed radically when he smiled. He knelt to introduce himself, and Eddie stoically ignored him. Scowling in an imitation of Shortie, he hoped he looked as tough as he tried to appear, because inside he was Jell-O.

"Eddie!" Startled at the sound of Inja's sharp voice, his face flushed pink. "You're being rude," she reminded in a softer tone. "Now shake hands."

He extended his fingers, but refused to meet the man's eyes. Shaking the dry, limp hand made his lower lip curl with distaste. Wiping his palm on his pantleg, he couldn't rub away the unpleasant sensation left by man's touch. He felt like he'd shaken hands with a snakeskin. Fighting an impulse to kick the man as hard as he could in the shin, he ran away from his sister's reproachful stare.

Shortie observed the verbal exchange from a distance. When the man in black took Inja's hand and brushed the back of it with a kiss, he saw red. Pushing through the crowd, he drew close enough to hear part of their conversation.

"Allow me to introduce myself. I'm William Anderson, major stockholder in the Lucky Spur." Gazing into her eyes, he added meaningfully, "My friends call me Bill."

Inja's cheeks flushed as pink as her brother's as she tried to withdraw her hand. Unsure of herself, she turned her head and directed her gaze away from him. Looking off into the crowd, she came face-to-face with Bert's frigid stare.

"Where are your loyalties?" Bert demanded. Guilt stained Inja's cheeks a bright crimson.

"I don't like the implication in your voice," she denied. "There's nothing wrong with being polite and showing proper social graces, which some of you need to learn." She tossed her head defiantly. "Haven't you heard the old saying of 'catching more bees with honey'?"

"Yeah, I've heard it, but I don't think it meant the two-legged kind," Bert sneered. Taking Inja's arm, she tried to drag the younger woman away, but was met with resistance. Shaking her head, she cursed Inja under her breath as she stormed away.

Over the next few weeks, the community grew accustomed to seeing one or more of the officials. They poked around the neighborhood and pried into everybody's business, asking lots of questions mostly about Shortie.

Every aspect of his life was scrutinized, and within a short time Frank Howard had a file over two inches thick telling all about him. Investigators knew where he worked and what shift, who his personal friends were, when he and Inja married and moved to the valley, and what church he attended. His friends were questioned about him repeatedly, and if stories didn't coincide, they were questioned again. Shortie remained calm and answered every question thrown at him with honesty no matter how personal. He figured they were on the same team and working toward the same goal. Who caused the explosion and why?

It became a game to see who had been questioned and who hadn't. If one person was asked for information another had not, it was cause for speculation. Some were insulted if their opinion wasn't consulted and complained loudly to Arden when they stopped by for a few groceries, to check their mail, or just to chat. Even though the community didn't like the intrusion, no further objections were voiced. Most tolerated their presence like bad medicine and for once agreed with Gabbie. "It's best ta' swallow and get it done with, 'cause holdin' back only makes fer' a bitter pill."

Frank Howard, chief inspector, traded his suit for blue jeans and a flannel shirt. He was often seen poking around in one of the many abandoned mine shafts honeycombing the valley. At the end of a long day, he met with the men as they gathered at Arden's for a cold drink. It was on just such an afternoon the first clue became evident.

Shortie, Blackie, Art, Tony, and of course Gabbie sat cooling their backsides on the cement step. Each of them sipped a cold drink, wiping beads of sweat from their foreheads as they rested in the shade. It was uncommonly warm for the middle of June, and they were worn out after a hard day's work. Frank pulled up in a dusty, black Ford. Climbing out of the car, he stretched stiff muscles. Taking the hat from his head, he slapped it against his knee, setting up a tiny dust storm.

"Having any luck?" Blackie asked. Reaching into a large, red cooler advertising its own brand of cola, he pulled out an orange soda. Reluctantly, he'd warmed to the man, and they each respected the other. Popping off the top, he handed it to him.

"Haven't found a thing," he replied. Snorting with disgust, he added, "Whoever had a hand in it hid their trail real well. You'd think I'd find some tangible evidence, but so far, nothing at all." He shook his head morosely, obviously disturbed. Taking a deep drink of his soda, he sighed with satisfaction, "Man, that's good." Two swallows later, the bottle was empty.

"There's got to be something you're missing," Shortie offered. Stifling a burp from gulping his root beer, he gazed steadily at Frank. "Is there anything I can do? I think I've proven my innocence and am willing to help in any way possible. If you need...."

"That won't be necessary," Howard interrupted. "What needs to be done, I've got to do myself."

"What do you think happened?" Art asked with emphasis on you. "Surely you have an opinion, or at least an idea."

"Just between you, me, and the fence post, I think the man we're looking for is a real expert. It had to be someone who knew the area and knew how to blast in mountainous areas. I figure he counted on opening one of the abandoned shafts to break into the Lucky Spur. There's a lot of gold in that mine if a man knows what to look for. He placed all the explosives in one spot and then, BOOM!" he explained with a flourish that took in the whole valley. "It went off, shook things up a little with the end result being a landslide ending up in Busch's backyard." Sitting back with a self-satisfied smile, he expected his explanation to be accepted. It sounded plausible to everyone except Gabbie.

"Never happened that'ta way." Smacking his gums together loudly, he sneered at the suggestion. He'd listened to the account but figured it was blind guesswork. "It would'a blowed a hole in th' mountainside, not a cave-in." Turning himself away from them, he slurped his coffee with a thoughtful expression.

"What do you know about it, old man?" Blackie teased. "Never mind him," he told Howard, "he can't resist adding his own two cents worth."

"Yeah, right," Frank responded. Taking a sip from his second soda, he contemplated Gabbie's comments. "Still, it won't hurt to humor him. Maybe he knows something we don't." He smirked conspiratorially at Blackie. "So, old man." He clapped Gabbie on the shoulder forcing him to turn and face him. "Let's hear what you've got to say."

Turning around slowly, he had a look of surprise on his grizzled face. It wasn't often anyone asked for his opinion. Blinking, he gathered his thoughts before speaking. Looking Howard in the eye, he decided to answer as truthfully as possible.

"It couldn'a happened the way you say."

"Why not?"

"'Cause the explosion wouldn'a done much damage if set off in a side tunnel. It would'a blowed into one of the mine's shafts and we'd of got less than a minor tremble. Now, the way I sees it, there were three old shafts. One, at Shorties place, was used fer' a root cellar and the other two were abandoned, and I'll bet they're connected somewhere's deep inside ta' mountain. Explosives had to've been laid somewheres near ta' base of the mountain where vibrations followed one shaft to the next an' then to the next. Echoin', they used to call it." Drawing a diagram in the dirt with a stick, he went on, "With the sound of that first explosion bouncin' off old shaft walls, it ricocheted up the mountain to Shortie's cellar. There, it met with methane gas from that old outhouse he uses fer' a tool shed. That's what caused the second explosion. There weren't but a few sticks of dynamite detonated, I'd bet'cha. It was gas mixed with heat from the first blast that set off a chain reaction. It foller'ed the only open passage straight to ta' nearest outlet and then BOOM!" Nodding with a toothless grin, he moved away from the shelter of the porch, gesturing for them to follow. Standing far out in the road so the hillside above could be seen above the trees, he pointed a gnarled finger to indicate a route from point A to point B.

As he followed the direction with a keen eye, realization swept over Frank with icy fingers. There was more truth than pretense to the old man's explanation, and it all made sense. Eyeing the older man suspiciously, he wondered what else he knew. Was it possible Gabbie set it off? Reading Howard's thoughts, Blackie spoke from the shade of the porch.

"You're on the wrong track, inspector. He's a harmless old man that wouldn't hurt a fly."

As if on cue, a horsefly lit on Gabbie's shirtsleeve. He flicked it off, and the stunned insect fell to the ground where it crawled about momentarily. Lifting a boot-clad foot, he stomped the bug into a sticky mass of goo. Wiping the sole of his foot off on some brush, he grinned at them with malicious delight. Shuffling to his place on the cool cement slab, he finished his coffee with a gulp.

Frank followed his every move with narrowed eyes. If ever a man appeared to be guilty, Gabbie certain did. Maybe they'd been investigating the wrong man, because Busch certainly had nothing to do with it.

"He's not your man, Howard," Blackie growled. He was angry, so angry his cheeks turned a mottled burgundy. He could have torn the old man's head off.

"How can one old man be so darned obstinate?" Shortie agreed. He understood his friend's anger and was getting a little riled himself. He was no longer under immediate suspicion, but felt little relief. Guilt could be pinned on any one of them, and especially Gabbie. His deliberate actions incriminated him.

"Besides, he don't move faster than ice flows, so forget whatever you might be thinkin'." The big Irishman didn't turn his head, but stared straight ahead. Tony stepped to the side, and Art moved away. Shortie placed a hand on his shoulder, warning him to remain where he was.

Gabbie, pleased at getting so much attention, added more fuel to the fire. "I know enough about nitro' to blow you and the whole shootin' match off the map," he bragged. Placing a wad of tobacco in his cheek, he chewed open-mouthed. He looked about as innocent as the devil.

"Quit the charade, old man, this is serious business," Shortie said through clenched teeth. "If there's something you know, tell us so we can end this thing. Do you know who hurt Inja?"

Peering into his cup regretfully, Gabbie left it on the porch as he stood to head home. Without a parting wave, he shuffled off with hands shoved deep in his overalls and shoulders hunched. It was hard to ignore his mocking laughter that floated to them on the warm, afternoon breeze.

"Don't pay attention to anything he says," Blackie repeated as he nodded at Gabbie's departing figure. "He don't know anything. He's just showing off."

"I suppose you're right," Howard replied with obvious skepticism, "but he sure talks like he knows his way around explosives."

"That's your first mistake, thinking the old man knows something. Don't matter what you think he knows or don't know because I know that old man had nothing to do with what happened here last April," Blackie argued.

"Don't get heated, Irish. Getting your dander up won't help matters." Shortie, always the peacemaker, tried to mollify the situation by appealing to common sense.

Shaking his head in exasperation, Blackie dared a wry smile. "I s'pose you're right."

Sighing, Howard placed his empty soda bottle in the metal rack next to the cooler. Setting his cap firmly on his head, he pulled a set of keys from a pocket, prepared to leave.

"At least I'm one step closer to solving this thing," he volunteered. "That old guy may have actually described the only way the whole thing could have happened, and that's more than I knew thirty minutes ago. Well, I'm tired and hungry, and tomorrow's another day. See you all another time." He gave a departing wave as he drove down the road.

The four watched the black car disappear. They were more than just surprised at Gabbie's knowledge of explosives. It was only on rare occasion the old man's talk made sense, and this, unfortunately, was one of those times. They glanced at each other, and Art was the first to voice their thoughts.

"You don't suppose...."

"Naw, he's just a crazy old man trying to make himself look important," Blackie stubbornly defended.

"He sure sounded like he knew what he was talking about," Tony added.

"Well, he should," Shortie interjected. "He was setting charges across the Arizona desert during the early uranium boom when you were still in short pants."

Heads turned at this unexpected piece of news. "Don't matter," Blackie huffed, "he's still a bothersome burr in my backside, but incapable of doing anyone harm."

In agreement, all went their separate ways. The next day would find them gathered together on the porch sipping cool drinks and hashing over today's turn of events.

Arden, in preparation to close for the day, ran hot water into the deep metal sink behind the meat counter. Adding soap flakes, he soon had a froth of suds to wash his meat cutting tools and customer coffee cups. Knowing full well how many cups were used, he cursed Gabbie for a lazy lout. How many times had he told him to return his dirty cup to the sink instead of leaving it wherever? Stepping outside, he spied the empty cup tucked in a corner of the porch. Calling down curses in Hebrew, he retrieved the cup and tossed it into the sink. Hearing it plink as ceramic hit metal, he wished it had been the old man's head.

Chapter 17

Shortie and Blackie walked to the Cleggs' driveway, and both men sniffed the air appreciatively. The enticing aroma of fried chicken drifted on the breeze, making their mouths water.

"Sure smells good," Shortie hinted.

"Why not join us for dinner? Bert cooks enough for an army." Patting his sizable abdomen and rolling his eyes heavenward, he tempted a hungry man's appetite. "Apple pie for dessert, and I'll bet there's homemade biscuits with honey."

A momentary twinge of conscience warred in Shortie's mind for a moment, but he couldn't resist the offer. His stomach had been knotted to his backbone for so long, he'd forgotten what "full" was like. Taking a quick peek up the hill, he hoped Eddie couldn't see him. He'd be a traitor if the boy were left to eat Inja's fixings while he sat down to one of Bert's sumptuous meals.

Entering the Clegg kitchen, Bert hollered from a bent position in front of the open oven door.

"Grab a towel off the counter and get outside to wash. I don't want any of that mine dust left in my sink. By the time you come back inside, dinner will be on the table." Standing upright, holding a panful of buttermilk biscuits in an ovenmitted hand, she grinned at their admiring looks, knowing they weren't for her. "Scoot," she ordered. "Won't take long for this stuff to cool. I'll set another plate at the table."

Shortie washed vigorously at the standpipe, splashing cool water over his head, neck, and arms. Toweling off, he stood back to allow his host access to the spigot. Spex, their big dog, greeted his master with huge, wet slobbers and dog licks. Standing on his hind legs, the animal was as tall as the Irishman. Man and dog wrestled for a moment, with the animal getting the advantage by pulling him to the ground by the arm. Standing over him, the dog growled savagely and shook his forearm as if to rip it to pieces. Then he sat his rump in the middle of his chest and cocked his head mischievously in anticipation of a head scratch and an ear rub. Expecting Blackie to wash away the dog's slobbery greeting, Shortie handed him the towel.

"No thanks." He wiped his hands on the seat of his pants. "I've had all the washing I can stand."

"Quit playing with the dog and get in here and eat," Bert ordered from the open door.

Inside the uncomfortably warm kitchen, the three sat down to a table laden with more food than Shortie'd seen in a month. His eyes rounded like saucers when he spied a bowl heaped high with fluffy mashed potatoes.

"You'd best eat up," Bert said as she handed him the potatoes. "You've been working so hard this summer, you've wore all the meat off your bones. If you keep it up we'll have to call you Bones 'cause you don't have enough meat to fill out your drawers." Laughing, she generously ladled chicken gravy over a mound of potatoes on his plate. She did the same for Blackie's and then her own, and they ate silently for a time as the chicken was passed along with creamed peas, biscuits, butter, honey, and a bowl of pickles. He ate so much, he groaned with an aching belly. Bert wrapped the remaining chicken and biscuits, already dripping with butter, in waxed paper.

"For Eddie," she said with a wink from her squinty eye. "He'll be hungry and wondering where you've been." Placing the food in a box, she added an apple pie. "You've got to have dessert," she explained. "I baked two, so there's plenty. I'm sorry there isn't any ice cream to go along with it."

"This is already too much," Shortie exclaimed. Thanking her profusely, he hurried home. With such a special treat, he wanted the boy to get it while it was hot.

Climbing the hill, he heard Eddie's greeting before he spotted him on the steps. The boy ran to meet him but stopped short before they collided. "What's in the box?" he asked, sniffing the aroma of the fried meat. "It smells like chicken; is there fried chicken in the box?"

Pausing, Shortie folded back the cloth cover to reveal the pie and several pieces of chicken. "And," he drawled, "biscuits already buttered." The boy's eyes lit up in anticipation.

Placing the box and its contents on the counter, he prepared Eddie's plate. The table was cluttered with the remains of a card game, which he pushed to the side. Dirty glasses littered the sink and an empty pitcher on the counter reeked of alcohol. Inja was nowhere to be seen, and he turned a questioning face to the child. Eddie pointed to the bedroom. His mouth was stuffed full, leaving no room to talk.

She was waking from a nap when he cautiously opened the bedroom door. Guiltily, she jumped off the bed to smooth her wrinkled dress and slip on her shoes.

"You're home early," she commented as she tidied her hair. Smoothing the coverlet on the bed, she put on an attitude of nonchalance. He knew she was trying to hide something. "I don't know what's the matter with me. I get so tired in the afternoon that I have to take a nap." Yawning widely, she stretched languorously and smiled, sleepy-eyed.

"What do you do that makes you so tired?"

"Oh, you know, the usual stuff. Today I did the laundry, and you know how tiring that can be." His eyebrows raised in question as he faced her with arms crossed. "I have to lug each load to the clotheslines," she pouted defensively.

"No more than an hour or so," he declared. Gazing at her in askance, he took in her rumpled skirt with a glance. "Is that another new dress?"

"So what if it is?" She allowed her lower lip to drop. "You didn't have to pay for it." As soon as the words escaped her, she clamped a hand over mouth.

"I don't care if I paid for it or not." His face darkened with anger. "Where did you get the dress?" he repeated. Stepping over to the closet, he yanked four more dresses off hangers and threw them across the bed. "For that matter, where did these come from, the dress fairy?"

"How dare you go through my things," she shrieked. Grabbing up the articles of clothing, she stalked away from him with her head high.

Something snapped inside him. Seeing red, he slammed a fist into the wall, leaving a good-sized hole, before he stormed after her. Grabbing her shoulder, he whirled her around.

"I want to know where you're getting all these new clothes!" he bellowed. "I also want to know who you're entertaining while I'm at work. There's something you're trying to hide from me, and I won't rest until I know what it is."

Her eyes widened and her face paled with fear. He'd never been so angry before, and she almost softened, ready to tell him everything and beg his forgiveness, but pride goaded her on. Shrugging from his grasp, she stamped her foot with indignation. She stuck her chin out in defiance and stubbornly refused to meet his gaze. He shook her by the shoulders until her teeth rattled.

"Well?" he demanded.

"Holly gave them to me, and why shouldn't I accept?" she said with cold deliberation. "She can't wear them anymore because they don't fit. She's eaten one too many slices of banana cream pie. See, there are some advantages to watching one's weight." Her mouth twisted into an ugly frown as she stepped around him.

He grabbed her by the wrist and swung her around. "Who gives a rip if you put on a pound or two?" he thundered. "You'd look healthier. You know how I feel about the Mayhews. There's something about the both of them you can't trust."

"Since when are you my keeper?" she snapped. Her eyes shot blue fire, and he involuntarily ducked when she raised her arm. "Who do you think you're talking to? You can't order me around."

His response was immediate. Releasing her, he regarded her strangely, as if he'd never seen her before. "Give them back and never accept another thing from them." His voice shook with suppressed rage. He'd had enough of her rotten behavior and expected her to obey. It wasn't a request. She took an instinctive step backwards, putting distance between them.

"I will not."

"Give them back or they'll go back in pieces." Selecting one of the dresses, he held it aloft, prepared to rip it apart at her next objection.

She studied him, searching for a weak spot or softening in attitude, but found only a wall she couldn't climb or get around.

"Why can't I have some nice things to wear?" she whined.

"You can have all the nice things you want, but not from those people. Not from him."

Realizing her tactics weren't working, she collapsed into tears of helpless anger. He pulled her into the kitchen and pointed at the remains of the afternoon's card party.

"You have all the time in the world to play cards and have drinks with company that disappears before I get home," his voice broke, tinged with bitter resentment, "but no time to prepare a decent meal for your family. Look at me, Inja, I've lost twenty pounds in two months. I'm working longer hours and working twice as hard to make enough to pay for all the things you want. The least you could do is cook a man's supper."

"Maybe I would if there was a man around to cook for. At least Leon knows how to treat a lady," she blurted.

"What did you say?" You could have made ice with the frost in his voice.

"I...I didn't really mean it the way it sounded. I only meant...."

"You've been seeing Leon Mayhew and you think he's the epitome of manhood? Well, have you? Have you been seeing Leon on the sly?"

For a fleeting moment, guilt flashed across her face. Trapped like a rabbit in a cage, she sought an avenue of escape. She had two choices. She could admit her guilt or deny everything. With either choice there was a chance she would lose everything that made her life secure. Truth was the only thing he would accept and the only thing she couldn't explain her way out of. Maybe a half-truth was better than nothing at all.

"Well, I'm waiting. Has something been going on between you?" His expression condemned her before she could answer.

"It isn't like you think," she started to say. When she took one tentative step toward him to plead her case, he pushed her back with the palm of his hand.

"I'll bet," he sneered. "It must have been real cozy for the two of you with Eddie in school all day and me at work. Well, I don't need to be told twice." The dress fell to the floor in two pieces, ripped from neckline to hem. Kicking it to the side, he grabbed his jacket and stormed out.

"Shortie, wait," she screamed as she ran after him. "You've got it all wrong. Please, give me a chance to explain." She tried to grab him by the shirtsleeve, but he yanked it out of her hands.

His parting words were, "Keep your hands off me."

Eddie was seated on the porch finishing his dinner when Shortie left the house. The expression on his face left little doubt there had been another fight. Eddie put the plate of unfinished food to the side, forgotten for the moment.

"Where you goin'? Can I come, too?" Rising to his feet, he started to follow.

"Stay here," Shortie responded without turning around. "You can't come this time, and you'd better listen to me, boy." Stunned at the gruffness in his voice, Eddie dropped back onto the step. Following the man's progress down the path, he decided it would be safer to remain right where he was.

With every angry footfall, Shortie envisioned Inja with Leon. Each step was deliberate, and he frequently kicked at the ground, cursing under his breath.

"If I ever get my hands on Mayhew, he's a dead man." Both hands doubled into fists clenched so tight, his knuckles turned white. Kicking a stone out of his path, it flew into the brush and startled a nesting swallowtail. The bird flew over his head, squawking in protest.

"Dang birds," he yelled, "always crapping on everything." Picking up a small stone to throw at the helpless bird, a moment of conscience made him chuck it toward a fallen tree. His pace didn't slow or falter when his feet hit the pavement. If anything, he walked faster and kept a running dialog with himself.

"Who does she think she is, and with Leon of all people. Just how much is one man supposed to take? First, I'm wrongly accused, then working all those extra hours just to make her happy and now this. Well, two can play that game." Clamping his lips together tightly, he continued down the road with arms swinging high at each step. He was so involved with his own conversation he didn't hear Jonesy's truck when he pulled alongside.

Rolling down the passenger window, Art leaned out. "Where you goin' this late in the day? From the way you're movin', I'd say you're spoiling for a fight." He started to laugh and then thought better of it. There was enough hate in Shortie's expression to put the fear in a man. "Want a lift? I'm headin' to work so I can drop you off somewhere."

"Yeah." Opening the door, Shortie hopped in and sat with one arm out the window. He didn't glance in Art's direction or even crack a smile. "Let's get movin'," he said impatiently.

"Sure, sure, we're goin'." Art nervously shifted gears and accelerated carefully. Casting a sidelong glance at his passenger, he had to ask, "You okay?"

"I'm just great, and not in a mood for conversation. Just drive and keep your mouth shut, okay?"

"Sure, Shortie, anything you say. Where you headed, though, if you don't mind me askin'?"

"Take me to Wallace."

"Wallace," Art exclaimed. "What do you want to go there for? There's nothing in Wallace, and besides I work up Big Creek. I can't drive all the way to Wallace; it's out of my way."

"I'm not askin' you, Art. Take me to Wallace and be a few minutes late for work. It won't be the first time."

"All right. I sure hope you know what you're doing."

"Shut up," Shortie ordered. The remaining distance was covered in silence. Every now and then Art glanced toward the man beside him to assure himself that it was Shortie Busch. If he didn't know better, he could have sworn he was riding with the devil himself.

Pulling up to the four-way stop in the middle of downtown Wallace, Art looked questioningly at Shortie.

"Take a left," he directed. Turning, they followed the road for two blocks.

There was only one street remaining at this end of town and it wasn't where nice folks went to play bingo.

"Take a right for two more blocks and then let me out."

"Aw, come on, man. You don't belong here, and for that matter neither do I. If Ellen knew about this, she'd boot me out for sure. Let me take you home and we'll forget all about it. Did you and Inja have a fight or something?"

"Mind your own business," Shortie snarled as he climbed out of the truck and slammed the door shut. Shoving his fists deep into his pockets, he took off without a backward glance.

Art followed for a few feet and then gave up. If he hurried, he'd make it to work with a couple minutes to spare.

Shortie heard the roar of Art's pick-up as he turned it around and headed out of town. He was alone with only a few cars parked along the street for company. Pacing the sidewalk for better than fifteen minutes, he finally came to a decision. Next to a two-story building was a recessed doorway set back in a little alcove. Looking up and then down the street, he turned the door handle and stepped inside.

For a few seconds he was blinded as his eyes adjusted to the subdued light. The room was small, like an entryway or coatroom and lit by a single bulb hanging from the ceiling. Directly in front of him was a menu that advertised a selection one wouldn't see in the local family diner. His eyes skittered away from it, refusing to read what the accompanying pictures graphically detailed. Changing his mind and wishing he'd never had the idea in the first place, he reached for the door handle. Turning it first one way and then the other, he found it had locked him in. The door allowed entry, but barred his exit. There was no other alternative than to follow the soft sound of music to an inner room beyond. He was surprised the second door swung open on silent hinges at the slightest pressure of his hand.

If his eyes needed to adjust to the anteroom, all of his senses reeled in this one. A red haze assaulted him, making him blink rapidly. Rubbing his eyes to clear his vision, he realized the red wasn't a mirage. The entire room was decorated in shades of red and pink. The couch along one wall was a hideous shade of pink, with ruffled red and black pillows decorating each end. Bright pink curtains hung at windows that couldn't be seen from the outside. Even the carpet on the floor was salmon pink, with big red roses in its center. The room made his stomach nauseous and his head dizzy. He made a mistake in judgment when he allowed emotion to take over common sense. He didn't belong here and looked around desperately for an exit. The faint aroma of cigarette smoke drifted to him, and a door opened above him. A staircase on the other side of the room led to the second story.

His eyes about popped from his head when he spotted her. Standing on the top step was a lace-clad figure. One hand trailed the railing while the other held a long cigarette holder. Putting the holder to her lips, she took a puff, allowing her breasts to rise dramatically as she inhaled. Her black lace bra strained against her flesh as she moved. She wore just enough to conceal the essentials, baring to the world what a lady kept covered. Her lips were painted a garish red and her eyes lined heavily with mascara. The smile on her mouth was engaging, and when she wet her lips, she promised a night of delightful experiences. But her make-up didn't hide the lines about her mouth and eyes. She was a young woman, already old.

"Hi," she breathed in a sexy voice, "my name's Sugar. What can I do for you?" When she touched him, his skin crawled as if something leprous had brushed against him. Jerking away, his head swam as if he was going to be sick. He had to get out of there before he puked all over her.

"Where do I, uh, you know, uh, wash up?" he asked. His head swivelled in every direction, seeking a way out.

"Oh, sure honey—right through the door to your right. While you're gone, I'll mix us a drink. What will you have? Whiskey? Bourbon? Scotch? We've got just about anything you could possibly want." Her intended meaning scorched his cheeks with embarrassment. Darting through the doorway, he found the men's room, and having no other exit, he squeezed himself through the open window above the sink. Finding himself in a back alley, he ran the length of it back to the street. Pictures flashed in his head: repeated images of Inja. Inja when she took care of him that time he was sick. The way she laughed when he did something funny. The way she cried when he made her sad. He also pictured Eddie seated on his lap with his arms wrapped around his neck as he told him he loved him. He almost lost it. Sobs of remorse tore from his throat as he ran away from temptation. Without a doubt, if he had succumbed, something good within him would have died. Berating himself for even harboring such thoughts, he ran all the way back to the highway. Gasping for breath, he thanked God he was saved before destroying himself. He firmly resolved to never allow anger to control him again, then stuck out his thumb and hitchhiked home. It's a funny thing about unresolved anger, however; Satan will find another avenue to use it once we open the door.

He didn't walk far before someone stopped to offer him a lift. The driver, an older man who drove with the radio blaring, raced along and chomped on a wad of gum as rapidly as he talked.

"Where you headin', Mac? Me? I'm headin' to my sisters for a few days R&R. She lives in Kellogg. You live near there?" I'm a salesman and I recently quit smokin'. Took up gum chewin' instead. Want a stick?" He pulled a package of gum from his shirt pocket and offered a stick.

"No, I don't think so. I've never cared for it myself."

"Suit yourself, Mac. I kind of like the stuff. It keeps me from eating so often. Say, you know anything about an explosion that took place somewhere's around here? My sister mentioned it in a letter a while back. Say, Mac, you don't talk much, do ya? If I'm talkin' too much, you just say the word, Mac. You say the word and I'll shut up." He looked at Shortie for a second, smacking his gum loudly. When he blew a huge pink bubble like some fourteen-year-old bobby-soxer, Shortie laughed.

"It's okay, I don't talk much. Besides, this is your car and I'm just a passenger, so if you want to talk, who's going to stop you?"

"You got a point there, Mac. Well, here's Kellogg comin' up. Can I drop you off at the corner, Mac? My sister lives on this same block."

"Sure, this is fine." Stepping from the car, Shortie waved the man away. He was tempted to tell him that his name wasn't Mac, but didn't. Setting a rapid pace, he was soon out of Kellogg and headed for the valley.

Ahead of him was a lone figure strolling down the hill. In the dark, he couldn't tell who it was until the guy stopped to light a cigarette. Leon Mayhew! All the anger he thought he'd left behind finally had an outlet on which to vent.

"Mayhew," he roared, "we need to talk."

Leon's head snapped up as soon as he recognized the voice. He turned to run, but Shortie pulled him off his feet. They rolled on the ground for a few minutes throwing punches. The struggle was over when Shortie's fist connected with Leon's nose. Blood spurted, and holding his face to protect himself from further blows, Leon begged for mercy.

"Don't," he begged, "don't hit me again. What's gotten into you? I ain't done nothin'." Shaking with fear, he closed his eyes, waiting for a final blow.

"I only want to know one thing, and now is not the time for lies. Have you been with my wife?" Shortie grabbed him by the throat, prepared to rip out his Adam's apple.

"We had a couple of drinks, a few laughs, but that's all. I swear it! It ain't that I didn't try, but she turned me down flat. Said she was waitin' for bigger fish."

Increasing the pressure, Shortie dug his fingers into the man's neck until gurgling came from his throat. A flash of light from a passing car lit them up for a moment. His hands were covered with blood and he sat astraddle the man's chest. Sickened, a sob escaped him as he released his hold. Compassion filled his heart, making him reach down and help Leon to his feet. "Stay away from my wife and don't ever let me see you in the valley again," he rasped. Leon nodded, grabbed his streaming nose and ran down the hill without a backward glance.

Chapter 18

More ashamed of himself than he'd ever been before in his life, Shortie made his way home. Inja sat on the porch waiting for him. Her eyes were red-rimmed and they searched his for a sign of forgiveness. Sitting beside her was a box filled with all the dresses wrapped carefully in paper sacks.

"I'll return them tomorrow," she said. "And dinner will be waiting for you tomorrow night." She forced a wobbly smile. "I've been neglecting my family lately and I promise to do better."

"It's okay." He fought the need to throw himself at her feet and beg forgiveness. All anger was gone, and inside, he felt empty, drained of all emotion. He embraced her for a moment and stroked her hair soothingly. The clean scent of her tickled his nostrils.

"It isn't so much the dresses, it's where they came from," he explained.

"I know," she admitted, "but me and Leon, we never...."

"Yeah, I know." At her quizzical expression, he broke down and confessed all he'd done that night. She didn't get angry, but shook her head in disbelief.

"So, you know it all," she said. "Did you really hit Leon?" Shrugging her shoulders, she took his hand and pulled him down beside her. "I'm sorry. It won't ever happen again." Resting her head against his shoulder, she cried softly. "I'm sorry," she repeated. Overcome with emotion, he nodded. There were no words to add.

A few days later, he returned home to find the TV blaring and no dinner prepared. Keeping anger in check, he snapped it off and turned to face her. "Instead of filling your time with useless activity, why not consider an addition to our family line?" She stiffened and refused to answer. He left the room with a sigh.

Eddie was eating a sandwich and brought his plate to the sink. Glancing from one to the other, he shrugged his thin shoulders in a gesture of resignation. Avoiding her anger at all cost, he trailed behind Shortie to the garden.

For the next two hours, Shortie pulled weeds and hoed around the scraggly plants. Even though the weather had been perfect, warm with just the right amount of rain, most of the plants showed little growth. Even the radishes, hardy in the worst of climates, appeared limp with yellowing leaves. Eddie watched as Shortie worked the soil.

"Huh?" he asked.

"I didn't say anything," Shortie responded.

"Yes you did. I heard ya'. You're arguin' with her, and she ain't even here," the boy insisted.

"Was I talking to myself again?"

"Yup."

"At least when I argue with myself, I don't lose."

Eddie glanced questioningly at him, clearly puzzled. Adults often send confusing messages.

"Eddie," Shortie continued, "don't ever try to match wits with a woman because you won't win. You either come out looking like the proverbial fool, or you end up feeling like the north side of a horse traveling south."

"Yup." He nodded as if he understood every word. Scratching the back of his head, he trailed a foot in the loose soil, making circles.

"Don't worry about it. You'll understand someday." Shortied chuckled as he tousled the boy's hair. "Now go play while I finish weeding." Studying the neat rows of plants, Eddie couldn't pinpoint an errant weed. If there were any, they were well hidden.

Halfheartedly, Eddie played a game of catch with himself, hoping Shortie would take the hint and offer to play. His loud sighs and deliberate fumbles of the ball were to no avail, because by the time he finished it would be time for bed.

Later, after tucking the child into bed, Shortie sat on the porch for a long while. Staring moodily at the star-studded sky, he marveled at the effect moonglow and starlight had on the ugly little town below. From his vantage point above the valley, it appeared almost beautiful, bathed in soft illumination.

"I'm going to bed," Inja said curtly, startling him from his reverie. Opening the screen, she peered at him, trying to make out his face in the dark. "What are you doing out here? It's not like there's anything to see."

"I'll be in—in a minute," he told her. Without responding to her question, he contemplated the scene below. He didn't want to go to bed yet and figured a few more minutes more or less wouldn't hurt.

Twenty minutes lapsed before he left the porch. Circling the house, he eyed the mountainside meditatively. Remembering that night in April sent shivers down his back. He was grateful the blast had been manmade and not nature gone awry, but the unidentified culprit troubled him. Someone set those charges, but why? The exchange between Gabbie and Frank Howard ran through his mind. Could one of his neighbors be the guilty party? Chuckling to himself, he pictured Inja storming into the store.

"Boy, was she something," he said to himself. Rubbing the back of his neck tiredly, he entered the kitchen and turned off the light. In the bedroom, Inja sat on the edge of the bed brushing her hair.

"You mad?" she asked with eyes averted. Placing the brush on the dresser, she studied his reflection.

"No, and to tell the truth, I still feel pretty foolish for letting my temper get away from me. I won't allow it to happen again." Letting down the suspenders of his overalls, he sat on the bed with his head in his hands. "I'm sorry, Inja; there's been a lot going on and I lost control. I don't want us to fight." Taking his Bible from the nightstand, he flipped through the pages until finding the right passage.

"In your anger do not sin. Do not let the sun go down while you are still angry...." he read aloud. "I think that just about says it all, don't you? This passage has been running through my mind for the past hour. Maybe it's God, maybe it's conscience, but I want to apologize again before we go to bed."

"Okay, fine, but can I ask you a question?"

"Sure," he said, "ask away."

"Just what exactly did you mean when you said I need more to do?"

"When did I say that?" he asked, confused at the new direction of their conversation.

"Don't you remember?" she added in an accusing tone, "you said I have too much free time. Will you please explain your comment?"

"I only meant you need more to fill your idle hours. Maybe if you had something fulfilling to do like caring for your own child you wouldn't chase after alternative forms of entertainment."

"Back to the same old gripe, aren't we?" she said in a tight voice. Keeping her temper in check, she softened, "I've told you before, it isn't that I don't want children; it's the fear of having them. What if I have the same problems as my mother?" Raising a tear-stained face to his, she wrung her hands, pleading with him to understand.

"It won't work this time." His voice sounded cold, detached. He'd seen the act many times before and wasn't moved to sympathy. "It there's something wrong, we'd best quit guessing and find out for sure. Have you seen a doctor and been checked out?"

"Not yet." Waving her hand in a vague, dismissive gesture, she added, "Doctors, what do they know? What did they ever do to help my mama when Eddie was born?" she hissed. "I don't think we should plan for any babies right now anyway. Living on this mountain is too dangerous." She studied his expression through lowered lashes. He wasn't accepting her explanation, and she was losing ground.

"Every time we have this discussion, you have a different excuse," he said gravely. "Is it children in general you don't want, or just my children?"

"You know that's not true."

"Then make an appointment and see the doctor."

"Why should I see a doctor just so he can tell me what I already know?" she asked.

"All right then," he folded his arms across his chest, "what do you already know? Explain it to me and don't tell me any more stories, just the truth. Can you or can you not have children?"

"Don't shout, you'll wake Eddie," she hissed. "What's gotten into you? You've never been like this before. How can I answer such a ridiculous question?" Real tears trickled down her cheeks, but whether from anger or hurt, he didn't know.

"Since when have you cared whether the boy loses a few hours sleep?" he mocked. "If I've never been like this before, then good for me because the truth has finally dawned. You've never wanted children, have you?"

"Your implication hurts," she said with an injured tone, "and I've never lied to you about my feelings. Someday I'll think about having kids, but not right now." Unwilling to meet his gaze, she bent to pull the sheet back on the bed.

"I want children," he said simply. "You've known it from the beginning, and I honestly believed you did, too." Taking her into his arms, he hugged her tightly. Something between them, something valuable was lost, and he desperately wanted it back. "You are my wife and I love you...." He didn't get any further because she wrenched herself away, glaring defiantly.

"I refuse to discuss this any further." Turning her back, she removed her robe, climbed into bed, and snapped off the light.

"Fine," he shouted, "we'll do it your way." Grabbing a pillow and a blanket, he stalked out of the room. "I'll make the appointment myself. Bert will drive you, so plan on it. Tomorrow, you will see the doctor."

She slammed the door in response. Angry footsteps pounded across the floor, and then there was silence. Throwing the bedding onto the couch, he picked up the phone and dialed before giving thought to the late hour. It was high time to find out what, if anything, was wrong with her. He needed to know for certain, one way or the other, if parenthood would be part of their future. After making the call, he wrestled with himself for the next couple of hours.

Unable to sleep, he twisted and turned until the sheets on his makeshift bed encased him like a mummy. Extricating himself, he tossed them to the floor. He hated that they'd argued and their angry words replayed in his head like an annoying gnat. He wasn't a man normally ruled by emotion and the depth of his feelings was frightening.

Forcing himself to think about other things he tried to pray, but the words wouldn't come. A disturbing thought came to mind. He hadn't prayed for his family or friends in so long, he couldn't remember when he had last knelt to speak to God. Closing his eyes, he tried to concentrate on the Lord's Prayer, but couldn't remember the last two verses. Angry with himself, he pulled a blanket around his shoulders and knelt by the couch. Try as he might, the words wouldn't come, and he soon found himself with head bowed to his knees.

"Help me, Lord," he groaned. Over and over again he repeated the same words, never guessing anyone heard. He was surprised to find tears moistened his cheeks and dripped off his chin as his injured soul cried out to the Master. As his inner pain ebbed, a great sense of peace soothed him.

Be still, and know that I am God.

He heard the voice from deep inside himself. "Thank you, God," he whispered brokenly. Suddenly, he was at peace and very sleepy. Yawning, he promised to set aside time for family devotions starting tomorrow. Exhausted, he lay down and turned over. His eyes closed immediately, but before he slept, a bright light flashed a message across the inside of his closed eyelids.

Forgive as the Lord has forgiven you.

Chapter 19

Bert, gritty-eyed from a sleepless night, poured herself a second cup of coffee. She hadn't been able to sleep since receiving Shortie's phone call the night before. When the ringing phone woke her from a sound sleep, her heart leaped into her throat. No one called in the dead of night unless it was bad news. Something terrible must have happened to someone. Her greeting was far from friendly.

"What's wrong?" she demanded upon answering. It had taken a detailed explanation before she understood there wasn't an emergency.

"Well, if there's nobody sick or dying, why'd you call me in the middle of the night? You about scared a body half to death."

"Bert, I need a favor, and you're the one person I can trust to do it. Inja needs to see the doctor tomorrow and I'm calling to ask if you'll take her. I'll make her an appointment as soon as his office opens in the morning. Will you make sure she gets there?" His voice sounded strained, and his anxiety frightened her.

"Of course, you know I will. Are you sure everything's okay? Will she be alright until morning?" Visions of broken bones and worse flitted across her mind. And hadn't it been on the nightly news about some new kind of plague killing people somewhere overseas?

"Everything is fine, I swear it," he responded with relief. "Sorry to wake you, but this was important. Bert, I owe you one."

After ringing off, she sat in a rocking chair for the remainder of the night, berating herself for giving Inja the cold shoulder. She hadn't spoken to her since the big hoopla at the store, and now she was sick. Why else would she need to see a doctor? It must be serious or he wouldn't have called. Maybe those headaches she complained about were the real thing! Maybe....

Rising, she padded barefoot to the kitchen and placed her empty cup in the sink. This was Wednesday and shopping day for all the girls. It wouldn't hurt to get an early start. Ticking off a mental shopping list, she reminded herself about their weekly lunch date. Every Wednesday, as regular as clockwork, Bert, Ellen, Inja and Maria shopped together, then treated themselves to lunch at the B&M. Bonnie and Mike's little café, conveniently located in the center of town, kept coffee cups filled and served the best pie in town—next to her own, of course. She looked forward to the midweek break and dressed carefully for the occasion.

After seeing Blackie off to work, she finished a few morning chores, arranged her hair as best she could, and then tinted her lips with a vivid pink lipstick. It clashed with her hair and coloring, but then, most everything did.

Leaving the house, Bert placed the key in the ignition of their yellow station wagon. Pumping the gas pedal twice, she prayed it would start. She didn't want Inja to be late for her appointment with the doctor. Slipping the car into gear, she gingerly accelerated and was pleased it took off without a problem. This was going to be a great day.

As she drove, she couldn't get Inja out of her mind. So what if Mayhew frequently parked below the house on the hill. There were plenty of reasons for him to be there, but did Shortie know? And why were his visits timed for only when the man of the house was at work? If Inja wanted to be friends with Holly, it wasn't a crime. It did prove one thing, though: her friends had abandoned her and she was lonely for company. "Humph, with friends like me, who needs an enemy?" Anxious to make amends, she gave the car a little more gas than intended and rounded a corner throwing gravel.

Feeling better, she shifted to climb the steep hill. Parking the car in front of the Buschs' steps, she honked the horn to let Inja know she was there. Expecting her to come running, she was alarmed when she didn't. Running up the wooden staircase as fast as her bulk and high heeled shoes allowed, she banged on the door, calling her name. There was no response so she invited herself in. It was obvious no one was at home and that Inja left in a hurry, leaving the kitchen a mess. Thinking the worst, she reached for the phone to call Shortie. There on the end table, however, was telltale evidence of an earlier visitor. Withdrawing her hand, she snorted contemptuously at an assortment of cigarette butts. Shortie didn't smoke and would be surprised to learn they owned an ashtray. Lots of people smoked store-bought cigarettes, including herself, but only one smoked that particular brand. Praying her suspicions were wrong, she left the house with fire in her eyes and dread in her heart. There had to be a logical explanation for the empty coffee cups and dirty ashtray that decorated her friend's home.

Expertly, she rammed the car into reverse and backed all the way to the main road. Stopping at the Martinez', she helped Maria into the car. Ellen couldn't go and volunteered to babysit. As she pulled into the Joneses' driveway to drop off Maria's little girls, children ran in every direction, happily running through a sprinkler. Eddie waved before chasing after James with the hose. Laughing at their antics, Ellen came to greet them.

"How much longer?" she asked as she held the dark-eyed two-year-old on her hip while grasping the older child's hand. She pointed at Maria's protruding belly.

"This one must be a boy," Maria laughed as she held up three fingers, indicating three more months. "He's much larger than both my girls and twice as active."

"You're big all right," she agreed. "Any chance of twins?"

"No," Maria gasped as she held her side in pain. "He kicks so hard, he knocks the wind out of me."

"Oh, is that all?" Bert's voice came out in a panic-filled squeak. She held her breath in fear every time Maria reacted to the movements of her baby.

"She'll be fine," Ellen reassured Bert with a pat on the shoulder. "You two have a good lunch," she said with a parting wave. "I'll be kept pretty busy here, I'm afraid." Running off to comfort a child with a skinned knee, she hollered, "Let me know what the doctor says."

After dropping off Maria, Bert parked the wagon and walked three doors down to the café. Maria's check-ups never took long, and a cup of coffee sounded good. Inside, she found Inja seated in a booth with Holly next to her. Opposite them was Leon, shuffling a deck of cards. She wondered where he got the black eye and who rearranged his nose for him, but decided to be polite and not pry. She approached the threesome with her usual forthrightness.

"Well, fancy meeting you here," she boomed. Smiling, she seated herself next to Leon. Waving to the waitress, she called, "Bring me a cup of joe and refills for my friends. Bring me one a'them doughnuts, too." Turning to the other three, she innocently asked, "You guys want anything? I'm hungry all of a sudden; I've had a busy morning."

Even though she kept her smile cheerful and her tone friendly, she couldn't hide her anger. As she chattered on about the morning's activities, she nailed Inja with her squinty eye and with the other, she watched Leon. Inja did her best to appear unconcerned and smiled animatedly.

"I'm sorry you made an unnecessary trip all the way up that hill to my place," she apologized. "You have to understand that when they came to invite me for breakfast, well, what was I to do? I couldn't be rude and refuse, now could I?" Waving her hands helplessly, she gazed from one to the other of them with wide-eyed innocence.

If she keeps batting those eyelashes, she'll work up enough wind to take off and fly, Bert thought. Rolling her eyes, she scrutinized the young woman with a certain amount of disdain. "Oh, I understand all right," she said dryly. Taking a huge bite of a sugar doughnut, she gave her mouth something to do besides telling Inja exactly what she thought.

"I guess our game's over." Leon shrugged his shoulders arrogantly as he placed the deck of cards next to Inja's cup. In doing so, he brushed against Bert's arm with his fingertips. Taking her free hand in his, he pressed her fingertips to his lips and smiled suggestively. "Would you, fair lady, mind moving I can excuse myself?"

Yanking her hand free, she wiped it on her dress. "Gladly," she said bluntly as she squinted at him as if he were a cockroach. "And don't be in a hurry to come back."

"Bert," Inja hissed as Leon made his way to the men's room, "you don't have to be rude."

Ignoring her, she turned to Holly. "You and Inja have sure been spending a lot of time together. I see your car there almost everyday."

"We are getting to be the best of friends," she agreed. "We share morning coffee together, and I've introduced her to everyone we know. They just love her, especially the men," she confided. "But she's been a good girl and informed all of them that she's already taken."

"Holly," Inja cried. Her cheeks flushed pink either from embarrassment or pleasure, Bert wasn't sure.

Waving away her admonishment with a careless gesture, Holly confessed, "I'm absolutely envious of her figure. I used to be her size and Leon bought me some of the most beautiful dresses. But, I've put on a few pounds and can't wear them any more, so I gave them all to her. Doesn't she look great?" Her gaze swept over Inja with fondness.

Leon returned, pulled a chair over to the table and leaned back comfortably, smoking a cigarette. As he gazed candidly at Inja, his knowing wink wasn't missed by Bert or Holly. Passing an ashtray, Holly glared as she slammed it down in front of him. Wishing to avoid a scene, he asked gallantly, "Would anyone care for anything to eat—a slice of pie perhaps?"

"I'd love a piece of banana cream," Holly volunteered.

"Nothing for me," Inja told him. "I'm still full from breakfast and couldn't possibly eat another bite."

"Perhaps another cup of coffee would satisfy you?" inquired an unexpected voice. Coming from behind and wielding a full pot of coffee was one of the officials Bert remembered seeing at the store.

"Why, you're the undertaker," she blurted out with surprise. At his quizzical expression, she stammered an apology and corrected herself. "I don't mean undertaker, I mean inspector, I think? You're one of them, aren't you? Weren't you wearing a black suit that day at the store?" she asked all in a rush.

Recognizing the connection between a black suit and an undertaker, Bill Anderson threw his head back and laughed heartily. She was thoroughly flustered, and her questioning expression showed it. "I'm William Anderson and known as Bill to my friends. And to answer your question, I'm not an inspector, I'm a stockholder, and yes, I'm guilty of wearing the black suit." Shaking her extended hand with his right, he poured coffee for Inja with his left. Setting down the pot, he allowed Holly to fend for herself. Lighting a cigarette, he smoked a few puffs, then snuffed it out in the ashtray. Pulling a chair over, he joined their little group.

"This is getting downright cozy, ain't it?" Bert asked. Suspicious bewilderment crossed her face. Both Anderson and Mayhew smoked the same brand, and it was obvious they both were making a play for Inja. Studying the foursome with a critical squint, she was glad to see Maria come in the door. Relief turned to genuine concern when she noticed the young woman's expression. Her naturally dark complexion was chalk white and her soft, brown eyes brimmed with tears. Jumping from her seat, she hurried to assist her.

"What's the matter? Is it the baby?" she demanded. Pushing the girl into a booth, she searched her face for some indication for the cause of her discomfort.

"The baby is fine, but please take me home. I need to lie down," she whispered. Bert noted Maria's fearful glance toward the four seated at the far table.

Inja squeezed past Holly to join them. "What's wrong? Is it the baby?" she echoed.

Maria shook her head, then collapsed into Bert's arms, crying uncontrollably. Helping her to her feet, she half carried the young woman to the door.

"I'll be back," Bert shouted. "As soon as Maria is settled, I'll be back to take you to your appointment. Don't forget, Inja, it's at two o'clock, so be ready."

"What was that all about?" Holly wanted to know. "Will she be all right? Shouldn't we go with them to help or something?"

Inja shook her head. She knew Bert wouldn't allow them within twenty feet of Maria. "She's in good hands—Bert will take good care of her."

"You didn't tell me you had a doctor's appointment this afternoon," Holly accused. "Is it anything to be concerned about?"

"It's just a check-up, nothing more than an annual physical. It's nothing really." Smiling brightly to alleviate their curiosity, Inja reached for the cards. "In the meantime, we've got time for one more game. Whose turn is it to deal?" Shuffling the cards, she laid them in the palm of Bill's hand. Behind her carefree façade, she had the sinking sensation that a trapdoor had opened in the pit of her stomach, spilling her guts out onto the floor.

Chapter 20

Shortie called Dr. Willom's office as soon as it opened. Speaking directly to the doctor, he explained what was necessary and was assured Inja would be given a thorough physical. If there was a problem, Dr. Willom would find it. Hoping she would understand why he took matters into his own hands, he worked close by the phone for the remainder of the morning. When Dr. Willom's office called with the results of Inja's tests, he didn't want to miss the call.

Every time the phone rang, he dropped what he was doing and rushed to see if it was for him. They were on lunch break when Tony received a message about Maria. He took the rest of the day off to go home and care for his wife. Reluctantly, Shortie left the bottling room and headed for the loading docks. Working alone, it would take him a couple of hours to load and unload the incoming freight from the incoming train.

The afternoon dragged on toward two o'clock before the locker room phone jangled again. Sprinting from the loading docks, he grabbed the black receiver and was surprised to hear the doctor's voice instead of his nurse. Butterflies fluttered in his stomach as he listened to the doctor's grave voice.

"I'm going through the data on your wife's tests and hope to have all the results by tomorrow afternoon. Can you come by my office about three-thirty or four? I'll set aside the time so can talk privately."

Swallowing a lump in his throat, he found it difficult to respond. Licking dry lips, he agreed to meet the next afternoon. The next twenty-four hours were the hardest Shortie had ever spent. Unable to think about anything else, his imagination went wild. Fearing something was seriously wrong with his wife, he pampered her by preparing her favorite dinner. He even tolerated a visit with Holly Mayhew just to please her. By four o'clock the following afternoon, he was a nervous wreck. Rushing to the doctor's office, he paced the waiting room nervously. Three pregnant women also waited and shared knowing smiles.

"Don't worry," one confided, "healthy babies are born every day; I mean, look at me, this is my sixth. Your wife is in good hands with Dr. Willom. He's delivered every one of mine." She patted his arm as if he were a child in need of reassurance.

"Yes, I suppose you're right," he mumbled. An explanation would take more time than it was worth, so he didn't bother. He about paced a hole in the floor before the nurse called his name.

"Doctor is ready to see you now, Mr. Busch." Following the white-clad figure to a spacious office, he looked around, admiring shelf after shelf of books. He respected educated men even though they intimidated him. His own education ended abruptly when he was eleven and just graduated sixth grade. His father had pulled him out of school and put him to work. Unable to resist the impulse, he pulled a book off the shelf and was leafing through it when Dr. Willom entered.

"Do you have an interest in anatomy? That book was written by one of the finest physicians in the world. You've made an excellent choice, but I must admit it makes for dry reading."

Disconcerted at being caught going through the doctor's personal library, he returned the book to the shelf, red-faced. "I apologize for making myself at home. I've always liked books, but seldom have time to read. The cover looked interesting," he said with a shrug. It was a lame excuse for going through a man's things.

"No apologies are necessary, and if you really think it's interesting, take it home to read. When you return it, we can have a long talk about the good doctor's theories about the evolution of man. Now quit looking like you just robbed Fort Knox and sit down. We need to discuss my findings."

As he sat where the doctor indicated, Shortie's knees turned to water and his mouth became dry as cotton. Prepared for bad news, he steeled himself to hear the diagnosis.

"Her blood tests show a low red cell count, typical for young women that frequently diet. Her blood pressure is normal, heart is strong, and all major organs are functioning normally." Systematically, he gave a detailed account of every test and his findings. A quick glance was enough for the doctor to know when he got too technical. Backtracking, he omitted medical jargon so there would be no misunderstanding his diagnosis.

Disbelief etched Shortie's face, and his eyes grew round and then rounder as he tried to make sense out of all the information.

"So, that's the long and the short of it, pardon the pun. Your wife is a perfectly healthy young woman and as likely a candidate for motherhood as

I've ever seen. Her bone structure and hip width are perfect; and except for normal scarring from an earlier pregnancy, there's absolutely no reason why she couldn't deliver several healthy children. In fact, I'm surprised a woman of her age doesn't have at least three or four by now." Eyeing Shortie covertly, he refrained from asking any personal questions.

"If I've understood you correctly, there's nothing wrong with my wife and she's been pregnant before?" Shortie's voice rose in anger. "She didn't share that part of herself with me." Heartbroken, grief brought tears to his eyes.

The doctor's brows lifted in surprise. "I think you need to have a long talk with your wife. Obviously, there are some things you both need to discuss." he said kindly. "If she's afraid to try for another child, she needs to come back and see me. I think I can put her fears to rest." Clearing his throat, he added, "I'm sorry, Shortie. I figured you knew about the pregnancy. The scar tissue is old, but certainly not enough to cause complications."

Leaving the doctor's office with a heavy heart, he walked home with grief for company.

"Is Eddie her son or her little brother as she claims?" he moaned aloud. "Or was there another child?" There were no answers in the soft sigh of the wind, and the very idea made him shake his head in anguish over the poor little baby that nobody wanted. By the time he entered his own front door, his mood was black and his thoughts even gloomier. Refusing dinner, he did the evening chores and then retired to the porch. Eddie sat silently beside him until bedtime. Instinctively, he knew something was seriously wrong.

"Are you sad?" he asked when he kissed Shortie's cheek goodnight.

Holding the child as if afraid to let him go, he answered as best he could. "Yes, Eddie, I'm very sad. I got some bad news today and it made my heart hurt."

"Will it get better?"

"In time, son, in time."

Chapter 21

As he bore the burden of Inja's secret in silence, Shortie's appetite dropped off and his usual jovial attitude turned surly. Worried over the change in him, Inja stayed close to home. She refused to accompany Holly to town on several occasions and instead put her spare time into putting their house in order. Cleaning out a closet one afternoon, she found her mother's old recipe book. If she could enlist Bert's help, Shortie would be in for a few surprises come mealtime.

Bert was suspicious when Inja first appeared on her doorstep begging for cooking lessons. But when she spied the old recipe book, she understood and couldn't have been more flattered. Her own mother had given her a book just like it filled with recipes for old favorite Irish dishes. Putting all grievances aside, she taught Inja to use seasoning and color to make foods look attractive and tempting. Tasty meals were prepared with sumptuous desserts to tickle Shortie's sweet tooth. She even learned to cook oatmeal. Bert was as disappointed as Inja when his lagging appetite did not improve.

Putting her energies into making their home more attractive, every closet, drawer, nook and cranny was neatened and rearranged. After an afternoon of mending a stack of items that had accumulated over the past year, she was exhausted. Placing a leftover beef pot pie in the oven, she sat with her feet up on the coffee table to enjoy her first cup of coffee since early morning. Sipping the hot drink, she sighed with satisfaction at the shiny floors and furniture, waxed to mirror smoothness. The windows fairly sparkled, and new curtains graced each one. Gingham ruffles puffed out like a little girl's petticoat, rustling gently with the breeze. Pleased with the effect, she hoped Shortie would notice. There wasn't much more she could do to make the place look good, and boredom was setting in fast. She deserved a little fun after all her hard work. Noticing the time, she fixed a bright smile on her lips. He would be home soon, and she didn't want the evening to begin with an argument.

Hearing the twang of the screendoor, she rose to greet him. Her smiling lips turned to a frown, however, when she spotted small, muddy footprints tracked across the floor. In the bathroom, Eddie turned from the sink, his face lit with excitement.

"Lock what I found." Pointing to the sink with a dirty finger, he admired a huge brown toad. A small stream of water ran over the toad's head, and it scrambled up the sides of the sink trying to escape a possible drowning. Proud of his find, he gazed expectantly at her.

"Did you do this all by yourself?" she asked in a low voice.

Misunderstanding her, he nodded his head. "I found him under the old water tank on the hill. Ain't he beautiful? Can I keep him? He don't eat much, just flies and bugs and stuff."

"I meant," she explained, her voice tense, "did you track all this dirt in here yourself?" Pointing to the tracks on the floor and the muddied sink, she went hot with anger.

"I didn't mean to," he mumbled. Nervously rubbing the back of his calf with the toe of his foot, the smile faded from his lips. Fixing his eyes on the floor, he tried not to cry.

"Look at me when I'm speaking to you, young man."

Eddie raised his head, and one skinny arm reached to cover the toad protectively. Her eyes glittered dangerously, and anger mottled her cheeks with red splotches. She stood in front of the door, barring the exit. Trapped, Eddie gazed at her in fear.

"I'm sorry, Inja. I'll clean it up," he pleaded. Struggling to control the quaver in his voice, he blinked rapidly, fighting back tears.

Her eyes narrowed as she regarded her little brother. Grabbing him by the shoulders, she shook him so hard he thought his head would snap off.

"What's the matter with you? How many times do I have to tell you to wipe your feet before coming into the house? Clean up this mess," she screamed. Taking a scrub brush from under the sink, she threw it at him as he cowered on the floor at her feet, sobbing. "Every bit of this floor better be shining before he gets home or else."

"Or else what?" Shortie thundered. "Is this what goes on when I'm not home?" Pulling her out of the doorway, he rushed to rescue the frightened child. Soothing him with reassuring words, he washed his dirty face with cool water and dried his tears. "Is this your toad?" he asked as he raised it out of the sink.

At Eddie's nod and sniffle, he examined the animal as if it were a real treasure, bringing a smile to the child's mouth.

"My, he's handsome. But, Eddie, I'm afraid Mr. Toad won't be happy living in our bathroom sink. He'd be much happier where he can be with other toads, catching flies and flirting with lady toads. I'm afraid if we keep him, he may die. You don't want that, do you?"

Concerned for the animal's welfare, Eddie agreed to return it to its home under the water tank. After a silent supper, the two climbed the hill and released the bewildered toad back to familiar surroundings. They didn't talk about the situation or discuss the cause of Inja's anger; it wasn't necessary. The boy clung to his side and shadowed his every move. Fear was evident in the furtive peeks he threw at her with eyes too large and face too pale.

Remorse ate at her conscience. It followed her around with accusations and images of the hurt in Eddie's eyes. Able to stand it no longer, she tapped on his bedroom door.

"Eddie?" He didn't answer, and she feared he'd already fallen to sleep. She opened the door a little wider, and light from the kitchen cut across the room. He lay on his side, facing the wall. His shoulders shook, and the sound of muffled crying reached her ears.

"Eddie," she repeated. Crossing the room, she gathered him onto her lap. Tears formed in her eyes as she recognized the hurt in his. "I'm sorry. I'm truly very sorry. I was wrong and should never have treated you like that." Hugging him fiercely, she held him on her lap, enjoying the feel of his heart beating against her own. The intensity of the anger she'd felt frightened her beyond belief. What if she had actually hurt him? Even though she spoke harshly at times, she cared for him in her own way. She needed his forgiveness.

Sniffling loudly, he drew back to look her in the eye. Cocking his head, he studied her expression somberly.

"I know ya didn't mean it," he said with a shaky breath. "Sometimes ya get so mad and ya gotta let it out. When I get mad, I run really hard until I can't breathe."

"Is that really what you do when you're angry? You must run very fast."

"Yup."

"I'll try that sometime," she promised. Smoothing his unruly hair, she couldn't resist hugging him before she tucked him snugly into bed. When he wrapped his arms around her neck and gave her a moist kiss on the cheek, she was totally overcome.

"I love you, Inja."

"I love you, too, Eddie. Is all forgiven?"

"All's forgiven, but Inja?"

"Yes?"

"Would ya really have done it?"

"Done what?"

"Would ya really have kicked me?"

A rush of heat filled her cheeks and then turned to ice as it skipped along her spine. She felt as if somebody had doused her with cold water. A startled gasp escaped her lips at his intuitiveness. How could she possibly answer such a question? "What makes you think I would kick you?" Unable to meet his steady gaze, she busied her hands by rearranging all the accumulated treasures on top of his dresser: four rocks, a stick of unusual shape, and a ragged, stuffed rabbit.

Sitting up, he studied her nervous movements for a moment before shrugging his shoulders noncommitally. The threat had been evident in her angry, contorted features. He didn't know how to explain what he'd read in her expression or even if he should. Lying down, he snuggled a stuffed bear close to his side. "I knew ya didn't mean it. Good night." Rolling over, his eyes closed, and within minutes he was sleeping soundly.

Visibly shaken, she shut the door. Coming face-to-face with herself in the darkened hallway, she vowed never to allow anger to take the place of common sense again. She had crossed one hurdle safely and geared herself up for the next. Shortie may not be as easy or as forgiving, but it was time to settle this thing between them and find out what bothered him. Opening the bedroom door, she crossed the threshold with lips pinched with determination.

As soon as the door clicked shut behind her, Shortie turned off the light, shutting her out at the same time. Changing into her nightgown, she climbed into bed. Lying on her back, she stared at the ceiling and tried to find the right words to approach the problem. He sighed. Feeling she'd go absolutely crazy if she had to listen to his silence another moment, she threw the covers off and snapped on the bedside lamp.

"It's no wonder I'm out of sorts. All you've done for days is mope around and sigh. Will you please tell me what's wrong so our lives can get back to normal?" she demanded.

Rising, he sat on the edge of the bed. Searching her face, his eyes accused her, and for what she didn't know. There was so much sorrow in his expression that an icy dart of fear jabbed her heart. What had she done to cause him such pain? Surely it wasn't about Eddie because an aura of sadness had been with him for quite awhile.

"Would you please tell me what's bothering you? I can't do anything to help unless I know what battle to fight," she said softly as she sank to her knees in front of him. Touching his arm tentatively, she invited his confidence, never suspecting the root of the problem. It was a secret that was supposed to be tucked away and never shared.

"Why didn't you tell me about the baby, Inja?" The question set her heart to beating frantically in her chest. She would have given just about anything to avoid the truth.

"Baby? What baby?" Unable to meet his gaze, she looked over his shoulder and was startled to see her own reflection in the mirror. Panic was written all over her.

"Have you forgotten so soon? You must have because you neglected to tell me about it. Dr. Willom's examination revealed more than I bargained for. I know you had a baby, and I need to know if it was mine."

Her face paled, and the fingers of one hand flew to her lips, stifling a denial. Startled, she frantically searched for an acceptable answer. Coming up blank, she suppressed an incriminating smile while nervously twisting the fabric of her nightgown into a ball.

"I don't know what you're talking about," she said with her usual feigned nonchalance. Caught in her own lie, she continued the charade. "That old man must be crazy. He must have confused my tests with someone else. Do you think a woman can hide that sort of thing from her husband?" Sniffing with an air of injured self-righteousness, she strode to the dresser and began brushing her hair with quick, angry strokes, being careful to keep her back to him.

"There's no sense in denying the truth. Doc went over all your tests with me. You've been pregnant before, and I can only assume one of two things: either Eddie is actually your son and you've lied about it for some reason known only to yourself, or there's a child of yours running around this world somewhere. Which is it?" The wounded look on his face knifed through her. It was time to tell the truth no matter what it cost her.

"I didn't know I was pregnant until it was too late. I didn't tell you because I.. .I didn't want you to be hurt. I wanted to protect you and the child, so kept it a secret all these years. I was seventeen and my boyfriend was still in high school when my little problem was discovered. He ran away and joined the Army, and Mama sent me to her sister's. I don't know what I had because I wasn't allowed to see it. The child was adopted through an agency ran by my aunt's church. It was a long time ago and I've never looked back." Exhausted, she dropped her head to her chest.

"You never tried to find your child?"

"What good would that have done? The final papers are sealed, and information about it will never be disclosed to anyone. It's over and done with." The bitter look on her face told him she was telling the truth.

"There should never be secrets between a man and his wife and especially ones as important as this. Never again, Inja, never again," he stated coldly. "Dr. Willom also told me about another one of your secrets. I don't know what you're using for birth control, but get rid of it. And I never want to see or hear you torment the boy again. I thought I knew you, but have discovered I never knew you at all."

"I've already spoken to Eddie and apologized and begged his forgiveness," she cried. "We made up, and I promise it will never happen again." Weeping, she was ready to promise anything as long as he didn't hate her.

Pity tore at his heart as he took in her bloodshot eyes and teary face. Gesturing for her to come closer, he kneeled at the edge of the bed. She stared at him, speechless and totally dumbfounded.

"What are you doing?" she sputtered.

"I'm going to pray for you, for me, for Eddie, for us. I'm going to pray unceasingly that the Lord will forgive our selfishness. Come and pray with me because our lives depend upon it." He extended a hand in invitation.

She remained where she stood with feet rooted to the floor. Gaping in stunned silence, she stared at him. Indignation filled her as she listened to his prayer for forgiveness. What right did he have to beg forgiveness for her? She regarded him with contempt. It was obvious her presence wasn't needed in this one-man prayer meeting. Turning on her heel, she left the room.

Making a bed on the couch, she tossed around uncomfortably. Sleep didn't come easy. Would *He* forgive her for the biggest lie of all?

Chapter 22

Waking with a favorite hymn on his lips, Shortie greeted the morning singing loud enough to wake the dead. Even though his vocalizations were slightly off-key, he had a pleasant voice which people enjoyed, but not at four in the morning. Slamming a pillow over her ears, Inja tried to ignore it. Finding herself humming along, she rose and stumbled into the kitchen to make coffee. He didn't drink the stuff, but she'd need a gallon to stay awake until he left for work. Eyeing him warily, she anticipated further questions about the child she allowed to be adopted. There were no questions, just a smile and an offer for breakfast. Deciding a night of prayer might have done him good, she pulled a chair over next to the stove to warm herself while waiting for the coffee to brew. Pleased, she watched as he prepared an enormous breakfast and lunch enough for two. Hiding a tiny smile that teased at the corner of her mouth, she hid behind her cup. His cheerfulness was contagious.

Opening the kitchen door as wide as it would go, he inhaled deeply. "Smell that, Inja, isn't it great?"

"Brrr, yeah, it's great all right, but cold on bare legs. Shut it, would'ya?"

"It rained during the night, did you hear it? The garden won't need watering today." Taking Eddie's baseball and tossing it up and down a few times, his expression turned boyish. "Maybe he'll want to play some ball tonight, what do you think?"

Astonished that he asked for her opinion, she returned a blissful smile. "I wouldn't be surprised," she chuckled good-naturedly. A stone born of deceit lifted from her heart as she admired his handsome features. As she stood with him to welcome the glory of a new day, the pinch of worry disappeared from between her brows.

Inja wasn't the only person who noticed a profound change in Shortie's attitude. At the dairy, his melodic whistling was heard all over the plant. Tony couldn't help but laugh aloud on numerous occasions.

"Things are gonna be different around here, I think," he commented to a co-worker. As if he'd overheard, Shortie chose that moment to glance over and wave. Their broad grins were no match for the smile that threatened to split his face in two.

He couldn't contain the overwhelming joy and peace God had put into his heart. It spilled over onto all those he came in contact with. At peace with God and himself, he hoped the sense of serenity would last forever.

All afternoon he gave thanks for the change in his heart. He had received more than he ever deserved and was doubly surprised when another blessing came his way. One of the delivery drivers quit and the job was offered to him. The new position meant a pay raise and all the dairy products he could carry home. He couldn't wait to share the news.

The Lord has done great things for us, and we are filled with joy.

When the shift ended, Tony and Shortie hurried to the corner, impatient to get home. Catching their breath, they had a few spare minutes before Blackie arrived. Seated on an elevated section of sidewalk, Shortie longed to share his previous night's experience with his friend. He wanted to describe the change he felt, but hesitated, afraid the words wouldn't come. How could he explain what he didn't comprehend himself? When Blackie pulled up, raring to get home to supper, the urge vanished.

Tony was eager to get home himself and encouraged a heavy foot on the gas. "Move this thing a little faster," he teased. "I want to get home before my son starts school." There was a standing joke between the two about "Fast Fords" versus "Crawling Chevys." Blackie drove a Chevy and swore they could drive any Ford into the ground. Shortie didn't see the sense in reckless driving and often admonished him to slow down. Today, however, he didn't mind the extra speed. Holding onto the door, he silently pushed for more as they barreled up the draw. He couldn't wait to tell Inja about his new position.

Tony was just as impatient. Maria hadn't been feeling well and needed him at home. The baby wasn't due for another couple of months, but she was already round as a barrel. She was sick a lot, her ankles and feet were swollen, and standing for any period of time was pure torture. Tony teased about the moose she carried and nicknamed their unborn child "Bubba." Aside from the teasing, he was very concerned. Her other two pregnancies had been without complication. They hadn't been prepared for morning sickness that lasted all day.

The truck slowed in front of Tony's place just long enough for him to scramble from the cab. Grinding gears, Blackie downshifted and sped up the hill. Thumbing his nose, he roared with mirth in response to Tony's return gesture. Chuckling, Shortie gave a good-bye salute and hurried home.

Taking the stairs two at a time, he burst in the front door, scaring the sleeping cat out of one of its nine lives. "Inja, you'll never guess what happened today," he gushed. Grabbing her around the waist, he waltzed her around the kitchen with more enthusiasm than grace. Laughing, she danced with him for a moment before pulling away and scolding him for such foolish behavior.

"Whatever has gotten into you?" she asked, dizzy from circling the room. "Look at this mess," she moaned. Dusting flour off her hands from the bread dough she'd been kneading, she grabbed the broom to sweep the floor.

"Never mind that," he laughed. Taking the broom, he swiped the floor a couple of times and then dropped it to the floor with a clatter. She couldn't have been more surprised when he seized her by the shoulders and kissed her passionately. When he released her, her eyebrows shot to her hairline and her chin dropped.

"My word," she whispered as she stared at him in shock.

"You'll never guess what happened. My boss offered me a new position and it pays a dollar more an hour. Come Monday morning, I'll be a driver with my own milk route."

"Did you say a dollar more an hour?"

With a screech, she threw her arms about his neck and danced around with joy. The bread was forgotten as he explained all about his new job.

"It's a blessing," he said rapturously. "Think about it; soon I'll be able to replace the savings I withdrew for the TV. We'll buy you a new dress, Eddie wants a new baseball glove and he needs new shoes. And for me," he added, "a couch without lumps."

"One without springs?" she asked as she rubbed her seat where an errant spring had poked her all night.

"Without springs," he agreed with an understanding chuckle.

After supper dishes were cleared away and four loaves of fresh bread were wrapped and placed in the bread drawer, Inja called Bert. Listening for a moment to her animated chatter, Shortie marveled again at God's goodness. The Lord had blessed him far beyond anything he'd ever imagined. So what if the picture-perfect ideal he had of her was slightly flawed? She was what made his world go around. Finding Eddie's baseball on the back porch, he went in search of the boy. It wouldn't take long to round up enough people for a rousing game before dark. His plans changed abruptly when Bert's yellow station wagon skidded to a stop in front of their steps. Prying herself from under the steering wheel, she climbed the stairs quickly. Inja met her halfway, squealing in the way women often do.

Clasping hands, the two climbed the remaining steps with Inja pulling the older woman along. They jabbered continuously, and he wondered when they stopped to breathe. Curiosity got the best of him, and he dropped the ball to investigate. Eddie appeared out of nowhere and picked up the ball to follow them. When Bert was around, treats usually followed. They found the women in the kitchen poring over a recipe book.

"Do you know how close the Fourth of July is?" Bert demanded when he entered the room.

Looking behind him to be sure she was addressing him, he put a finger to his chest and inquired, "Are you asking me?"

"Of course I'm asking you, Shortie Busch," she said haughtily. "The fourth is only two weeks away, which means we've got to prepare for the bake-off. It's a good thing I checked my calendar for Maria's next appointment," she sniffed. Turning to Inja, "We've got two weeks to teach you the art of cake decorating with and without frosting," she declared. "That means experimentation with different recipes until you find a favorite. Then you practice until you make it better. Are you game?"

"I'm game," Inja responded. As if to prove the truth of her statement, she gathered together a mixing bowl, spatula, and spoon. For the next couple of hours, Inja worked happily in the kitchen with Bert as her tutor. Shortie and Eddie were kept busy running to the store for more eggs, then a gallon of milk, and then a third time for vanilla. By the time bedtime rolled around, they were exhausted. The last thing Shortie heard before sleep claimed him was Bert explaining something about a wolf in sheep's clothing. Sleepily, he wondered what kind of recipe that entailed.

Chapter 23

By six AM on the morning of the 4th, the day promised to be a scorcher. Thermometers showed a warm 77 degrees with the red inching steadily upward. The entire community anticipated the Fourth of July picnic like kids do Christmas. It was sponsored by the local mines, and no one willingly missed it. Even though the morning was warm, kitchens of bake-off participants were 20 to 30 degrees warmer. While chickens fried, fresh bread was set to rise in the overheated air. Cakes cooled along window ledges, and flaky crusted pies browned in hot ovens. The competition had begun.

Inja hummed to herself as she added more molasses to her baked beans. Her beans had to be extra special this year. A self-satisfied smile crossed her lips as she tasted the sauce and found it perfect. She anticipated the compliments she was sure to receive and shoved the beans back in the oven.

The bake-off was the most important event of the year. Lucky finalists won a ten-dollar prize, and their recipes were published in the paper along with their photograph. She was positive she'd win one of the prizes and spent the winnings on a new dress. Still fuming over Shortie's recent tithe, she spent the money out of spite. The amount he so casually had tossed into the offering plate would have bought the dress and new shoes for Eddie. Since he'd promised to buy her a new dress anyway, he certainly wouldn't begrudge her the few extra dollars. Wiping beads of perspiration from her forehead, she giggled aloud. The cake was flawless. Tiny pink rosebuds graced the top, connected by pale green vines that swirled and looped beautifully throughout the flowers. The snowy white frosting set off the decorations perfectly.

"Wait till Bert sees this," she said to herself. Bert baked for the picnic, too, but had never brought a frosted cake to the judging. "I wonder why," she mused. Admiring her handiwork a moment longer, she placed the cake in the keeper and secured the lid with a loud snap. Turning back to the stove, she turned the chicken before mixing the potato salad. Everything was going according to schedule, and she would tolerate no interruptions.

Eddie watched from a safe distance. With chin in hands and elbows resting on the table, he followed her movements hungrily. Everything smelled so good. His mouth watered and his stomach was rumbling loudly before he worked up the courage to ask a question.

"Is it time yet?"

"No, it isn't," she answered impatiently. Turning to face him, a frown of displeasure creased her forehead. "I believe you can see the time as well as I. It's barely past seven, and I still have several things to do, so keep out from under foot."

Brushing his hair back out of his eyes, Eddie studied the hands of the clock. He wanted to remember what seven o'clock looked like.

"Have you made your bed, washed your face, or brushed your teeth?" She didn't wait for an answer, but turned her attention back to the frying pan, turning the chicken once more.

"We won't leave for another three hours. If you're hungry, eat some bread and butter. There's cold milk in the ice box and you know where the glasses are."

Sliding off the chair, he took a plate, glass, and knife from the cupboard. Clumsily, he sawed off a thick slab of bread, which he smeared with butter and huckleberry jam. Leaving a sticky trail between the jar and the bread, he wiped up the purple sweetness with an index finger. Popping the finger in his mouth and with bread in the other hand, he made a hasty exit. Glancing nervously over his shoulder, he checked to see if she noticed the spilled jam and then escaped to the front porch with a sigh of relief. He could eat his breakfast in peace now that he was away from her watchful eye. Squinting against the bright morning sun, he took large, thoughtful bites of the bread.

Huckleberries dripped off the side and ran down his fingers, and with no one around to tell him not to, he gleefully licked it up. He devoured the remainder in four huge bites.

Standing, he searched the road below for a sign of Shortie. Milk was delivered even on holidays, and he'd left for work hours ago. Impatiently, he paced the yard, pausing frequently to scan the path. Finally, he spotted a lone figure striding up the hill, and yelling excitedly, waved his arms in the air. Taking off like a shot, he ran to meet him and hurry things along. Now that he was home, the day could be enjoyed.

"Did ya get'im?"

"You bet'cha. Look at all the firecrackers we've got." Pulling a handful from his pocket, he allowed Eddie a quick peek before hiding them back in his overalls. With a devilish expression and gleam in his eye, he tossed one up and down. "What's Inja doing?"

"I wouldn't if I was you. She might throw somethin' at ya'," Eddie warned.

"Yeah, you're probably right," he admitted, but the temptation to fire one off was great.

When he and Eddie climbed the stairs, there was Old Joe, sunning himself on the porch. Stretching out his legs, the cat lay full length on the welcome rug in front of the screen door. He looked too comfortable, and Shortie acted without thinking. Lighting a blackcap, he threw it behind the sleeping cat. The explosion was magnificent, but the cat's reaction wasn't. Jumping straight up, his long legs galloped in midair, suspended by his own momentum. His huge saucer eyes looked ready to pop out of his head. Coming to earth, he landed on lightening feet with hair puffed and his stump of a tail sticking straight out behind him. Yowling, he twisted his body around and leaped onto the screen with all claws extended. The delicate mesh, not meant to hold thirty pounds of cat, tore from its moorings. The poor animal crashed through the doorframe, taking the screen with him. Caught, he gave a blood-curdling howl and took off. He shredded most of the netting and half the couch before running for refuge beneath Eddie's bed.

"What on earth...." Inja exclaimed. Startled, she ran to investigate the commotion and was drawn up short by the cat running pell-mell with half the screen door hanging over his head. She stood in the doorway where the screen had been and glared at the two culprits. They were laughing so hard they hung onto each other to keep from falling down. Tapping a foot angrily, she shook a wooden spoon at them.

"That was a real stupid thing to do," she yelled. "Who's going to fix this door before the flies get in?" Her question was met with another fit of hysterical laughter. Opening her mouth to really tell them off, she closed it in exasperation. They wouldn't listen, and if they wanted to stand there braying like jackasses, well, who was she to stop them? Storming off to the kitchen, she struggled to keep her own laughter in check.

Contrite, Shortie tried to make up with the cat. Old Joe ignored his pleas and refused to budge from his position of safety. He promised to fix the door as soon as new netting was purchased, and grudgingly, Inja accepted his apology.

Coming into the kitchen, he hinted, "That chicken sure smells good. I hope you fried extra because my stomach's hammering against my backbone."

"There's plenty and more frying, so help yourself." Pouring him a glass of milk, she handed him a loaded plate. Sitting down, he slapped his cap down on the table and ran his hands through his hair. He'd covered a full milk route that morning and had completed a full day's work in just a few hours. He was hungry, not tired, and looked forward to the holiday with enthusiasm. His face smiled in all directions as he wolfed down the food, savoring each bite.

"You'd better slow down," she admonished him with a laugh, "or you won't have room left for the picnic."

He grabbed her around the waist and pulled her onto his lap. Kissing her on the lips, he suggested his hunger was for more than just food.

Holding her with one hand, he snuck a hardboiled egg with the other. Stuffing the entire thing into his mouth, he tried to chew and swallow, but couldn't. His mouth was full of too much egg. She chose that moment to goose him in the ribs, and egg spewed across the table in one loud guffaw. Standing abruptly, he choked down the remaining egg and dumped her to the floor, where she landed on her backside, laughing hysterically.

Eddie came running when he heard Inja cry out. Shaking his head, he wondered why she was on the floor rubbing her backside while Shortie stood above her with food dripping off his chin.

"Adults," he grumped.

Back in control of himself, Shortie righted Inja to her feet. He grinned candidly at her for a moment, and they each admired the other. He loved everything about her—from her frosting- smudged nose to her pink-slippered feet. The mood was broken when she whisked out a towel and wiped his chin.

"Look at the time. Help me get this mess cleaned up before they get here." Handing the dishrag to him, she ordered, "You wash while I finish getting things ready." Giving himself a quick rinse, he filled the sink with sudsy water, then dumped in what dirty dishes he could find.

"You'd better hurry; they'll be here any minute," he reminded her. Art and Ellen Jones were driving them because Blackie had to work. The Joneses lived close and could easily transport them in the back of their pickup. The picnic, held up the Northfork of the Coeur d'Alene River, was a scenic 40 miles or so away, so there would be plenty of time to visit while en route.

As Inja packed the food, plates, and other paraphernalia, she kept up a steady stream of chatter which required little response. Enjoying the sound of it, Shortie tidied the kitchen while she finished.

"They're here, they're here," Eddie called, so excited he literally jumped up and down.

Hearing the Joneses' pick-up pull up the grade, they packed the remaining items in a box with the cake-caddy placed carefully on top. She hadn't allowed him to see the cake, wanting it to be a surprise. Jonesy bounced from the driver's seat and stretched his lanky frame. Grabbing Eddie, he positioned him safely in the back of the truck. Shortie was pleased to note Art was sober and there wasn't a beer bottle in sight.

"You don't mind sittin' with the kids, do ya? I saved the front for the wife, Inja, and the twins," he apologized.

"You know I won't. I like sitting in the open air, and besides, I'll be closer to all this good food," Shortie joked. Chucking the twin girls under the chin, he seated Inja inside and then jumped in the back, situating himself with an arm around the smallest child. Sitting in the midst of five overly excited kids, the Joneses' two lazy hound dogs, picnic boxes, blankets and a bald spare tire, there wasn't much room to stretch his legs. Grinning at the children, he hollered, "Are we ready?"

"We're ready," they shouted. Slapping a hand against the side, he signaled they were set to go.

Climbing into the truck, Art started it with a roar. Ellen handed one sleeping twin to Inja, then grabbed onto the dashboard.

"You'd best hang on," she warned when Art gunned the motor. The old truck took off with a cough and it stalled out twice before speeding off down the road. The kids roared with approval, thrilled with the speed and rush of wind. Shortie hung on for his life, cursing Art under his breath.

As the pickup left the dirt road and turned onto pavement, it slowed to a more sedate speed. They followed the main drag down Division to Main, and then from Main to Hill Street past Teeter's Field where several kids were setting off firecrackers. Turning off Cameron Avenue, a sharp left led them onto the highway. As soon as Jonesy merged with traffic, he switched gears and jammed his foot into the accelerator. The old truck shimmied all over the road before settling into gear. Backfiring and complaining loudly, it enveloped the occupants in a fog of thick black smoke before smoothing out to rattle down the road with just an occasional tremble. The children thought this was great fun, and every time the truck belched smoke or threatened to jump off the side, they shrieked and hollered for more. Hanging on the littlest ones so they wouldn't get bounced out on their heads, Shortie grasped the side of the truck bed frantically and prayed they'd all make it one piece.

Inside the cab, the women jostled the sleeping babies while keeping up a steady stream of chatter. Inja learned to quickly grab onto something every time Ellen reached for the dashboard. Several times she saved herself from smashing painfully into the door panel or worse yet, into Ellen, by following her example. A steady rhythm of grab, tense, and sway with the movement of the truck kept them occupied for the remainder of the ride.

By the time the truck came to a stop, Shortie's eyes were watering, his ears rang, and his stomach wasn't where it was supposed to be. The two hounds came to life as soon as the truck slowed and their baying added to the pounding in his head. The dogs lumbered toward the tailgate with tongues lolling. Wet drops rolled off their tongues onto the picnic boxes, bare legs, and an ill-tempered Shortie. Shoving the sweltering animals away with unintended force, he launched them from the back of the truck. The dogs gave a rather disgusted backward glance and then disappeared into the trees. Jonesy didn't fear losing them because they always appeared at mealtime with an uncanny timeliness.

Inja and Ellen searched out a suitable picnic table while the men unloaded their supplies. Finding one shaded between two stately pines, they quickly set up for the day.

"We've certainly got enough food," Ellen commented as she surveyed the loaded table. "You boys better work up a good appetite or we'll be eating leftovers for the next month."

"I don't mind leftovers, but a person can only eat so many baked beans. They seem to have an effect on some people, and there are just so many windows a person can open." Inja glanced meaningfully toward Shortie and rolled her eyes. Laughing together, the two enjoyed their little joke at his expense. He busied himself by spreading blankets on the grass for the little ones to lie on. His cheeks were scorched scarlet clear to the tops of his ears.

Inja took the cake-caddy out of the box and carefully snapped up the cover. Turning it all around, she checked it minutely for signs of damage.

"Not even a crack," she said smugly.

"I've never seen a more beautiful cake," Ellen admired. "It's almost too pretty to slice. Are you entering it in the bake-off?"

"I certainly am, and for all the work I've put into it, it better win first prize."

"It might." Ellen looked the cake over with a doubtful expression. "Aren't the entries supposed to be unfrosted?"

"Nowhere does it say cakes or pastries must be unfrosted," Inja objected.

"Now, let's find the tables and get entered." Placing the twins in a double stroller, the two rushed off. Ellen's loaf of beautifully browned sourdough bread was a surefire winner. The men followed, with Shortie taking command of the stroller.

After signing in and receiving their numbered tickets, Inja placed her beans among the other casserole dishes. Ellen's bread was marked and displayed in the proper category, but when the cake was placed with the other baked goods, one of the judges felt inclined to comment.

"Don't you want to keep it covered until time for the judging?"

"I certainly do not," Inja replied indignantly. "I want it left out for everyone to see." Turning the cake, she beamed at it fondly, "This cake," she added with a proud flourish, "needs to be seen and admired in order to be judged fairly."

"Okay, I hope you know what you're doing." The judge shrugged off her comments and moved on to the next table.

Surveying the assortment of pies and cakes, she smirked, "Look at that, not a single one is frosted or even decorated with colored sugar. Mine is sure to win first or at least second place." Ellen didn't respond, but gave a patronizing smile usually reserved for children.

"I hope they judge this table first," Shortie said as he admired all the desserts. "I don't know what I want a piece of more; the spice cake looks fit to eat, but so do those berry pies. Mmmmm, I've made up my mind," he said with mouth watering. "Here's my favorite, apple pie."

"Strawberry rhubarb for me," Art pointed out. Inja was slightly miffed at their lack of enthusiasm for her entry and turned to flash a welcoming smile to the couple coming to join them.

"Holly, Leon, I'm glad you decided to accept my invitation." Linking arms with Holly, she guided her over to the judging tables to admire the entries.

"How's it goin'?" Leon greeted Art but eyed Shortie warily.

"To tell the truth, it was better a few minutes ago." Art ignored Leon's outstretched hand and turned away.

"What are you doing here?" Shortie fumed. He resented the intrusion and eyed the younger man suspiciously. "This is a family gathering, and we're not exactly the type of people you usually hang out with. I don't know what you're up to, but stay away from me and my family." Spying Eddie running across the field, he raised a hand and waved. "If you'll excuse me," he said curtly, "my boy and I have things to do."

Boys, with fathers in tow, converged on the open field where the games were held. It was hard to tell who was more excited, the children or their fathers.

"Come on, Shortie," Eddie urged, pulling him along. "We gotta sign in ta' enter the race." So far, he had signed up for the baseball game, the foot races, and a greased pig contest. Shortie entered the wood splitting contest, the baseball game with Eddie, and the tug-of-war. Signing in for the three-legged race, they joked with Art and James, who entered with them.

While waiting for the games to begin, they wandered around the park hoping to spot the Cleggs. They promised to join them as soon as Blackie was off-shift. Already there was a huge crowd gathered, and a steady stream of cars was pulling into the parking lot. Greeting everyone they knew and even those they didn't, they stopped to speak to Frank Howard. He was with other representatives of the miner's union, and in honor of the fourth, had discarded his official duties. Union reps attended the picnic for the same reason as everybody else—to have a good time. Spying another familiar face surrounded by a crowd of children, Shortie wandered over to say hello.

"Did you bring the entire store with you?" he marveled at the stack of candy boxes, melons, and crackers.

"Nope, just a few things I figured would sell," Arden replied as he handed out a licorice stick. "I didn't expect this much business, though." Children with pennies, nickels, and dimes clamored for attention. Candy boxes emptied quickly, and some feared he'd run out before they obtained their treat. Serving the last child, he turned his attention to Shortie.

"What can I do ya for?"

"Do you have any soda pop?"

"What kind of fool do you take me for? Do ya think I'd leave my real profits at home?" Pulling a tarp off the rear of his blue delivery truck, he proudly revealed enough beer, soda pop, and ice to satisfy even the thirstiest participant. Handing over a dime, Shortie bought a root beer. He'd just put the bottle to his mouth when Eddie called.

"Hurry, the races are startin'."

Chugging down the soda, he hurried after the boy. Shortie stood on the sidelines with Inja and Ellen, and they cheered Eddie on in the foot races. He took the blue ribbon in the first race, but lost the second. Shortie cheered himself hoarse.

"My throat's drier n' an ole' corn cob," he quipped. "Anyone else want something to drink? Arden's set up his store and he's selling just about anything to quench a body's thirst."

The ladies deferred, but Art came along. He hoped Arden was selling beer because he'd worked up a thirst himself.

"You want another beer?" Arden joked with a teasing laugh. Shortie nodded as he offered up another dime and took a root beer from an ice chest. He sized up Art's state of sobriety and then stated, "I'm going to tell you right now that the beer is limited. It's three to a customer, so do you want them all at once or one at a time?"

"Well, since you're offering and I'm dry enough to make dust, I'll take all three," Art countered. Placing the money in Arden's outstretched palm, he grinned sardonically. Chugging down the first, he drank the second in three swallows. The third he sipped slowly under Ellen's watchful eye. All the while he searched hungrily for another outlet to quench a growing thirst. Shortie watched as his probing gaze came to rest upon Leon. He found his mark.

"Take it easy on that stuff," he growled. "This is a family get together and I won't babysit a drunk." Smiling at Ellen and Inja across the field, he added, "You'd better stay sober, because if you don't...." Increasing pressure on Art's upper arm grew intense, sending a message loud and clear.

"Funny thing," Art winced. Just last night Blackie suggested something along those same lines. You know what they say about like minds...." Extricating his arm, he grimaced with pain. "I will not drink too much, scout's honor," he promised with a three-fingered salute. "But this is the Fourth of July and a man's got a right to drink a beer if he has a mind to. Isn't that what the Fourth is all about? Men have fought and died for freedom of speech, the right to assemble, and the right to bear arms, and I have the right to drink a beer once in awhile if I want to." Leon laughed, sharing in Art's little joke. Arden and Shortie remained stone-faced. Their solemn expressions followed him as he walked away with his new friend.

Hurrying to the field for the next event, Shortie spotted Blackie across the way. He waved a greeting but didn't stop to visit. His event had been called.

As soon as the announcement was made, the open area around the participants filled. Onlookers were cautioned to keep back and away from where entrants held sharp axes, poised to begin. Lying before each man was a log they were to chop into firewood lengths and then stack. Child's play! Shortie had chopped and stacked wood all his life.

"I'm bettin' on ya, Shortie," Blackie yelled.

"Show 'em what you're made of, Busch," Art called. Waving a bottle of beer in one hand, he weaved around with the other arm looped around Holly's neck. There wasn't time to worry about the extent of his sobriety, however, because the starting gun went off with a blast of black powder.

As each axeman threw their weight into the task, the bite of the blade went deep. Chips flew high as the rhythmic beat of it filled the air. At each thud of the blade, logs split and cracked, echoing off the surrounding mountains. Stacks of cordwood grew beside each wood splitter, and the crowd cheered them on. Shortie, hurrying to stack the wood he'd split, stumbled when his bad leg buckled under him. Regaining his balance, he staggered under the massive armload he carried to a growing pile. Throwing down the wood, he stacked it neatly and with lightening speed. He finished a full minute and a half before his closest competitor. Holding the axe high above his head, he saluted the other woodcutters before accepting the first place trophy. The little bronze woodcutter would grace a shelf in his front room for at least one more year.

"Could ya use a cold one?" Blackie asked as he rubbed Shortie's shoulders as his once were before a fight. Boxing was his forté, but unfortunately, the picnic sponsors didn't think a boxing match was fit family entertainment. At Shortie's nod, he slapped an icy bottle of root beer into his palm. He took a deep drink, enjoying the fizzle as it went down his throat.

"Where'd Art take off to?"

"He went somewhere with his kid. Don't worry, if he's with James, he'll stay out of trouble. Man, you were somethin'. You handle an axe like it was part of you. It was really somethin' to see," Blackie repeated, awed by the power and finesse of true axemen at work.

"Thanks." Flattered by such high praise, color flooded Shortie's already reddened cheeks. There wasn't time to search for Art before another game started. Eddie was already pulling him to his feet.

The baseball game was a rapid play that took less than forty-five minutes. Blackie and Shortie played on the same team, but lost anyway. After a defeat of two runs, they wandered over to Arden's for another drink. Blackie bought one and then Shortie reciprocated.

"What's next?" Blackie asked. Wiping his lips with the back of a hand, he swiped a trickle of sweat from his brow with a shirttail.

"The three-legged race starts in a bit, but I'd better find Inja. She's competing in the bake-offs, and if I'm not there for the final announcements, I'll never hear the end of it.

"Yeah, I know what'cha mean. Bert entered a cake or pie or something. Last year I wasn't around when they announced the finalists and she wouldn't speak to me for a whole week. She made me eat canned beans for supper. How was I supposed to know she'd win first prize?"

Sauntering over to the tables spread with every kind of baked, canned, pickled, fried, and stewed food, they found their wives huddled together for moral support.

"It's about time you showed," Inja said, relieved to find him behind her. Grasping his arm tightly, she held her breath as the judges tasted her beans. "Bert won second for her pickled watermelon, but first for her strawberry jam. Isn't this the most exciting thing?" she exclaimed.

"Yeah, exciting," he said as he removed his arm from her clutches. She was cutting off circulation and his fingers had gone numb.

"Shortie," Eddie whispered. Eddie stood beside him with a woebegone expression. "Ya gotta come over here," he pleaded. Beyond him stood James; he was pacing nervously and motioned for his immediate attention. Thinking Art was in real trouble, he made an excuse and promised a quick return.

"You'd better hurry, they'll judge the cakes next," Inja told him.

Shortie followed the boys as they led him not away from the bake-off arena as expected, but straight to the dessert table. There on the far corner was Inja's three-layer cake iced with fluffy white frosting, pink roses, and chocolate sprigs.

"So, what's the problem?" he asked. Leaning closer, he examined the cake a little closer to see what the boy's were so upset about. He was surprised to see one of the chocolate bits move. Stepping to the side, he examined it from the back and then all sides and realized they were all moving. His hand flew to his mouth to stifle his shock.

"Oh my gosh. Has she seen this?" He cast a worried frown in her direction.

"Uh uh," the boys chimed in unison. "What should we do? They'll be over here in a just a few minutes.

He didn't think twice. He took the cake, plate and all, and dumped it into the nearest garbage can. Finding a pile of pine needles and loose soil, he covered the sticky mass puddled beneath the table. Who would have thought ants could climb so well?

"Don't ever tell," he admonished both boys with a finger to his lips.

"I'll never tell that ants got into it," Eddie declared, "but what happened to the rest of it?"

"The sun done it, I'll bet," James volunteered. "The sun melted the frosting clean off, didn't it?" James looked to Shortie for confirmation of his hunch.

"I'm afraid so, but we'll never tell her, will we?" Both boys promised with crossed hearts. Worried about the consequences when she finally did find out, he stopped for another root beer to calm his nerves. He drank it while the judging continued. Inja took second for her baked beans, but Ellen took a first place ribbon for her sourdough bread. Blackie enjoyed a huge slice of it after the judging and topped it off with a bowl of beans. He was still eating when the judges approached the next table.

"Where's my cake?" Inja asked. Studying the crumbs on Blackie's plate for a condemning hint of frosting, she satisfied herself that he hadn't eaten it. Bewildered, she scanned all the tables, but there was no sign of it. "Wait a minute," she yelled as the judging began, "you can't start until I find my cake."

"Oh no," Shortie groaned. "Inja, calm down. Are you sure it was on this table?" He pointed to the desserts and tried not to appear guilty. It was a lame charade.

"Am I sure? Do you think I've suddenly gone senile?" she bellowed. "I put a three-layer frosted cake on this table, and I want it back and I want it now," she screeched.

"She's right, she's absolutely right," agreed a little fellow with a red, white, and blue striped bow tie. "I was here when she brought it in and I distinctly remember asking if she wanted keep the cake covered. She was quite adamant in her refusal, and I wouldn't be surprised to find that it was eaten."

"Eaten?" she lamented. "Eaten by what?"

"Ants," he replied. "That's why we request no frosted cakes be entered and that entrants keep their baked goods covered. Timber ants will go over water or climb trees to get to sugar. That cake was loaded with sugar," he reminded.

"Wait just a minute," Inja wailed. "The rules don't say anything of the kind." She dug a wad of papers from her purse and searched through them until finding the rule sheet.

Removing his own copy from a shirt pocket, the judge pointed out the fine print at the bottom of the page. He read it aloud for everyone's benefit, then turned on his heel and walked off.

Inja half-heartedly cheered Bert's first place spice cake. She never forgave whoever tossed her cake in the garbage can. When it was discovered, ants snaked through what was left and the frosting had disappeared.

Relief etched Shortie's features when the three-legged race was announced. Art didn't show up to race with James, so Blackie filled in. Racers had to run to the end of their lane, pick up a baton, and return with it. Laughing and falling over each other, runners picked themselves up several times before they reached the baton and raced back. Blackie cheated! In his enthusiasm, he picked James up off the ground with one arm and ran all the way to the finish line.

"We won," James yelled as he threw his arms around the big man's middle. Accepting the ribbon, he proudly showed it to his mother and then to Bert. Blackie's eyes were mysteriously moist as he caught Bert's eye over the boy's head.

"Ain't it time to eat?" he complained over a rumbling stomach. Shortie drank another root beer and whole-heartedly agreed.

Tables were moved together and spread with cloths. As food was spread out, seats filled and voices stilled. It became so quiet, bird song and the buzzing of insects could be heard above the roar of the river. The surrounding trees spread a green, canopied roof above them as a prayer of thanks was said. Startled birds swept from tree limbs in a rush when "Amen" echoed from over a hundred throats. Dishes passed up and down the tables and plates filled several times before even the heartiest appetite could eat no more.

"I need something to wash this food down with," Shortie puffed. He was so full his bloated stomach hung over his belt, but still he was thirsty. Someone slapped another root beer into his hand and he drank it down greedily. His stomach was feeling some distress by the time dessert was served. Cakes and pies of every variety were cut, with plenty for seconds and thirds, and Arden served free ice cream for as long as it lasted.

"You thirsty?" Blackie asked with a stomach as bloated as Shortie's. "Let's take the kids over for ice cream," he suggested. "I've got to move around or I'm gonna bust."

"That's what you get for eating like a pig," Bert scolded. Patting his protruding belly with a heavy hand, she shook her head. "One of these days you're going to absolutely pop. By the way, while you're out and about, see if you can find Art. Ellen's worried because no one's seen him all day."

They herded all the kids they could find to Arden's and watched over them while scoops of ice cream were passed around. They licked fast because the stuff melted quickly in the heat of the day.

"Want another soda? It's free and I don't offer something for nothing very often so you'd better take me up on it." Handing another root beer to

Shortie, Arden gave Blackie a welcome cup of hot coffee. Drinking a cup himself, the three stood in companionable silence as the children chased each other among the trees.

Reluctantly, Shortie lifted the soda to his lips. He was beginning to have a real distaste for root beer. It was upsetting his stomach something awful.

The children's giggles stopped abruptly when angry voices drifted to them from a stand of poplars. Going to investigate, they found Art. Empty bottles littered the area, and his drunken state told what he'd been doing all afternoon.

"Take it back," he yelled. Staggering, he squared off opposite Leon who appeared to be straight and sober.

"You're drunk; go home and sleep it off. A man that can't handle his liquor shouldn't drink," he taunted.

"Drunk or not, a man don't talk about another man's wife," Art bellowed. Putting up his fists, he swung and hit air.

"Hey, get hold of yourself." Blackie grabbed him by the shoulders and pulled him away from Leon. "What's been going on here all day, and who's sayin' what about whose wife?" Shooting a keep-your-mouth-shut look over his shoulder, he tried to make sense out of what Art was saying.

"I'm drunk, but not so drunk I don't know what's going on." His eyes smoldered with some inner rage as he glared at Leon and warned, "You stay away from her and don't ever show your face around my place or so help me, I'll kill ya."

Shortie grabbed Leon before he could run off. "What's he talking about? Have you been bothering Ellen?" Prepared to finish the job he'd started a few weeks before, he doubled up his fist.

"He's drunk and talking crazy. I ain't done nothin' I need to explain to you." Squirming out of his grasp, he edged away. When Shortie advanced with both fists clenched, he turned tail and ran.

"Once a coward, always a coward," he crowed. Jeering Leon's retreating figure, he turned back with a jubilant grin.

Blackie helped Art to his pickup, where he immediately passed out. Dark was coming on, and the fireworks display would start soon. He'd be better off left alone to sleep it off.

Blankets were spread as close to the open clearing as possible. Shortie ate a second slice of pie, and Ellen brought him another root beer while everyone was ooohhhing and aaawwwing over the fireworks. When the last starburst faded in the sky, they loaded Bert's car for the ride home. She drove the wagon loaded with sleeping children, Inja, Ellen, and Art's smelly hound dogs. Blackie and Shortie loaded all the picnic items into Art's truck and managed to drive all the way home without so much as a single backfire.

The house was sweltering after the heat of the day. They opened the front and back door to let the evening breeze cool the air to a more comfortable level.

"Do you think it could get any hotter?" Shortie mopped his face with a handkerchief as he handed Inja the last of their picnic supplies.

"I don't know; summer's just begun and it's bound to get a lot hotter come August," she reminded him. They had no idea how prophetic her statement would prove to be.

Inja was putting Eddie to bed when Shortie stuck his head in to say good night. He wasn't feeling too sharp and wanted to get to bed himself.

"I don't feel good," Eddie mumbled. Placing a hand over his forehead, she found him too warm.

"You're probably coming down with 'toomuch.'" At his quizzical expression she explained, "Too much sun, too much food, too much ice cream, and too much soda pop will make anyone sick. I know just the thing to settle your stomach if I can only remember the ingredients." Wandering into the kitchen, she mumbled to herself, "Let's see, was that spirits of peppermint and sugar or was it honey? Cayenne pepper, water...I can't remember, oh yeah, now I've got it." She mixed a concoction that looked deadly. Returning to Eddie's bedside with a spoon, she ordered, "Open up."

His lips clamped together tightly and his eyes rolled up in his head.

"Now Eddie, don't be such a baby. This stuff will make you feel better, and besides, it's good. Watch, Shortie will taste it first."

Shortie's eyes widened in alarm when she held the spoon to his lips, but at her demanding gaze obediently opened his mouth. The spoon clacked against his teeth as two full tablespoons were poked in.

"There, you see, it's good, isn't it?" she asked. He couldn't answer because his tongue was on fire. Gasping, he involuntarily swallowed the stuff and holding a hand to his searing throat, ran for the door.

"What's the matter? Was there a tad too much cayenne?" Shrugging her shoulders, Inja gave her brother an encouraging smile. Filling the spoon again, she held it out to him. Eddie jumped and dove under the bed.

"Get out from underneath there," she demanded. "Shortie," she called, "come get Eddie out from under the bed." He didn't answer. He was busy out behind the shed. Standing in the dark among the bushes, his stomach rolled and emptied, leaving him gasping for breath.

"What the sam hill!" he exclaimed.

Chapter 24

Things were quiet around the neighborhood the day after the Fourth and as it was Sunday, many napped the afternoon away. Shortie planned to work in the garden after church, but wasn't up to it. Instead, he and Eddie browsed through an old family album until they both fell fast asleep on opposite ends of the couch. Inja spent the afternoon thumbing listlessly through an old magazine. The day ended with a cold supper of leftovers and an early bedtime.

At work the following day, Shortie readied for the early train and drove the delivery van to the depot ahead of schedule. He was helping Tony unload freight when Gabbie stepped from the train. They waved a greeting and watched him shuffle off after his daughter with shoulders hunched.

"He's been gone quite a while, hasn't he?" Tony inquired.

"At least four or five days," Shortie replied. Taking up a heavy milk canister with a grunt, he speculated, "I wonder where he's been. You don't suppose that daughter of his tried to pawn him off on some hapless relative, do you?"

"Who knows? Lately, I've had a hard enough time trying to figure out Maria without worrying about anyone else," Tony said with a sigh.

"How's she doing? We missed you at the picnic on Saturday. Was she sick?"

"She wasn't feeling well enough to go, but went swimming with me in the afternoon. She even took the girls wading in the pond. Women, who can figure them?"

"Where's your sense of humor?" Shortie asked. "It will all be over soon, and you wait and see, as soon as that baby is born, Maria will get back to her old self."

"I certainly hope so," he worried.

Lines creased the younger man's brown face, and Shortie noticed he laughed less as each day passed.

"How long has it been since you flexed your muscles for the ladies or enjoyed a good laugh? You'd better ease off or you'll be a nervous wreck by the time she goes into labor. She's still got two months to go, and the worst is yet to come. I remember when my sister Evie was pregnant with her first. Oooocweee, was my brother-in-law in for a surprise. My sweet sister became an absolute tyrant." He laughed at the memory. "Don't worry so much; it will get better."

"I know, but I feel there's something bothering her. She doesn't sleep at night, and she cries all the time. I sometimes wonder whether she even wanted this baby." As he shook his head, his troubled, dark eyes gazed into the distance seeking a solution.

"Try not to worry. Everything will work out, you'll see." Shortie clasped Tony's shoulder with fatherly affection, and they finished out the shift in silence.

When Blackie drove up, they scrambled aboard, eager to escape the sweltering heat. "Hot enough for you?" he asked. "I swear, it's gotta be at least a hundred or better. Thought I'd melt clean away before I got here."

The big man did appear to be melting, with big damp splotches under his arms, down his chest and across his shoulders. "Guess who's on the wagon?" he laughed. "Jonesy's in the doghouse and Ellen's got him housebound, and if he doesn't walk-the-talk, she threatened to leave him—not that she ever would, but he believes it. He had the shakes so bad today I thought he'd fall clean off the lift and fall to the bottom of the shaft. He ain't drank a drop in two days and that's something for a man that's drank every day for the past ten years." When he glanced at the solemn expressions of his passengers, his laughter fell flat.

"You two are sure a barrel of laughs. What's the matter, did somebody curdle your milk?" When neither man responded, he tried again. "Surely those solemn expressions aren't because you're missing ole' Jonesy! Seems to me the dairy couldn't wait to get rid of him, and he's doin' swell at the mine."

"Naw, it's not that," Shortie explained. "We're happy Art's doing well. It's Maria—Tony's really worried about her."

Blackie nodded sympathetically. "Women," he consoled, "you can't live with them, and it's pretty lonely without them."

"Gabbie's back," Shortie interrupted, changing the subject.

"He is?" brightened Blackie. "You know, I been missin' that old man. When'd you see 'im? Is he okay? Where'd he take off to, anyway?"

"Didn't see him to speak to, but saw him get off the train. He looked fine to me. Did he look okay to you, Tony?"

"Yeah, fine. He looked just fine," Tony said indifferently. His mind was on other things and wasn't following the conversation.

Blackie accelerated and drove straight to Arden's, anxious to see if the old man was there. Gabbie was seated in the rocking chair, sheltered by the porch awning. The three piled out, and cold drinks were emptied from the cooler for everyone except Shortie. He opted for a tall glass of ice water. He'd sworn off soda pop since the Fourth. Arden brought a hot mug of coffee sweetened with fresh cream and sugar for Gabbie. Clasping the old man's shoulder, Blackie greeted him affectionately. "Where you been old man?"

Click.

"I thought for awhile I'd finally be rid of ya. But here ya are, showin' up just like a bad penny. Now where you been?" Shortie cringed at Blackie's welcome home. Anyone else would have taken offense at the big man's words, but Gabbie beamed as if given the finest compliment.

Click.

"Well, where you been, Gab?" Blackie prodded. Seated on the edge of the porch, he turned to Gabbie and waited for an answer. The old curmudgeon took a swallow and shrugged noncommittally.

Click.

"Fine, you don't have to tell if ya' don't want to, I was just tryin' to be sociable." Turning to Shortie and Tony, he teased, "He probably went to one of them old folk's homes to admire the ladies. What'sa matter Gab, couldn't get one interested in your scrawny bag-of-bones?" The older man's black eyes flashed as he took another sip of coffee.

Click.

"What's that old man? I didn't hear ya."

Gabbie stubbornly refused to answer. Shortie was puzzled by the old man's continued silence. He usually talked your ear off, but so far hadn't spoken a single word. His week-long absence and sudden reticence was mysterious. There were several reasons why a man might go out of town, but it wasn't like Gabbie to be close-lipped. Covertly, Shortie studied the old man's grizzled face, searching for a clue to explain the sudden change. There was something different about him, but he couldn't put a finger on what it was.

Gabbie raised the cup to his lips and...click.

The subject of conversation switched to Tony and his difficulties when another "click" interrupted them in mid-sentence. Turning, the men searched for the source of the noise, but found nothing unusual. Resuming their conversation, Blackie threw a comment in Gabbie's direction every now and then, but not once did the old man's lips crack wide enough to utter a word.

Except for an occasional dainty sip of coffee, he remained silent. The "clicking" continued with uncommon regularity until Blackie couldn't stand it any longer.

"What's that a'clickin' an' a clackin' back there, old man? Is that you?" As Blackie peered closely at Gabbie's face, surprised registered in the big man's expression. "Hey, how come your cheeks are all swelled up? You ain't got somethin' contagious do ya'? It'd be just like ya to get the mumps or somethin' and then come share them with me." He scooted as far away as he could get and still remain seated.

Curious, Shortie and Tony rose to examine Gabbie at close range. Sure enough, his gaunt, sunken cheeks were fuller, and his lips were below his nose, instead of sunk into his mouth like a prune. Scratching their heads, they couldn't figure what would change a man's appearance so. Sudden realization dawned on Tony's face.

"It's teeth—he's got new teeth." Whooping with delight, he pointed at Gabbie's plump cheeks. "What else?"

"Is that it, old man?" asked Blackie. The three gaped in stunned silence as he pulled back his lips and grinned. His smile revealed a perfect set of pearly whites that filled his mouth to overflowing. When he took another dainty sip of coffee, the clicking sound was determined. Blackie's guffaws echoed up and down the valley as he rocked back and forth.

"So that's where you went," he chuckled. "You went to Spokane and had your snags pulled." Sobering, he studied the older man's swollen cheeks and thoughtfully inquired, "Do they hurt?"

"You haven't got much room in there, do you?" Shortie stared at Gabbie in awe. The new set of dentures filled the old man's mouth. "Can you eat?" he asked. As he peered into his mouth to examine further, the older man pushed him away.

"Can you eat?" roared Blackie. "That's the funniest thing I ever heard. Old man, you got more teeth than sense. How you gonna eat anything with a set of choppers big enough for a 'gator?"

Gabbie didn't appreciate being the butt of their humor and glared with black eyes spitting blue fire. Unable to talk over the swelling in his mouth, he gestured rudely before shuffling off in a huff. He hadn't gotten far before he turned with a smile tugging at the corners of his mouth. It was good to be home.

Blackie watched over his retreating form. He snickered, unable to contain his laughter.

"Do ya think he's mad?" he asked Shortie.

"Oh I don't know. Do dogs howl? Do chickens lay eggs? I have a good idea he's mad enough to boil his own coffee."

"Good," roared Blackie, enjoying the moment. "Well, that's one mystery solved. At least we know where he went and why, and that's more than we know about other things."

No one needed to ask what other things he referred to. The cause of April's explosion was still a point of concern and the culprit still at large. Loud noises still caused hearts to stop and children to cry out in fear. He wondered if the guilty party would ever be found. And for the first time in over a month, he wondered what had become of Ben Schultz. The last time anyone had seen him, he was in the custody of a federal marshal. A grey pall settled over the three as they glumly made their way home.

A few days later found them at their usual gathering place. Blackie was unusually subdued; his mood matched Tony's perfectly.

"What makes you so happy this afternoon?" Shortie teased.

"Aw, it's Bert. She's been real depressed lately. I know she's been dreamin' about all those babies she wanted and never could. I don't know what do for her."

"You, my friend," Shortie patted his arm for emphasis, "should do nothing. Put this one in the Lord's hands. Someday, He'll fill her arms with children. The Lord will provide. You've just got to have faith."

"Do you really think so?" An expression of delighted anticipation crossed his face. He imagined Bert with her arms full of babies. Feeling better, Blackie turned his attention to his empty stomach.

"Want a cold one?" He offered an icy bottle of root beer. Shortie's stomach rebelled at the sight of it.

"No thanks. I don't think I'll ever be able to look at another bottle of the stuff without getting sick. Water suits me just fine." Lost in their own private thoughts, they remained in the shade of the porch with elbows on knees. Shortie studied the hillside opposite them until movement caught his attention.

"I wonder who that is?"

"Who what is?" Blackie asked.

"There, on the hill by the old mine—don't you see him? Is it Howard or someone else? It sure don't resemble Frank."

"You must need glasses. I could tell who that is even in the dark. Now, what do you suppose that old man is doing up there? He's been wandering all over the countryside since he got his new teeth. I don't know what his teeth have to do with anything, but...he's looking for something. Do you s'pose he lost his choppers up there?" Snorting derisively, he added, "Crazy old man's probably trying to find the tooth fairy. Yeah, he probably wants a reward for his snags. Now, he'd better watch himself or he'll fall off that mountain and break his fool neck." Rising to his feet, he watched Gabbie descend until he was safe on level ground.

"He's seen us. Watch out because here he comes. I wonder what's gotten into him?" Shortie mused. "It isn't like him to willingly walk anywhere, so he must be up to no good."

Even in the distance, Gabbie's shuffling gait was recognizable. As he approached, he waved and grinned like a Cheshire cat with his store-bought teeth gleaming brightly in the sun.

"You'd best close your mouth before you blind somebody," Blackie teased. "What's with you, anyway? You've been crawling around these mountains for the last couple of days and it's beginning to make me nervous. Now, what are you up to and don't tell me nothin'."

Spitting out his teeth, Gabbie wiped a stream of spittle from his chin before stuffing them into a pocket. Blackie's lips curled back in distaste, and Shortie's sensitive stomach rolled. He enjoyed their reaction for a moment before answering.

"I been lookin' fer the cause."

"Cause of what?" Rolling his eyes, Blackie cast a knowing wink at Shortie. Gabbie's eyebrows peaked in surprise.

"Now what do you suppose ever'body's been wantin' to find? Seems to me you two should'a been lookin' round yer'selves. That missin' dyn-o-mite is hid 'round here somewheres and it needs to be found."

"Who would hide anything up there?" Shortie pointed toward the old mine.

"Did I say it was up there? I didn't say anythin' of the kind. Up there," he said as he pointed to the far left of the mine, "I was lookin' fer movin' rock."

"Moving rock? You've got to be kidding. Have you been stealing Arden's liquor again?" Blackie smelled the old man's breath, but detected nothing. "How much hooch you been drinkin'?" He found the notion of rocks moving about the hillsides by themselves hysterically funny. Shortie didn't, and for once gave the old man his full attention.

"What exactly do you mean by moving rock? Did you find something up there?" He scanned the hillside, searching for something he might previously have missed.

"Nope, but I found somethin' ta' do with rockslides." Gabbie looked from one to the other of them with satisfaction. Shortie's head snapped around, and his eyes about popped from his head.

"Come on, old man, you've been shinin' us on, admit it. You've had your little laugh, now knock it off," Blackie ordered. Gabbie turned on the big man in anger.

"You'll be gettin' the horse laugh before this thing is over," he screamed with exasperation. Pointing a finger, he accented each word with a poke to Blackie's chest. As he advanced, Blackie retreated. He'd never seen the old guy so angry and had never heard him raise his voice.

"Hold on, Gab," he said. Raising both hands defensively, he prepared for another onslaught.

"Humph," Gabbie snorted with disgust. He left without a backward glance or a parting word.

"I didn't mean to upset him, honest I didn't." Twirling his cap in his hands, Blackie made it obvious that he wanted to apologize.

"You know he'll be back tomorrow and will act like nothing happened. He sure told you though, didn't he?" Smiles tipped their lips at the memory of it.

"He sure did," Blackie said wonderingly. "Do you think he meant it?"

"Every word, Irish, every word; that old man is mad enough to chew you up and spit you out. He'll be looking for you, though, if for no other reason than to gloat." Shortie didn't give him an opportunity to respond, but followed Gabbie's route down the road and then turned to go home. He turned back once and was surprised Blackie stood where he'd left him with a puzzled frown creasing his forehead.

Chapter 25

With Independence Day over, the days following drifted by uneventfully with little to mark the passage of time. Somnolent summer days remained hot under cloudless skies and clear nights. The only event worth lifting a few eyebrows was Holly and Leon's sudden move. No one expressed much concern, but found it odd they packed only their necessaries and left several items of value behind. Inja moped around for a few days, but her tearful expression brightened after awhile, and life went on.

Coming home late one afternoon, Shortie was surprised to find his house full of women. They were involved in planning a baby shower for Tony and Maria when he walked in. Making a hasty exit, he escaped to Arden's until the coast was clear. He would check the mail, pay their grocery bill, and then have a nice long visit with Arden. He wasn't surprised to find several others gathered on the cement porch nursing cold drinks.

"What's going on at your place? It's a fine thing," Blackie grouched, "a man works all day and expects to come home to a hot dinner. Instead, I come home to an empty house."

"Keep your shorts on, Irish. You know as well as I do that your house is rarely empty and your dinner is usually waiting for you. A few ladies have planned a baby shower for Maria. They should be finished soon and will be home directly."

"Yeah, I s'pose. It's women's stuff." Blackie shook his head as if totally bewildered by the entire female race. "I don't know what all the fuss is about. You know, those women in Africa have babies right out in the open fields. They just squat down and plop, there it is. I'll bet they don't throw parties or keep a man from his dinner every time a kid is born."

"You think you know so much about it," Shortie fumed. He couldn't believe anyone could have such a cavalier attitude about the birth of a baby. "I'll bet they do celebrate their births, and how do you know where they have their babies? I didn't know you were such an expert. Maybe I should tell Tony not to bother with a doctor, but to bring Maria to you, Dr. Clegg. Just how do you plan on delivering their child, with a crow bar and a pair of tongs?"

"Aw, I didn't mean a word of it and you know it," he atoned. His expression grew serious. "You know, my Bert's a good woman. She always wanted children; in fact, she'd give her right arm to have one. But for some reason the good Lord never gave us any. She cries about it sometimes." Hanging his head, the big man looked about ready to cry himself.

"Do you want to know what I think?" Shortie placed a comforting hand on the big man's shoulder. "There aren't many women in the world like Bert. She has a loving heart and a giving nature and maybe she's meant for bigger things. We don't know His ways, and His timing isn't our timing. Pray about it and then leave it with the Lord. If it's meant to be, it will happen. Do you know how old Sarah was when she had her baby?"

"Sarah? Sarah who? Is she married to that fella' with the big soup-strainer?"

"No," Shortie laughed, "she was married to Abraham, the Bible's Abraham. Sarah had a baby when she was in her nineties. Think about it: what are the odds? If God gave her a baby, He can do anything. Bert has an advantage because she's only in her forties."

It wasn't long before women were seen leaving the house on the hill. One by one, men drifted off the porch to make their way home. Blackie didn't comment and had been thoughtfully quiet after the short sermon. Shortie hoped he'd think seriously about what was said.

Plans for the shower were finalized and the date set for the following week. Husbands were coerced into helping by keeping Tony away from home the day of the shower. It rained the night before. The welcome moisture cleansed the air and invigorated the soul, dropping the sweltering temperature to a more comfortable degree. As Bert drove off to retrieve Maria from a doctor's appointment, she honked the horn loudly. It was the signal to start decorating the house. Cars full of women with children in tow converged on the little place, and it was quickly transformed from a plain living area to one festooned with paper streamers, storks, diaper pins, diapers, bottles, and dried flowers. As the women stood back to assess their handiwork, even Inja found nothing to fault.

"Ooooh, this looks great," Ellen raved. "I wish someone would decorate my nursery like this. Those dried flowers are the perfect touch."

"I hope she'll be surprised," Inja said. "It took us a long time to make those paper storks, and I'd hate to think she wouldn't like them."

"We could stand here and admire all day, but there's more we need to do.

Let's get the punch ready and set out the cake. They should be back soon." Women scattered in different directions to finish the refreshments. Everything was beautiful, and all that was missing was Bert and the expectant mother.

"They'll be along any minute now," Inja said as she checked the time on the kitchen clock. As if on cue, a car horn sounded in the distance.

"Here they come, hide somewhere," Ellen ordered as she dropped behind the sofa. Bert's wagon pulled into the driveway just as the rest of them hid behind chairs or in closets.

Bert jumped out of the car and rushed around to help a weeping Maria inside. The young woman had been in tears since they'd left the doctor's office, just as she had the month before.

"Quit that crying," she fussed, "it's not good for you or the child. You want a healthy baby, don't you?" The question only upset Maria more, and she cried all the harder.

Just as Bert opened the door, "Surprise," female voices yelled as they leaped from their hiding places. Their excited expressions fell flat when Maria put a hand to her mouth and rushed off to the bedroom, sobbing. They looked to Bert for an explanation, but she knew less than they did.

Ellen rushed after Maria and found her lying on her side across the bed. She tried to comfort her.

"When I was pregnant with Art Jr., I cried an ocean before he was born. The tears didn't stop until he was almost two months old."

Her sobs quieted and she sat up to take Ellen's hand. "I don't mean to be rude," she sniffled.

"It ain't being rude," Bert's husky voice said from behind the door. Entering the room uninvited, she pulled Maria to her feet and escorted her to a place of honor in the front room. "We're having a baby shower for you whether you want it or not." She wagged a finger in front of Maria's nose. "You might just as well plan to sit and enjoy yourself for the next couple of hours."

Drying her eyes, Maria rewarded Bert with a wobbly smile. Her large, expressive eyes didn't reflect the smile on her lips, and a deep sadness could be detected in their depths. The women worried about her, and a damper fell on the party atmosphere.

"What did the doctor say?" Bert asked. "Is everything okay?" Maria nodded that everything was fine, but looks were exchanged between them. To get her mind off whatever bothered her, they all began talking at once.

"I had the baby blues after my last one was born," another volunteered. "My husband was ready to walk before I finally got over it."

"Oh, I can beat that one. During my last pregnancy, all I did was cry. And over the silliest things, too; it like to drive me and everyone else crazy," another shared.

"Tears and babies seem to go together, so don't worry about it. If you want to cry, then you go right ahead and cry."

With the ice broken, the party atmosphere was restored. As gifts were handed to her, she held up each item for them to admire, but seemed reluctant to actually accept them. Bert and Inja exchanged bewildered expressions. This was not the same Maria who tore wrapping off packages with childlike squeals. Bert was slicing the cake when the problem was discovered, or so she thought. Maria stood to go to the bathroom and then doubled over in pain. Before anyone could reach her, the poor woman was standing in a puddle of water.

"My water broke," she moaned. Biting her upper lip to keep from screaming, she panted, "Get me to the hospital and call the doctor. Oh my God, he was right—what shall I do? He was right."

"Well, of course the doctor was right," Bert boomed. "You're having a baby and from the look of it, real soon." Picking Maria up, she carried her to the car. Inja jumped in the back to time her contractions. The car took off with a roar that nearly jolted her off the seat and when Maria moaned, Bert's foot jammed the gas pedal. They made it to the hospital in record time.

Once there, Maria was whisked off, cleaned up, dressed in a gown, and placed in a delivery room. Bert tried to follow, but the head nurse, another bullheaded Irish, barred her path.

"Listen Red," Nurse Targhee addressed her, "you ain't going in there unless you're family. Are you her mother?"

"You know I ain't her ma."

"Then, go to the waiting room. It won't be long now, anyway. Has the father been called?"

"Yeah, we called him." For the first time in her life, Bert was intimidated by her surroundings. Lowering her voice to a whisper, she obeyed the nurse's orders.

"You've done all you can; now if you'll excuse me, we have a baby to deliver." The door shut with a soft whoosh, leaving Bert and Inja to worry and wait.

Tony and Shortie arrived and came running down the hall. Dr. Willom entered the delivery room, then returned a few minutes later to speak with Tony.

"What do we want this time, a boy or another girl?"

"It's a boy," Tony stated without hesitation. "Maria told me so."

"Well, I can't guarantee a boy, but I can tell you it won't be much longer. I told her the baby was due in August, but she insisted it wasn't due until late September. It's a big one, so she might have a little trouble. We'll take every precaution of course." After a short conference with his nurse, they both entered the delivery room leaving the little group, now joined by Blackie, to worry together. They paced the hall, each praying in his own way.

Two cups of coffee, three trips to the bathroom, and a walk around the hospital finally brought the response they all waited to hear. A husky wail filtered to them through the thick, heavy door. Minutes later, Doc Willom exited the room and pulled off his surgical cap to wipe his streaming brow.

"She was right. Young man, you've got a son. A healthy baby with a head of hair like I've never seen before. Congratulations," he said. Extending his hand, he clasped Tony's in a handshake. "By the way, Maria's fine, too." He chuckled at the young man's beaming expression and then left.

Shortie gripped Tony's shoulder, and Blackie, more excited than he'd been in years, bear-hugged him in a rib-cracking grip.

"Congratulations," he growled in his deep bass. "Did you hear that? It's a boy! We'll have to teach him how to fish, won't we, Bert?"

Maria was released from the hospital one week later. Bert and Inja cleaned her house from top to bottom and set up the crib in preparation for her homecoming. Tony brought the two little girls to Bert after the baby was born and they trailed after her wherever she went. Both of them had Tony's almond-shaped eyes and deep, soulful gaze. Their solemn expressions were deceptive, however, because behind their innocent expressions were two little imps that managed to get into everything. She had the time of her life playing substitute mom and loved dressing them up and curling their hair with ribbons to match frilly dresses. Teresa, the older child, loved playing dress-up, but the younger girl, Anna, thought ribbons were for sissies. She pulled them from her hair as soon as Bert's back was turned. The only thing the girls had in common was their total devotion to her. Their shining, dark eyes followed her every move.

Maria was released the following Tuesday, and Tony borrowed Bert's car to bring her and the baby home. She received several gifts while in the hospital, and the wagon was filled with flowers, stuffed animals, diapers, and other gifts that remained unopened. While Bert helped Maria from the car, Tony carried the baby himself. It was his first opportunity to hold his son without a nurse hanging around. He didn't want to put him down until absolutely necessary.

"Proud wouldn't do justice to the expression on your face," Shortie chuckled. Tony beamed radiantly, and a grin split his face from ear-to-ear. Moving the blankets away, he motioned to his daughters to come see their little brother. For Teresa, it was love at first sight, but Anna's expression betrayed a hint of jealousy.

"Don't you worry, you'll always be Daddy's *cielo niña*—angel girl." Pulling one of her pigtails, he reassured her by teasing in the way he always had.

"What's his name?" Blackie asked. "You're not going to tie one of them mile-long names on the little fella are you?" Touching the baby's tiny fingers, he was delighted when a little fist clamped onto his finger. "Look at that grip, would you?" he exclaimed.

"His name will be Hosea Anthony, after my father; Mario, after Maria's grandfather; and Miguel, after my grandfather. Hosea Anthony Mario Miguel Martinez is his full name, but we'll call him Tony after me." Silence fell over the room.

"That's an awfully big name for such a tiny baby, but I guess he'll grow into it," Bert remarked. "He's already got a pretty good start at over eight pounds and ten ounces."

Shortie ached to hold him, but figured it wouldn't be polite to ask. His gaze rested on Inja, who showed little concern or interest. When she glanced his way and found his gaze upon her, she smiled, but ignored the pleading in his eyes.

Little Tony began to fuss, which signaled the welcome home party was over and time for guests to go home. Inja helped Maria into bed and placed the baby beside her. The new mother looked at him listlessly and then rolled over, ignoring his cry for nourishment.

"The baby's hungry, Maria," Inja reminded. "He needs to be fed, and you're the only one who can."

"I will break him to a bottle as soon as possible," she replied in a distant, wooden voice.

Bert placed the child in Maria's arms, hoping to see a spark of interest. Waiting expectantly, she was relieved when Maria opened her blouse and allowed him to nurse.

"You must be tired," Bert excused her. "Gosh, look at the time, no wonder you're wore out. We've been here all afternoon keeping you from your rest.

We'll leave so you two can get acquainted." Bert ushered Inja out ahead of her, and they exited the bedroom as quickly as possible.

Tony, listening at the doorway, was horrified at Maria's response to their son. She'd always been so protective and loving with the girls. Her lack of interest cut him to the quick. When he entered the bedroom, his grim expression softened when he saw the child nursing at her breast. Humming a little tune, she held the baby close. It was a tender picture of mother and son, and it would have been perfect except for the tears that rained down her cheeks.

Chapter 26

Little Anthony was eleven days old when Shortie raced home after work and ran into the kitchen to find Inja. He whirled her around the room until her giggles matched his mood and he laughed with her.

"Put on your prettiest dress, your high-heeled shoes, and fix your face. We're going out," he announced.

"Do you mean it? What should I wear?" Rushing to her closet, she threw dress after dress onto the bed. Discarding each one, she finally settled on a blue silk swing-skirt with matching blouse—her latest acquisition. "Is there time for a bath?" she asked.

"Don't you want to know where we're going? Guess what the Inn is having this weekend?" he shouted through the bedroom door.

"You don't mean it! Are they having a fish feed?" He peeked his head in and nodded. She squealed with joy, gathered up her clothes and scurried to the bathroom. Stopping her headlong rush, she turned to ask, "What about Eddie? Who will watch him while we're gone, and what's he to eat for dinner?"

"He's going with us. I'll find him and get him cleaned up. If you're going to bathe, you'd better make it snappy. Blackie and Bert will pick us up in an hour, and guess what? Tony and Maria are going, too." Opening the bathroom door a crack, she thought she'd heard incorrectly.

"Did you say Maria is coming? Isn't it too soon for her to be going out?"

"I don't think so. I just saw her and she's the picture of health. Now hurry or we'll be late."

While Shortie washed at the kitchen sink, Inja bathed, fixed her hair, and put on fresh make-up. Fastening the pleated skirt at her waist, she assessed her reflection in the mirror. She looked great, and the color of the blouse brought out her eyes. When she returned to the kitchen, she looked at Eddie with dismay. His hair dripped water from a hurried washing, and he wasn't wearing a shirt or shoes and socks.

"He's not ready, and the Cleggs are already here. We can't go into a restaurant with him looking like that."

"Who says?" Bert hollered from the front door. "Bring him just the way he is and finish getting him dressed on the way."

"Yeah, we can hang him from the antenna by his ears so he can flap like a sheet on a clothesline. He'll dry in no time." Blackie chuckled at the horrified expression on the child's face.

"Come on, Inja." Shortie ushered her out to the car and plopped Eddie onto the seat beside her. Climbing in himself, he combed Eddie's hair and dressed him in a neatly pressed white shirt complete with shoes and socks. By the time they parked in the Inn's crowded parking lot, Eddie was as neatly put together as any of them.

Helping Inja from the car, he admired her slim legs under the swinging skirt. "Have I told you how beautiful you look tonight?" he asked. Pulling her close, he kissed her while Bert and Blackie looked on.

"Wow, you'd better watch out, Inja. That's the sort of stuff that babies are made from," Blackie teased.

The Inn, the finest restaurant in town, held a huge fish feed twice a year. One was held in late summer and the second in early spring. Fresh seafood was shipped in and extra staff hired to accommodate the huge number of hungry customers.

Standing in line, they moved steadily along to the door where their money was collected. For a reasonable price, a person could eat all he wanted as long as he ate all he took. It grew unbearably hot with so many bodies standing close together, but nobody complained. As they moved at a snail's pace to the open doorway, the aroma of fried fish, fresh bread, and clam chowder mingled with the mellow odor of whiskey and beer and wafted out to titillate the nostrils and make stomachs growl. Finally, they paid their fee and entered the darkened room to find a table, but Tony had arrived before them and already had one reserved. Pulling out chairs, he seated the ladies.

"It's sure good to see you out and looking so well," Bert told Maria. "I hope you're not trying to do too much too soon."

"Maria's strong and doesn't lay around like some women," Tony bragged. He beamed at her. "She's doing fine, and the doctor says she can do anything she wants as long as she doesn't get too tired."

"It sure isn't taking you long to get your figure back," Inja praised.

"Well, I don't know about anybody else, but I'm so hungry I could eat leather. If nobody minds, I'm going to get me a plate of that seafood before they run out." Shortie took his plate and left to stand in line by the seafood and salad bar. Soon, everybody followed and returned to the table with plates loaded. Eddie ate until Shortie thought his stomach would pop and then went back for more.

It was after their third trip to the fish bar that the band entered. Shortie wasn't much of a dancer, but Blackie and Tony were virtually Fred Astaires. Inja wouldn't sit through the evening without an opportunity to dance with good partners. The first tune was a jitterbug with a rhythm that kept toes tapping. Watching a few couples take the floor, Tony grabbed Inja's hand and pulled her to her feet.

"Come on, let's show them how it's done." They both knew all the fancy steps and really put on a show. When the music ended, claps of appreciation followed them off the floor. Taking their seats, they were both out of breath and flushed from the heat of the dance.

"I didn't know you could dance like that," Shortie whispered in her ear and leaned close to kiss her cheek. The hackles on the back of his neck sprang to life when a familiar voice interrupted their good time.

"Well, that was a real pretty picture. Inja, you dance like a professional, and brother, have you got legs!" Leon admired with a whistle. Shortie looked into his smirking face and wished he could put a fist right in the middle of it.

"Our table's full and there's no room for you," Blackie growled.

"Don't be rude," Inja pouted. "Do you want to sit down for a minute?" she invited as she pulled her chair to the side to make room.

"No, we're finished eating and ready to leave. Boy, that dress sure looks swell on you. It never looked that good on me." Holly spoke to Inja, but her eyes never left Maria's.

"Did she give you this dress?" Shortie's question went unanswered. In fact, he didn't get an answer until much later. Bert placed a warning hand on his arm and motioned for silence.

Maria stared at Holly as if she were a snake ready to strike. Her hand trembled as she reached for a glass of water.

"Your baby came early, I see. I thought it wasn't due until late September, but you can never tell about babies, now can you? I'd love to come around and take a peek at the little fellow someday. Would you mind?" she asked. Her eyes narrowed, assessing her response.

Maria froze with the glass halfway to her lips. Shaking her head, her face turned pasty white and she appeared ready to faint.

"Okay, this party's over," Bert announced. Jumping from her chair, she helped Maria to her feet. "She's had all she can handle for one night. It's getting late and this little mama needs to get home and get her beauty rest."

"But it's still early, and the band just started," Inja protested.

"It's late," Bert stated firmly. "We're going home, so grab your purse and come along. Besides, Eddie's asleep on his feet." She walked Maria to the car with Tony following behind.

"Something's wrong here," Shortie thought. "Is Maria just tired, or did something just happen that I missed?"

Late that night, someone pounded on the Cleggs' front door, waking them both from a sound sleep. Bert threw on a robe and tossed Blackie his pants.

"I hope nobody's died," she said as she hurried to the door.

"Don't open it yet; I've got to get my pants on," Blackie said as he stumbled from the bedroom.

When she opened the door a crack, Tony almost fell into the room. His eyes were red-rimmed and he reeked of alcohol. Holding the baby against his chest, he looked liked someone had kicked him in the teeth.

"Take him," he slurred. "Maria won't feed him, and he just keeps crying and crying." Bert reached to take the baby from his arms before he collapsed. Blackie stepped to his side and helped him to a chair.

"I'll be glad to watch little Tony. Did Maria get sick after her night out? I just knew she was rushing things," she clucked. Holding the child in the crook of her arm, she was embarrassed when the baby's head turned to her breast, seeking nourishment. "No, you don't, little one," she said as she laid him over her shoulder, "I don't have the equipment you're looking for. Did you bring a bottle or anything to feed him with? This little fellow is starved to death. Look at how he gnaws on his fist."

"Watch your temper, Bert. If I can hear it in your voice—so will he. Do you want to scare the little guy?" Blackie patted the baby's back clumsily, trying to soothe his angry cries.

Tony rose and staggered to the door. "It's out here."

Pushing him back onto the couch, Blackie opened the door and found a large suitcase lying in the driveway. He brought it in and placed it at Bert's feet.

"Well, open it. Is there a bottle or not? I wonder if he could have found anything bigger to pack this stuff in," she complained as she searched one-handed through a pile of diapers, receiving blankets, and baby clothes all wadded together in a tight ball. In a side compartment, she found three bottles, a full can of formula, baby lotion, powder, extra diaper pins, and a tiny hairbrush. Selecting one of the bottles, she found it was warm to the touch. After testing it to be sure it wasn't too hot, she put the nipple to the baby's lips. Within seconds he quieted and nursed contentedly.

"She won't take care of our son. I don't understand because I know she loves him. A mother always loves her children, doesn't she?" Tony's despairing look searched Bert's for an answer. Having none to give, she was helpless to offer any suggestion that might ease hhis pain.

"You been drinking, son?" Blackie's usual gruffness was softened with concern.

"Yeah, I've been drinking, but it doesn't help." Rising, he threw Blackie's restraining hand from his shoulder. "I've got to go, but will be back tomorrow. If you need something, call me at the dairy." Caressing his son's smooth cheek, he stumbled out the door.

Blackie turned on the outdoor lights and watched as he staggered down the road. He didn't go back inside until Tony was safely home.

"I've never seen him drink before," he told Bert gravely. Shutting the door with a click, he leaned against it. "Something's been seriously wrong between those young people for a long time, and it's tearing him apart. Tomorrow, go and talk to Maria; talk some sense into her before she loses her husband." Shutting off the porch light, he stepped to her side.

"In the meantime, I guess we won't be getting a full night's rest around here for awhile." Gazing at the sleeping infant, he chuckled, "I guess a few hours of missed sleep won't kill me."

"You sleep too much anyway. And as far as Maria goes, I've tried to talk to her several times, and the more I talk the less she hears. She's withdrawn and refuses to listen." Shaking their heads regretfully, they made a makeshift bed for their guest in an empty dresser drawer. Tomorrow was soon enough to get his crib, but only if necessary. They both hoped Maria would come to her senses and send for her son. Little Tony needed to be with his own family even though Bert was thrilled at the prospect of caring for him, if only for a few hours.

Early the following morning Bert went to Maria's to talk some sense into her, but she refused to answer the door. Frustrated and angry enough to take the young woman's head off, she drove home fuming and muttering to herself. The baby was beginning to fuss by the time she let herself into the house. A bottle was heated immediately, and she sat in the rocking chair to feed him, repeating the words to a tune she'd heard somewhere. Watching the baby's jaws work as he nursed, she was enthralled with everything about him. His hair was almost three inches long and refused to be smoothed down, but stuck up in downy wisps all over his head. He had small hands with long, graceful fingers and big feet. His dark eyes weren't shaped like Tony's or Maria's, but were narrower, closer set and shadowed with a heavy upper lid.

"Someday, girls will think your eyes are sexy. Don't you listen to a word they say." The baby seemed to study her, putting a face with the voice. Laughing, she burped him before lying him down for a nap. She waited all afternoon for Tony, but he never showed. He didn't come the next day either, or the next. She was beside herself with worry when he finally called.

He planned to visit baby Tony the following Monday afternoon as soon as he got home from work.

"Well, what do you make of that?" she asked aloud.

Chapter 27

After the fish feed, Shortie and Inja argued again about starting a family. They finally called a truce, ending the cold silence between them. It was a mutual decision that the subject would never be brought up again. Shortie was too worried about Tony to argue anyway. The young man looked worse everyday. Shadows filled the hollows of his face and his clothes hung on him.

"Have you seen Maria?" he asked Inja one evening.

"No, and I've tried on several occasions. I saw the little girls playing outside and went to say hello. She refused to come to the door and locked it so I couldn't go in." Sighing, Inja curled up on the couch to read. "If she's an example of perfect motherhood, then count me out."

"That's not fair. We both know she's always been good to the girls. She was sick a lot during this pregnancy, and maybe that explains why she has a hard time accepting the baby.

"Make all the excuses you want. All I know is I don't want any part of it."

"You've made that point abundantly clear," he snapped. Stepping out on the porch to cool off, he was immediately sorry for speaking in anger. Remorse tugged at his heart until he decided to make amends.

"I'm sorry—I didn't mean to snap at you."

"Yes, you did, but I accept your apology anyway. You must know I'm in no hurry to be a mother. I like things just the way they are."

"Yeah, I can see that you do," he said sarcastically.

"Why don't you go find Tony or Blackie? While you're gone I'll fix dinner, but not until I finish reading this chapter."

Feeling like an inconvenience, he wandered the yard aimlessly. With little else to do, he decided to head to the store and see if anyone was hanging around. On the way, he encountered Gabbie headed home after another one of his trips around the mountainsides. There were cobwebs in his hair and beard. Dirt smudged his cheeks and forehead with streaks of gray. Spitting out his teeth, he hurried a few steps to catch up.

"I found 'em," he pronounced as if Shortie would know what he was talking about.

"Found what?" he asked. He wasn't interested in hearing any of the old man's stories.

"I found the dyn-o-mite, that's what. And if'n someone don't move it soon, it might blow up agin. It's gettin' wet and nitro don't take kindly to baths."

It took a moment for his words to sink in, and when they did, Shortie spun around to face the old man.

"What did you say?"

"You heard me plain as day and I don't stutter," he said with irritation. "Now will ya help me out or not? I got to git hold of that investigator fella'."

"Do you mean Frank Howard?"

"Yeah, and the other fellar that's been hangin' around, that Bill Anderson. They'll know what to do."

Hurrying to the store, they placed a call to Anderson's office, and Anderson in turn called Frank. In less than thirty minutes, both men arrived, bringing an entourage with them. Blackie followed when the long line of cars stirred his curiosity.

"Okay, old man, we're here, and your story better be good. You say you found the dynamite, so where is it?" Anderson's voice was cutting, mocking Gabbie and everything he said.

"Ya don't think I'd carry it around in muh' pocket, do ya?" Gabbie asked innocently. He refused to play the fool for a man in fancy pants with hands softer than a baby's butt.

"Tell 'em, Gab," Blackie encouraged. "Tell where the stuff is so we can all sleep better tonight."

"I'll show 'em if'n they've a mind to follow," he replied as he headed down the road. "We got to go through some brush so their fancy pant cuffs might get wet." Cutting through wet brush, milkweed, and long-stemmed grass, they headed toward the hillside at the base of Shortie's mountain.

"We could have taken the road," Shortie whispered. He slowed, matching his pace to the older man's slow shuffle. Gabbie nodded. A glint of amusement lit his eyes like candles.

"You'd best not be fooling around, old man, and this better not be a wild goose chase." Gabbie rolled his eyes and then grinned, showing shriveled gums. Anderson cursed after catching his pantleg on another briar. If they didn't come to the end of their search soon, his pants would be in tatters.

Coming to a small clearing, Gabbie pushed aside the branches of a stunted tree growing out of the hillside. Behind the tree was a hole that was obviously manmade. Deserted years ago, it had been hidden and undisturbed until recently.

"Well glory be," Blackie breathed. Sticking his head into the hole, he was stunned to find it led into a long shaft leading into the depths of the mountain.

"I've been over every inch of this place and never knew this was here. How did you find it?" Shortie asked. He was as stunned as Blackie and was curious to know where the shaft led.

"I follered a path and here it was. Now, it's wet in thar' and a section of the support beams have fallen in, but I believe it's safe enough. Thar's a second shaft off to the side ready to cave in; stay out of that'n." Squeezing through the opening behind him, they followed his flashlight to the rear of the first shaft. Their feet sank in yellow clay mud, and their heads dripped with yellowish water that ran off the ceiling. The dank odor of rotting vegetation grew stronger as they went deeper into the shaft. Stomachs rolled when they nearly stepped in the rotting carcass of an animal that had crawled in there and died. The only complainer was Anderson. His alligator shoes were ruined.

Stopping abruptly, Gabbie flashed a beam of light over a wooden crate held above the slippery floor of the shaft by two lengths of pine. "Thar' it is and don't be for thankin' me all at once," he hooted. Thumbing his nose at Blackie, he grinned, showing all his teeth. "Who's got the horse laugh now, big man?" Sure enough, the box held all the missing dynamite, plus some unaccounted for. Peering closely, faces paled at the beads of moisture collected on each one.

"We've got to defuse them things before they go off," Frank said as he stepped away from the box. The blood drained from his cheeks, making him appear ghostly in the dim light. Two men skilled in explosives stepped forward. The others hurried to the exit and pushed each other through the tight opening in their haste as they went to work. Shortie paced the clearing and prayed for the safety of the remaining two. It seemed an interminable length of time before a head poked out. Pulling himself free, the first helped the second out and then handed the box to Bill.

"This stuff is harmless, but if it would have blown, this mountain wouldn't be here. It'd be somewhere between here and the Montana border," the taller one told them.

"I don't know who set it in there, but they either didn't know what they were doing or did it deliberately. Most of the fuses were so wet you couldn't have lit them with a blow torch," the other laughed.

"How long do you think it's been in there?" Shortie asked.

"Hard to say," he shrugged.

"Do you mean to say this stuff couldn't have caused the explosion last spring?"

"There's two sticks missing from a case. It wasn't enough to do serious damage, but could've tore things up a bit. The other stuff is so old it crumbled in our hands. It's probably been there since before Washington crossed the Delaware."

"You can breathe easier now, Anderson; the dynamite's found. All we have to do now is find who put it there. Old man, do you have any ideas who that might have been?" Frank asked expansively.

"Well, maybe I does and maybe I doesn't," Gabbie retorted. Scratching at some hidden flea bite beneath his beard, he studied their faces for a moment. Yawning widely, he turned on his heel and headed for home.

"Aren't you going to help us find who did it?" Anderson sputtered indignantly.

"I'm goin' to take a nap. I'm tired and I'll be darned if'n I'm gonna' do all your work fer' ya."

Later, Blackie and Shortie chuckled on their way to Arden's. They explained to the investigators that forcing information out of Gabbie would be pointless. He'd volunteer what he knew when he was ready and not a minute before. They convinced them to return the following day when the old man might be in the mood to talk.

Chapter 28

Hurrying through the pasteurizing room to the sanitizer, Shortie loaded the machine rapidly. Without pausing, he raced to take the empty milk cans to the depot. Tony was late again, and he was doing all he could to cover for him. This was the fifth day of it, and his work was beginning to suffer.

Returning from the depot, he hurried to load the van.

His customers were used to getting their deliveries before sunup, and it was already past eight. Pulling out of the parking lot, he almost ran into an oncoming car, and waving an apology, drove much slower throughout the remainder of the day. He completed his deliveries and was able to return to the dairy in time to punch the time clock before the office closed. There would be overtime in his pay packet the following week. Taking his lunch box, heavy with his uneaten lunch, from the shelf, he headed for the door.

"Would you come in here a minute?" His boss stood in front of the office. He followed Shortie inside and shut the door. This was not a good sign.

"Sit down, take a load off. If anybody needs a rest these days, you do." Shortie blinked with surprise but didn't comment.

"I don't know what's going on with your partner, but you can't cover for him any longer."

"Tony and his wife just had a baby, and things have been a little rough lately," he tried to explain.

"The company knows about the baby; in fact, the dairy sent her a bouquet of flowers and a check for twenty dollars while she was still in the hospital. The point is, you've got to attend to your own duties, or we'll be forced to remove you from delivery. Customers are complaining, and we can't afford to lose their business."

"I'm sorry, I was only trying to help...."

"I understand and might have done the same thing if in your position, but Tony has got to pull himself together. You've got a family of your own to worry about, and friendship or not, a man's family must come first."

"Is he going to lose his job?"

"No, not at this time," the employer hedged. "However, we might put him in sanitation until he gets his head on straight. He's been ordered to take the rest of the week off, without pay of course. Now go home and we'll see you tomorrow." Smiling, he shook Shortie's hand in dismissal.

After such an exhausting day, Shortie also missed his ride. He didn't relish the idea of walking all the way, but figured he wouldn't get there any faster by stewing about it. Doggedly, he trudged up the road to the top of Corduroy Hill and with only a few blocks more to go, gratefully accepted a lift from Frank Howard.

"Worked late tonight, huh?"

"Fourteen hours." Closing his eyes, he rested his head against the door panel. Even the idea of conversation made him tired.

"Your friend, the one called Gabbie, is finally ready to talk. I'm headed to his place now. Do you want to come along?"

Shortie was tired, but curiosity won out. "Sure, I'll go with you. I'd like to hear what he has to say."

Gabbie led them back to the hole in the hillside. "Whomsoever put that dyn-o-mite in thar' didn't know the power they was 'a dealin' with." Ducking into the shaft, he gestured for them to follow. Crawling through on hands and knees, Shortie remembered a story about a little girl falling down a rabbit's hole. The idea wasn't very appealing.

"You told me you didn't think the explosion was caused by the stuff we found. Do you have any proof? Have you evidence to support your theory?" Howard asked.

"Proof? You want proof?" Gabbie's voice cracked to a falsetto in his excitement. "Look down that side shaft. Notice anythin' funny 'bout it?"

"It isn't very deep, and there aren't any support beams to hold the roof," Shortie noted.

"Thars' muh proof. Dyn-o-mite blasted that hole from this existing shaft. The one thar' is new and weren't thar' a'fore. Go ahead and check it fer' yerself. You'll find I'm tell'in ya the gospel."

"If dynamite didn't cause the blast, then what did?" Shortie asked sarcastically. Gabbie ignored him and spoke bluntly.

"Didn't ya say thar' were two explosions? Well, one was caused by this here, kind of like a backfire if you will," he gestured to the recently blasted hole. "The second came from somewheres inside ta' mountain."

"Old man, I follow you up to a point, but there's no way you'll make me believe a mountain exploded all by itself." Frank scrutinized the older man's features trying to discern truth from story.

Gabbie didn't waver as he looked him in the eye. "Mountains don't explode by themselves; this one had a little help from nature. Methane gas," he announced, "just like I tried ta' tell ya a'fore." Folding his arms across his bony chest, he dared them to dispute his findings. He'd done his duty and without further discussion, crawled out the way he'd come. Frank and Shortie had no alternative than to follow. They didn't know whether to believe him or not because there was still too many unanswered questions.

A few days later, Tony appeared at Shortie's front door. He was sober and acting more like himself. As he grinned at Inja flirtatiously, his dark eyes were as bright as candles.

"Has the wife of my best friend been behaving herself?" He laughed as she squirmed under his appraisal. "I need to talk to Shortie. I hope you don't mind if we speak in private." Nodding, she refused to meet his eyes.

"We'll be out back," Shortie confided as he led Tony outdoors. "Do you want something, some coffee maybe?"

"Coffee, it sounds good." Sheepishly, Tony shuffled his feet. His complexion took on a shade of plum. "I'm not a drinker and I've made myself the fool. I want to apologize for shirking my duties, and I swear that it won't happen again." His repentant expression about tore Shortie's heart out.

"Think nothing of it; what are friends for? I don't think we need to mention it again, do you?" Tony grinned thankfully as he took the cup Inja handed him. "Things are better at home aren't they?"

"*Si.*"

An overwhelming sense of gratitude filled Shortie's heart. He was certain everything would be resolved if given enough time.

"Thanks," he said with uplifted eyes. Tony searched the clouds with a puzzled expression.

"Do you thank the sky, the air, or what?" Realization dawned and his eyes grew round. "Oh, you talk to Him, to *Dios*. Thank you for including me in your prayers." He stared at Shortie for a moment in awe. "It's a wonderful thing to be valued so highly."

"Is Maria better? Will you bring the baby home soon?"

"That is why I came here today. I need a favor. Maria has agreed to see baby Tony tomorrow at the café. I'm sure she'll want to bring him home after she sees how much he's grown. Bert and Blackie are bringing the baby, and she's asked if we can all have lunch together."

It was a strange request but they agreed to meet around one o' clock the following afternoon. Tony, too excited for words, shook his hand and leaped into the air. As he ran down the hill, he turned once, gave a parting wave and flashed a triumphant grin. His exuberance lifted the heaviness in Shortie's heart.

The rear of the station wagon was crammed full by the time they finished loading all the baby's things. Bert, snuffling loudly, struggled to hold back tears. Patting her clumsily, Blackie didn't know how to console her. He was far more comfortable with the tough, brassy side of her than the soft, female side that surfaced now and then.

"You're really attached to the little fellow, aren't you?" Tickling the side of the infant's cheek, Shortie was rewarded with a gummy smile.

"It doesn't take long for such a sweet little guy to work his way into your heart. I'll miss him almost more than I can bear." Hugging the baby tightly, she reluctantly handed him to Shortie. "You take him. It will be easier if someone else hands him to his mother. I'm afraid I might say something I won't be sorry for."

They rode in silence with the radio for company. There wasn't much need for conversation.

"We're here," Bert said needlessly. At the sound of her voice, the baby cooed and waved his arms excitedly. She broke her own promise and lifted him from Shortie's arms. Unable to help herself, she kissed his chubby cheeks soundly.

Inside, extra chairs were pulled over to a table where Tony and Maria waited. Gathering in the tiny alcove, they squeezed around the table as best they could. An uncomfortable silence ensued as each glanced to the other, waiting to see who would speak first. The waitress broke the silence when she came to take their order.

"We have fresh apple pie, baked this morning, berry pie, and chocolate cream. Our lunch special is a hot beef sandwich and all the coffee you can drink. What'll you have?" She rattled off the menu mechanically, as if she'd repeated it so many times it bored her.

"We'll have coffee all around except for him," Inja said as she pointed toward Shortie. "He'll have a cream soda, and we'll all have a slice of apple pie.

"Coming right up." She hurried away to fill their order. She returned with a tray balanced against her hip that was loaded with several slices of pie. The coffee and pie were served first, and a bottle of cream soda was placed before Shortie. He found the new taste delightful.

Tony took the baby and examined him from head to toel. "You have taken good care of my son, Bert." Hefting the child like a sack of flour, he joked, "He's gained at least ten pounds. I'll have to farm him out just to pay for his groceries."

"Seems to me you already have," she snapped. Raking Maria's face with a glare from her squinty eye, she dared the girl to make a wrong move.

"Now Bert, keep your girdle on." Blackie gripped her arm tightly and flashed a look of warning.

"Do not be angry with her," Maria pleaded, her soft voice a whisper. "She is right, I have neglected my son and should be ashamed. I pray someday he will forgive me." Reaching out her arms, she took her son and held him for the first time in over two weeks. Her face flushed with happiness when baby Tony smiled behind the fist stuffed in his mouth. Any reservations she might have had faded as she renewed the mother-son relationship. Tossing aside his blankets, she delighted in every toe, finger, and dimple of his body. Holding him in the crook of her arm, she smoothed the hair on his head as she gazed at him with adoration.

"Well, if this ain't a sight. It's about time we got a look at that kid." Leon stood behind them with his arm slung carelessly around Holly's waist.

"And you aren't getting a look now, either. This is a private party and I don't recall inviting you." Covering the baby with a corner of a blanket, Tony shielded the child from further scrutiny.

"Suit yourself—just trying to be a good neighbor."

"Neighborly, my Uncle Sam," Shortie sneered. "You've never had a neighborly thought in your life. Tell me, Leon, why is it you're always showing up where you're not invited?"

"Who says we weren't?" Leon glanced toward Inja.

"Did you call them?" Bert asked.

"Oh, what's the harm? It seems to me if they're friends of mine then they should be welcome." Inja defended her actions with icy defiance.

"It's okay," Leon laughed, "we were just leaving."

"Coffee?" the waitress interrupted as she held the pot aloft. She poured a fresh cup for Blackie and freshened Bert and Inja's. "I've been just dying to see the baby," she gushed. Placing the coffeepot on the table, she came round to stand by Maria.

"What a handsome little guy." Pulling the blanket off, she chucked the child under the chin. "Coochy-coochy-coo," she babbled.

"Coochy-coochy. What language is coochy-coochy?" Tony asked with a comical expression. Ignoring the sarcastic remark, she admired the baby's full head of hair.

"How old is he? Look at all the hair; why, he'll need a haircut before he's six months old," she remarked.

Maria didn't respond, but turned away from the woman. Her complexion turned suddenly ashen, and a tiny white line formed above her upper lip. Refusing to lift her head, she sat stiffly, holding the child too tightly.

"Can I hold him?" the waitress prattled on.

"No," Maria shouted.

"Maria, what's the matter with you? Of course she can hold him. She won't hurt him," Tony admonished. Taking the child from her, he placed him in the waitress' arms.

"He's heavy, ain't he? He sure doesn't look much like you, Dad."

"Yes, he does," Tony retorted defensively. "See, his eyes are dark and his hair is black like mine."

"Well, I suppose, but he resembles his mother more. Humph, look at that! He's got a birthmark on his neck shaped just like a little strawberry. Isn't that cute?"

"What's that you said? Did you say he's got a strawberry birthmark?" Holly was suddenly very interested in the baby and inspected the mark hidden in the folds of his neck.

"Do you have a birthmark like this?" Her tone demanded an answer from both parents. Tony shook his head silently with an expression of suspicious bewilderment on his face.

"Oh, now isn't this just too ironic?" she said. Stepping to Leon's side, she jerked his head back to reveal a similar mark on his neck.

Deathly silence fell over the table. Bert paled visibly and had a hard time meeting Tony's stunned gaze.

"I think it's time to go." Shortie jumped up from the table and pushed Inja from her chair. "Now Tony," he warned, "don't make something out of nothing. Let's go to your place and hash this thing out."

Bert reached for the baby, but Maria refused to relinquish him. Tony's swarthy complexion paled, and a muscle jumped involuntarily in his cheek as he clenched his teeth.

"Give me my son," he ordered savagely. Placing the child in his arms, Maria left the restaurant without raising her head. The waitress gawked after them. She didn't notice until later the five-dollar tip left on the table.

The drive home was full of stilted conversation with everyone talking, but saying nothing at all. Shortie remained silent, too upset for words. He didn't respond to Inja's questions or pay attention to Blackie's comments.

When the ignition was switched off, Blackie hurried to open the passenger side for Bert. Nervously, he studied his wife's inscrutable expression for storm warnings.

Inja slid over the seat and hopped out. "I'm going to Ellen's," she whispered to Shortie. "If there's a fight, I don't want to be here." Giving a polite wave to Maria, she hurried away.

Opening the front door, Tony motioned for them all to follow. Inside, he did an odd thing. Gazing into a hand mirror, he scrutinized his reflection, comparing his own to little Tony's. Shortie and Bert shared troubled glances. Trouble was brewing, and neither of them could stop it.

"Does he look like me?" he demanded as he shoved the child into their faces.

"You watch what you're doing there or you'll answer to me." Bert wouldn't hesitate to beat the young man senseless if she had a mind to, and they all knew it. Her voice was as cold as death, and her ruddy complexion high-colored in anger.

"Of course he looks like you," Shortie lied. "You can see the resemblance for yourself if...."

"Do not lie, my friend," Tony interrupted, resigned to the inevitable. Much to Shortie's consternation, he began to weep.

Gesturing helplessly, Maria stared at them for a moment with a hopeless expression. Unexpectedly, her legs folded beneath her. She sobbed brokenly as she dropped to her knees and begged for forgiveness.

"Forgive me. Please say you'll forgive me. I can not bear the thought of losing you. He came here at night when you worked late. I thought he was being nice, he brought wine, and...." Her expression dissolved into itself. There would be no more tomorrows, and the realization was more than she could stand.

"I will not hear this." Gripping her viciously by the shoulders, he snarled into her upturned face, "What evil is this you have brought into my house?" Releasing her, he tossed her aside. Unable to bear the sight of her, he turned away from her crumpled form while tears of grief streamed down his cheeks.

"You have shamed me, yourself, and our children. From this moment on, you are dead to me, Maria. Do you hear me? You are *los muertos*, dead."

Throwing her head back, a high-pitched keening rose from her throat as if coming from the very depths of her tormented soul. Covering her face with her hands, she rocked back and forth and sobbed brokenly.

His face twisted in agony as he hugged the baby to his breast. Kissing the infant's forehead one last time, he shoved the child into Bert's arms.

"Take him. Take this child that is not my son. I never wish to see him again. He will forever be a reminder of my wife's shame."

"No," Maria screamed, "do not send him away; he is not to blame. The blame is mine, mine and Leon's."

Shortie placed himself between the struggling couple and motioned for Blackie to get Bert and the baby out of there. Placing a hand on Tony's shoulder, he tried to get the young man to listen to reason. Shrugging him off, Tony ran out the door with the sound of Maria's screams resounding in his ears.

Bert ran for the car, shielding the baby with her body. Locking the door behind her, she sobbed into the blankets. Little Tony sensed his world was not as it should be, and his lower lip quivered. When she hugged him too fiercely, he howled at the top of his lungs.

Blackie followed after Bert, leaving Shortie to deal with Maria. She ran to the bedroom and locked the door, and the sound of her weeping carried eerily through the thin walls. Tony was already halfway up the street, running like a man possessed. Unsure of what to do, Shortie's shoulders slumped in defeat.

"What the sam hill," he said in despair. Rubbing the back of his neck with a trembling hand, he couldn't rid himself of an overpowering sense of loss.

Chapter 29

Deciding that action was better than reaction, Shortie ran after Tony. Cursing Leon and vowing vengeance, he covered every inch of ground between town and the top of the draw. Exasperated at his inability to find him, he headed back to the Martinez home, hoping Tony would return. Recognizing a familiar figure plodding slowly up the road, he waved to Gabbie.

The old man was out of breath by the time he was close enough for Shortie to hear him. "You better get down to ta' bar. Tony's been in thar' all afternoon, talkin' crazy. Keeps sayin' he's gonna kill somebody. Blackie and Art been talkin' to him, but he ain't wantin' to listen. You better come quick...."

Gabbie didn't have to say any more. Rushing off, Shortie ran the remaining distance, ignoring a tearing pain in his left leg. Bursting through the door, his senses were immediately assaulted. Stale cigarette smoke burned the sensitive membranes in his nose and throat, taking his breath away. The yeasty, pungent odor of beer and sour whiskey was over powering. Pausing, he breathed shallowly, giving his eyes time to adjust to the dim lighting and his nose time to acclimate to the absence of fresh air. Spotting Tony at the end of the bar, he was relieved to find Blackie and Art seated on either side of him. Taking a deep breath, he collected himself before approaching. What he said in the next few minutes could make all the difference.

Closing the door with a loud slam, he strode purposely across the room. "It's about time I found you. I've been looking for you all afternoon and here you are."

Pulling up a stool, he eyed a bottle on the counter. A cork lay beside the near empty fifth of whiskey. It was obvious Tony had drunk most of it.

"Why'd she do it? Why?" Tony asked them over and over again.

"I don't know why, but I do know sitting here, getting drunk and talking crazy won't help. Why don't you let me take you home? After you've slept awhile you'll feel better." Taking Tony's arm, Shortie tried to pull him to his feet. Tony twisted away, refusing to budge.

"I ain't leaving. I'm not drunk enough yet to do what I've got to do."

A silent message was exchanged between Blackie and Shortie.

"What do you have to do? Maybe we can help," Shortie coaxed. Tony studied their expressions through unfocused eyes.

"A man couldn't ask for better friends. Especially you," he slurred. Throwing an arm around Shortie's shoulders, he smiled lopsidedly.

"Yes, we're good friends. And because I'm such a good friend, I'm taking you home." Moving the bottle out of Tony's reach, they forced him off the stool. Pinning his arms to his sides, Shortie dragged him to the door. The others trooped out, relieved the situation had been taken care of. Gabbie trailed behind, wringing his hands in worry. Apologizing profusely, Art left for work.

Shortie and Blackie kept up a steady stream of conversation as they escorted the young man home. Desperate to get Tony's mind off his problems, Shortie talked about the future. He told him God loved him and had a hope and a plan for his life.

"Was it part of His plan that my Maria have another man's child?" he asked brokenly. The bitterness in his voice tore at Shortie's heart. How could he explain that people sometimes make bad choices for which there can be painful consequences? How could he tell him infidelity was okay when God's plan for marital happiness was so clearly stated in the Bible?

"I don't believe God had anything to do with it, but He is in the middle of every situation and can make something good out of this if we let Him."

Tony appeared to listen until he heard Blackie's snort of disbelief. Sobering in the cool, fresh air of early evening, he shook his head to clear the fog away. "No, this sin can never be made good." Looking toward the mountaintops, his eyes misted. "It's over. All the good things I had in this life are over, wiped out in a single night of one man's pleasure with my wife. What is there left? How can such a thing be made right?"

Feelings of inadequacy swept over Shortie. He didn't have words strong enough to wipe away Tony's pain. Seeking assistance from Blackie or Gabbie, he was disappointed to see they had nothing to offer. Knowing he should say something, no words of consolation came readily to mind.

"Things will look better after a good night's sleep. I know how bad you must feel, but...."

"No, you do not know how I feel. But if you don't wake up, my friend, you will."

"Shut up, kid, you don't know what you're saying. Don't spout off about things you might be sorry for later," Blackie growled. Shaking the young man's shoulder, a peculiar look passed between the two.

Opening the front door hesitantly, they found the house empty. Maria had taken the girls and left, leaving drawers and closets ajar.

Stumbling into the house, Tony looked around for a moment. Trying to appear indifferent, he shrugged his shoulders.

"Just as well," he said drunkenly. "Never want to see her again." Weaving, he lost his equilibrium and fell to the floor. "Maybe a little nap ain't such a bad idea."

Blackie lifted him effortlessly and carried him over his shoulder to the bedroom, where he dropped him onto the bed. Removing his shoes, Shortie pulled a blanket up to his chin. He was out instantly and breathing heavily.

"Maybe he'll sleep it off," Blackie suggested.

Sighing, Shortie pulled up a chair and sat with his feet propped on the edge of the bed. "Don't matter; I'm staying right here until he wakes. A man shouldn't be alone at a time like this."

"You're about dead on your feet, man. I'll stay with him and if anything happens, you'll be the first to know. I never thought I'd see the day when I'd have to baby-sit the man instead of the kid," he exclaimed.

Gratefully, Shortie relinquished his chair. "Stay till he wakes up, would you? Get him to eat something."

Nodding, the big man seated himself with arms folded across his chest. "He won't be going anywhere for quite a while, so go home and get some rest before you fall down. Don't worry. I'll call as soon as he wakes up."

At home, Shortie sat at the kitchen table with his head in his hands. His body ached with exhaustion and his eyes were gritty from lack of sleep. Strain showed on his face in lines of worry that furrowed his brow. Eddie, always sensitive to Shortie's mood, sat next to him with his head resting against his shoulder.

"Well, what happened after I left? Was there a big battle or what?" Inja's eyes blazed with curiosity.

"Nothing."

"What do you mean nothing? You've been gone all afternoon and you say nothing happened?"

"I'm not telling you a single word, Inja. What's happened is a horrible thing that has destroyed the lives of several people. It isn't something to be bandied about."

Miffed at his rebuff, her mouth quirked in annoyance. "Sit up, Eddie, can't you see he's tired?" she said gruffly, needing a victim to vent her anger on.

Hugging the child to his side, Shortie regarded her coldly. "Leave the boy alone."

Clamping her lips shut, she opened the refrigerator and removed the makings for a sandwich. "The least you can do is eat something. I'll make you a sandwich, and then you go to bed. No wonder you're so crabby; it's been a long day."

The phone rang while Shortie was eating. Hurrying to answer it, he listened to the message, then hung up. Smiling, he returned to the kitchen and fixed himself a second sandwich. The call was from Tony, not Blackie. The boy was sober, or sounded like he was, and promised to eat a good meal and then go back to bed. He said he was feeling better and would see him in the morning. The black cloud of worry should have lifted, raising his spirits, but a niggling shred of doubt lingered in the back of his mind.

A short while later he went to bed. He planned to rest for an hour or two and then return to Tony's place. The young man shouldn't be left alone through the long, and what could be lonely, night. Losing the battle, however, he soon fell into a deep, dreamless sleep. Inja didn't wake him when she came to bed, but snuggled close making a warm cocoon around them.

Waking suddenly, Shortie's eyes snapped open and immediately searched for the clock. It wasn't quite midnight. Something had woken him, but what? Hearing a series of soft pings at the window, he sat up and threw off the covers. Peering through the window, he was startled to see a face peering back.

"Shortie. Shortie, wake up," the voice begged. Gabbie stood at the window, striking the pane gently with pebbles.

"I'm awake," Shortie whispered angrily. "What are you doing looking in my bedroom window in the middle of the night?"

"You gotta come. You gotta come quick."

"Come around to the door. I can't understand half of what you say without your teeth." Throwing the door open, he fastened the suspenders of his overalls while Gabbie talked.

"Blackie sent me to fetch ya. The boy's got a gun and won't let anyone in the house."

"Where'd the gun come from? Was he left alone?"

"Not fur' a minute. The boy outsmarted him. Waited till he fell asleep, then poked that gun in his face. He made Blackie leave tuh' house by threatening to shoot him. And Shortie, he's cold-stone sober."

Hurrying down the hill, Shortie left Gabbie far behind. Nearing the Martinez home, he heard Blackie yell, "Open the door. Don't do something stupid. Think of your kids. Come on, Tony, open the door and talk to me." Hastening his steps, his heart nose-dived to the pit of his stomach when a single shot pierced the quiet of the night.

Breaking into a run, he covered the remaining distance. Taking the steps in one leap, he was knocked to the ground by a solid black shape. Blackie ran from the house as if the hounds of hell were behind him.

"He's crazy, the kid's gone crazy. He darn near shot me." Shaken, he helped Shortie to his feet. Raking his hair back, he paced the yard nervously. The muscles in his chest twitched with every step.

"Break down the door," Shortie screamed. Frantically, they beat on the door, using their shoulders and combined weight as a battering ram. When the door splintered, breaking away from the casing, they fell into the house. An eerie silence made the hum of an electric clock seem uncommonly loud. The small hairs on Shortie's arm stood on end, causing his heart to race.

"Tony," he called. Approaching the bedroom, his steps slowed. The smell of gunpowder lingered in the air. "Tony, are you in there?" Reaching out to grasp the doorknob, he forced himself to turn it until the latch clicked. Wiping his sweaty palms on his overalls, he glanced over his shoulder to Blackie.

"I'm scared to open the door. What if...."

"Don't say it, man." Blackie's eyes were huge in the dim light. Raking his hair back, he paced the floor, but refused to come closer.

The door opened easily, and he stepped into the darkened room. Feeling for a light switch, he groped around until finding a lamp with no bulb.

"Tony," he whispered, "you in here?" Tiptoeing across the room, he pulled the window shade. It rolled up with a loud snap, making him jump involuntarily. Moonlight flooded the room, glinting off something metal lying on the floor near the bed. Kneeling down, he felt around until his fingertips touched something warm and sticky. He found Tony on the far side of the bed in a pool of his own blood.

"Tony...Tony," he cried. Clasping him to his chest, he sobbed his name over and over again. "No, oh, dear God, not this boy. Call an ambulance," he called to Blackie.

Sobbing incoherently, he frantically searched for a pulse. Holding the limp wrist, he detected the weak thrum of a heartbeat that weakened to a flutter as he held Tony's lifeless body.

"Don't you die on me, boy. Dear God, don't let him die," he begged. He continued to hold Tony's body even after the faint breathing stilled to silence.

When the ambulance arrived, he wouldn't allow them to place the boy's body on a gurney. He wrapped him in a blanket and placed him on the gurney himself, then covered him with another blanket. The ambulance left without sirens and without a flashing light.

"Oh God, no," Gabbie wailed. Clasping a hand to his chest, he would have fallen if Blackie hadn't caught him. Supporting the old man, Blackie carried him away from the grizzly scene. Gabbie was transported to the hospital and treated for cardiac distress.

Collapsing onto the porch, Shortie sat without feeling or thought. His clothes were blood-soaked and his hands red-streaked and sticky.

"This shouldn't have happened," he mumbled over and over again. "My God," he despaired, "How could You allow this?" He fell silent, his face glazed in shock. He had no idea when Bert and Blackie took him home. He spent the rest of the night seated in the dark kitchen staring at nothing.

The funeral was held three day later. Standing at graveside, Shortie clasped his hands in front of him. He had remained dry-eyed since the night Tony died and was unable to shed a single tear. Bitter anger raged within him, spilling over and out of control.

It was during the sermon delivered by a priest at graveside that the rage inside him flamed to a tempest, consuming all rational thought. The image of dark, hooded eyes mocked him, even in his sleep. When the service ended, the fire in him raged at the unfairness of it all. Pacing the scrap of yard in front of his house, he blamed Maria and then God for Tony's death. When the rage inside flared to include the bloody images of Tony's head with a gaping hole in the back of his skull, something inside snapped. A dark, menacing hatred stole over him as he strode purposely down the hill in search of the one person really at fault. Blackie saw him coming and met him where the dirt road met pavement.

"Where you going to, Rand? You look like you need some company." One look at Shortie's face spoke volumes. Blackie knew what he had in mind and had no intention of interfering, because God help him, he'd had the same idea himself.

Jumping in the pickup, the two drove off. Stopping at the post office, they wheedled the address out of the postmaster and followed his directions to a little side street off the main drag. Shortie didn't wait for the truck to come to a stop, but jumped out to beat upon the door with his fist.

"Open up, Mayhew. Come out and face me and stop hiding like the yellow cur dog that you are." Next-door neighbors peered out though screened windows, and when they saw the two of them, bolted their doors and latched their windows.

Blackie beat on the door with a beefy paw, as eager as Shortie to vent his grief and anger. "Come out and face me, Mayhew; it's about time we had it out—that is if Shortie doesn't get to you first." His mouth fell open in surprise when the door suddenly opened and a weeping Holly stood before them. Trembling like a leaf in the wind, she bravely faced them.

Wiping her streaming eyes with a tissue, she sniffled, "You're too late. He's gone. When Leon read the article in the paper about Tony, he got scared and was afraid you'd come looking for him. He remembered all too well the first beating you gave him and didn't want another." Blowing her nose, she allowed the door to open slightly.

"Where is he? Where did he go?" Shortie demanded ruthlessly. Eyeing the suitcases standing just inside the door, he figured she was on her way to meet him.

"By now, he's in Spokane County, being arraigned for the explosion last spring and for theft. The coward decided facing the law would be easier than facing you. Ben Schultz came forward and confirmed that Leon was the one who set off the dynamite last spring. He didn't say anything before because Leon threatened to turn him in for stealing it." Stepping back so they could see into the house, she gestured toward the packed bags. "I'm leaving, as you can see. I'm getting as far away from this place as I can go. He lied to me, too, you know."

"We're sorry," Shortie said curtly. "But you asked...."

"No, I didn't ask for all his lies or his cheating. I always thought it was Inja he was seeing. That's why I went out of my way to befriend her because the best way to rid yourself of an enemy is to make a friend out of them. I never asked for any of this." Her face dissolved into a mask of tears. "All I wanted was for him to love me," she whimpered.

The two men shuffled their feet, unsure of how to handle the situation. If what Holly said was true, it certainly put a new slant on things.

"By the way," she said before stepping back inside the house, "if it's any consolation, Leon took advantage of Maria. He told me all about it before he left. He didn't rape her, but took advantage of her just the same. Your friend shouldn't have done what he did because it wasn't her fault." Shutting the door firmly, she slid the bolt into place.

The morning's headlines blazed with the news of Leon's arrest and Ben's statement to the local news. It seems Ben had found an old mineshaft hidden in the hillside near his home. He explored it and found a box of old dynamite that had to have been left there years before. Wanting to deepen the shaft, he thought the dynamite was quite a find until he realized it was rotten and quite useless. So he decided to take a couple of sticks from the supply room at the mine, but Leon spotted it hidden in his lunch bucket and eventually put two and two together. Accusing him of stealing dynamite to blow up one of the seldom-used shafts owned by the Lucky Spur, he threatened to turn him in if he didn't pay him off. Ben showed Leon the old shaft and told him what his plans were. He thought a new shaft could be opened off the existing one and figured to mine it, hoping it would pay off with a little silver. Leon got greedy and set off the explosives, which caused the cave-in. Reading through the article, Shortie's anger only intensified. Where was God in all of this? Why wasn't Leon stopped before the damage was done?

A few days later, he stormed into Pastor Adams' study. Startled at the interruption, the pastor waited patiently for his anger to run dry.

"How can you preach that God cares when He allowed these things to happen?"

"Did God tell your friend to commit suicide?" he asked calmly. Shortie's eyes blazed murderously as he pounded the desk with his fist.

"No, but He didn't do anything to stop it either. I prayed for Tony, just as the Bible says, and this was my answer? Oh God," he cried, "why? Why did Tony do it?" Pacing the room, he fought back tears of grief and anger, and with every step slammed a fist into the palm of his hand, bruising the flesh without feeling the pain. For over an hour he raged at God, Pastor Adams, and Tony until the heated exchange broke him down. As Shortie sobbed out his grief, the healing process took a tenuous first step. In the weeks following, the two shared similar sessions, and as they prayed and talked together, Shortie took control of his anger. When he shared his inner pain, the floodgates opened and all the fear and guilt over Tony's death poured out in great wracking sobs. And lastly, after keeping it a secret for over a year, he shared his suspicions about his wife. All the bloody wounds in his heart were brought out into the open where they could begin to heal.

He bore his soul to the one man he knew could be trusted and nonjudgmental. He didn't want biased advice but needed the pastor's listening ear and the power of God's word. The last conversation he'd had with Tony haunted him and played over and over in his mind.

"Was there something more I should have done? Maybe if I hadn't left that night, Tony would still be alive," he wept.

"What more could you possibly have said? You must understand it wasn't your fault. Once your friend made the decision, he was dead already. There was nothing you could have done to stop him, short of locking him up to prevent him from hurting himself. It is a tragedy, but certainly not your fault."

"I can't get it out of my head. He died alone, how could God let him die alone?"

"How do you know Tony died alone? Have you asked the Lord about it?"

"Ask Him? How can I? It isn't as if I can call Him on the phone," Shortie said sarcastically. Bridling at the pastor's senseless remark, he rose to leave before he said or did something he'd be sorry for.

"Wait, don't go. I'm not talking crazy, and I mean what I say. Ask God about Tony and in time He will answer all of your questions. I frequently hear his voice, and usually when I need it most. Our God is an awesome God, and please be assured He is very concerned about your well-being."

Remembering Tony's warning about Inja, he wondered what other secrets were yet to be revealed. Did Tony find a source of comfort in his final moments? Was *God* with him in that darkened room and did *He* weep when Tony pulled the trigger? Behind the closed doors of the pastor's study, he worked through the heartache until able to handle it on his own.

Chapter 30

With the coming of fall most people expected cooler weather, but as the days passed without the usual night frosts accompanied by rainy days, it was accepted that an Indian summer was upon them. Eddie was back in school, and Harvest Night and Halloween were only a couple of weeks off when Shortie became aware of how much time had passed since Tony's death. Getting ready for bed one night, he was instantly alert to something Inja said.

"Can you believe it?" she asked as she tied the belt of her robe snugly around her waist. Hanging her dress in the closet, she turned to face him with hands on hips. "Well, say something. Don't you think it's just awful? The owners plan to rent the house without telling what took place there." Shivering, she wrapped her arms around herself. "You wouldn't catch me in there. The place gives me the willies."

"What's that? Did you say Tony's house is to be rented?"

"Well, that's what I've been trying to tell you all evening," she said angrily. "Honestly, you've got to snap out of it, Shortie. I know he was a good friend and you miss him, but you hardly speak two words to anyone any more and," she smiled shyly, "I miss you. Eddie misses you, too and it's time to get on with living, don't you think?" Wrapping her arms around him, she rested her head against his chest. "I've been worried about you. I want our life back."

"You're right," he sighed, "I need to get past it, and I'm sorry for being so moody, but bear with me. You go on to bed and I'll be there in a little while. All of a sudden, I'm not very tired." Sighing with irritation, she climbed into bed. Snapping off the bedside lamp, she fumed as he left the room.

"Hurry back, okay?" she called after him.

"Yeah, I'll come to bed in a few minutes." Closing the door behind him, he sat on the couch gazing into the darkness. After awhile, he went outside and stared into the valley for the longest time. Once he made the decision, he turned abruptly and went back into the house. Picking up the phone, he dialed a number and waited impatiently for an answer.

"Irish, this is Busch. Have you heard? I can't let it happen, and I think you know what I mean. Meet me in ten minutes." Hanging up, he left the house through the back, being sure to shut the door quietly. In the dark he made his way to the shed to find what he needed by touch and feel. Lifting a metal can by its handle, he made tracks to a hidden path behind the shed that led into the Martinez backyard. Switching the weight of the container from one hand to the other, he hurried down the hill to meet Blackie. He paid little attention to the shadow that followed him through the night.

Spotting the five-gallon container in Shortie's hands, Blackie knew immediately what he had in mind. "You aren't serious, are you? I mean, you're Mr. True-blue, Mr. Decency himself; are you sure about this?" At Shortie's answering nod, he stepped back, allowing him to pass by.

Eddie watched in amazement as gasoline was spread throughout the little house and along the outside walls. When a match was thrown and it ignited with a whoosh, he came out from his hiding place to stand beside Shortie. A single tear trailed down the man's face as the flame spread, engulfing the house in a raging fire.

Blackie stood on his other side and threw an arm around Shortie's shoulders. The three of them watched in silence as flames engulfed the building.

Their faces blistered from the heat, but they didn't leave until the wail of fire engines was heard in the distance. Illuminated as they were by the light from the fire, they knew they could be identified, but didn't fear the wagging tongues of neighbors. Too many of them wished they had thought of it themselves.

"It's done," Blackie stated. Turning to face Shortie, his face scorched from the heat of the flames, he ordered, "Go home now. It's time to rejoin the living."

Nodding, Shortie took Eddie's hand and they climbed the hill together. "I'll never tell," the boy whispered in Shortie's ear as he tucked him into bed. And he never did!

Chapter 31

When Inja came into the kitchen the following morning she wrinkled up her nose with distaste. "Whew, it stinks in here." She pecked Shortie's cheek and backed away with a hand over her nose. "You absolutely reek. Are the dampers on the stove open? We need to air this place out." She opened the back door and opened the damper on the stovepipe.

"It isn't the stove. You know there's never been a problem with the dampers and it has excellent air circulation. There was a fire last night," he said evasively. "Tony's place burned to the ground."

"Tony's place! They didn't own that house and everybody knew it. I wonder what caused the fire though. Do you suppose the new renters left a burner on or forgot to turn off the gas heater? It's a good thing it happened before they moved in. Boy, were they lucky."

"Yeah, lucky," he agreed. "It was probably a short in the wiring or something," he answered glibly. He didn't know why he was impelled to lie, but one lie followed another. "Smoke and heat rise you know, and our bedroom window was left open last night. I guess that's why I smell of smoke since I sleep right next to it. I'll take a bath and wash my hair. That'll get rid of it. You smell a little like smoke yourself so maybe you'd better wash your hair or something."

Sniffing the sleeve of her robe and then a lock of her own hair, she detected nothing. "I don't smell anything, but you and I won't sit down to breakfast with that horrible stench upsetting my stomach."

"Okay, I'll bathe now instead of later." Running water into the tub, he opened Eddie's bedroom door and stuffed both their clothes out the window. Waking the boy, he hurried him into the bathroom for a quick bath. After Eddie was dressed in clean clothes, Shortie stripped off his overalls and chucked them out, too. Eddie didn't ask any questions. He accepted the strange behavior with a conspiratorial smile. Shortie held no fear that the boy would betray a promise of secrecy. All evidence of the previous night's adventure was quickly washed away and swallowed by the drain, and when breakfast was over, he washed all trace of smoke and ash from their clothing using the strongest lye soap he could find. When the local police came by later that afternoon, Shortie was found on the front porch calmly reading the paper.

"Have you noticed anyone hanging around the empty Martinez place?" the officer asked.

"Nope, can't say that I have," he answered lazily as he leaned his chair back against the wall.

"Did you see anything last night? My gosh, there was a tremendous fire and the blaze should have woke most of this neighborhood."

"Well," Shortie drawled, "we live up so far, nothing much disturbs us. I didn't hear or see anything last night," he chuckled. "I sleep so sound it'd take more than a little ole' fire to wake me." He turned the page of his paper, making it obvious that further questioning would be pointless.

Scratching his head, the officer stuck a notepad back in his shirt pocket. "Seems to be a lot of sound sleepers here in the valley," he sneered as a parting shot as he stepped off the porch. "Must be something in the water that makes everyone deaf and blind, too."

The city police and fire department made a half-hearted attempt to find whoever set the fire. They knew it was arson because the remains of a gas can had been found in the rubble, but without a witness, their investigation came to a dead end. The owners of the place collected the insurance money, then took an extended vacation. Within a few days, the entire episode was swept under the carpet. Towners believed most of the houses in the valley were eyesores and should be burned or torn down, and besides, the burning of one place wasn't cause for alarm.

Shortie's reticence ended the night of the fire, but he remained quiet and thoughtful. Something Tony had said bothered him, and he puzzled over it until deciding to meet the problem head-on.

"We need to talk," he announced one day. Seated on the sofa next to Inja, he moved her stack of magazines to the floor.

"Okay, what about?" Her blue eyes gazed innocently into his.

"Are you happy? I mean, have you been happy since you married me?"

"Why of course. I'm as happy as I'll ever be and I'm glad we married. Whatever brought this on?" she asked, suddenly impatient with the conversation. As she smoothed a fold in her skirt, her eyes skittered away from his.

He took her hands and forced to face him. "Inja, I need to know who comes here to play cards twice a week, smokes imported cigarettes, and drinks beer. I've seen the evidence hidden in the trash, and the cards, pardon the expression, on the table."

Her eyes widened and then narrowed in anger as she edged away from him. "I have other friends besides them," she gestured toward the valley. "Some of my friends are from town and they bring their husbands with them. So what! Do I need your permission to have friends over during the day?"

"Don't get so defensive. I have no reason to believe you aren't telling me the truth. But please tell your cigarette smoking friends to keep it outside. The stink permeates the house and chokes Eddie up something awful. Will you do that?"

"Sure," she said grudgingly. "Is there anything else you're dying to know or can I get back to my magazine?"

"Sorry to have interrupted, but a man's got a right to know who comes into his house. It's pretty suspicious when your company never sticks around long enough to meet me." His mouth tightened to a stubborn line as he yanked the door open angrily. He paced the porch, muttering to himself for over an hour before he was calm enough to go back inside. Needing something to do, he decided to fix dinner. He was washing the dishes when he noticed a huge pumpkin drawn on the calendar in a childish hand.

"What's this? Is Halloween that close?"

"It's the first Saturday after Harvest Night, and Eddie wants you to take him trick-or-treating. He's been looking forward to it for weeks. It's funny you find it so surprising because he asked you about it just the other night."

"I guess I've been a little preoccupied, but I'll make it up to him. He'll have the best Harvest Night and trick-or-treat of any boy on the block."

Harvest Night was held at the school either on Halloween or the closest Friday. The entire community was invited, but only families with children in school attended. There would be games, prizes, food, a cakewalk, and pumpkins to carve. Remembering the fun of the year before, he almost looked forward to it.

Walking to the school holding the hand of Inja on one side and Eddie on the other, Shortie felt better than he had in weeks. He still ached over the loss of a good friend and avoided the area where the house had stood, but was overall better. Surprised at himself, he was eager to see friends and neighbors again. He had the oddest feeling, like he'd been away for a long time and had just recently returned.

The basement of the school was festooned with paper streamers and colored jack-o-lanterns of all shapes and sizes. All decorations were made by the children or supplied by their parents. Eddie wanted to buy a ticket for the fishpond, so a dollar's worth was purchased. Tickets were ten cents apiece so he could participate in just about everything. Handing him a fishing pole, Shortie threw the attached string over a cardboard wall. The line was jerked several times with false alarms before it pulled taut and jerked three times signaling a catch. Reeling in the prize, Eddie's eyes sparkled when he saw the toy derringer. Shortie blanched when light reflected off the barrel. He grabbed the gun to throw it back when a strong arm pulled him back.

"That's a fine catch if ever I saw one," Blackie bellowed good-naturedly. "Ain't that fine?" he asked him. "Put it behind you, man," he whispered. "Look at the boy's face and then try and tell him he can't have it. It's a harmless toy that can be used to teach the boy a valuable lesson in gun safety."

Releasing the toy from the line, Shortie laid Eddie's catch at his feet. "Do you want to go fishing again or do something else?"

As a family the three bobbed for apples, participated in the cakewalk, carved a pumpkin, sampled cookies and apple cider. When the music started, they joined in the square dancing and clapped along with everyone else when Bert and Blackie danced an Irish jig. Shortie's hands burned from clapping when Blackie hollered across the dance floor.

"Guess what? We're getting little Tony back. We're going to adopt him. We'll be seeing you in church every Sunday from now on, because a promise is a promise."

After the party, Shortie shook Bert's hand and congratulated Blackie on their decision to adopt the abandoned baby Anthony. Maria left him with a friend after Tony's death and never returned. He was happy for them, but when he came under the subdued light of a streetlamp on the way home, he couldn't hide his sorrow.

"You were a good friend to him. You've been a good friend to all of these people," Inja defended.

"Some friend. I let him down." The bitterness in his voice shocked her.

"It wouldn't have mattered if you were there or not. Tony had his mind set to do what he did because he couldn't handle the truth. Maria had an affair and...."

"She didn't have an affair, that man used her."

"Leon wouldn't take what wasn't given. He didn't rape her."

"How do you know so much about it? There are other ways to abuse a woman and he knew them all. How can you continue to blindly defend that man after all he's done? What kind of relationship did you have with him anyway? It sure makes a man wonder the way you bristle up every time his name is mentioned."

"Leave my friendship with Leon and Holly out of this." Taking a deep breath, she let it out in a deep sigh. "Let's not argue. I know you've been hurt, but it's time to put it behind you. The holidays aren't very far off and I want them to be special for all of us."

Later, long after Inja slept soundly beside him, Shortie lay wide awake.

Why Lord? Why has everything gone so wrong? What have I done to anger You? Please Lord, don't take my family away like you took Tony. Why did You let him die alone?

His prayer was interrupted by a voice he recognized.

Be still and know that death is the destiny of every man and the living must take this to heart. I was there; he did not die alone.

Peace such as he'd never known stole over him and he finally slept reciting the Lord's Prayer.

Chapter 32

The following Saturday was Halloween and Shortie spent most of the afternoon helping Inja decorate jack-o-lantern cookies, chocolate cats, and popcorn ghosts. They were so engrossed in the activity that they lost track of time until shadows fell across the kitchen. Glancing at the clock, he was astonished at how late it was.

"Oh my gosh, it's almost four and I haven't started on Eddie's costume. Can you finish without me?"

"I think I can manage," Inja answered dryly. She didn't look up from the cookie she was decorating with eyes, nose and mouth. The decorator's bag was plump with orange frosting that she squeezed to make realistic faces. He was proud of her artistry.

He washed the stickiness from his hands and then called Eddie. He was surprised to find him on the porch with a glum face and chin in hands. Sitting down next to the boy in the fading sunlight of a brilliant fall day, he placed an arm around him. "Why the long face? Did you and one of your chums have a falling out?"

"Nope."

"Can you tell me about it?"

Shrugging his shoulders, he swiped his nose with the back of a hand. "You forgot," he mumbled.

"Forgot? What did I forget?"

"You promised to help me with my costume. You forgot and trick-or-treat starts soon," he wailed.

Laughing, Shortie ruffled the boy's hair and picked him up with a toss in the air to make him forget his troubles. "I didn't forget," he reassured him. "You're going to have the best costume of all. I've planned it all day, so wipe that frown off your face and let's get busy."

Eddie ate a hurried dinner and then raced to the shed where Shortie waited for him. With the help of a few stuffed potato sacks tied to his spare frame and three coat hangers bent into a brace to hold one leg stiff, he soon resembled a hunchback. Throwing an old blanket over his head, he cut a hole big enough for it to slide over his shoulders. His skinny arms protruded awkwardly but were covered with a stolen pair of Inja's nylon stockings. A third stocking was pulled down over his face to distort his features grotesquely and then tied snugly at the top. The final touch was a flashlight attached by wires around his chest and hidden under the blanket. Its beam illuminated his face giving him an appearance any spook or goblin would envy. Shoving Inja's hand mirror at him so he could admire himself, he was gratified to see the shocked look on the child's distorted features. The costume would be a great success.

Eddie, so excited he fairly danced down the steep hill, played the part of monster hunchback perfectly during the evening's raid for trick-or-treats. By the end of it, Shortie wasn't sure who received more, Eddie or himself. He'd eaten more candy, homemade cookies, popcorn balls, doughnuts, and cupcakes than any one man should in three years. His stomach ached, accustomed to all the sweets. When he carried Eddie to bed, the child fell asleep almost instantly. Afterward, he joined Inja on the porch where she was enjoying a last cup of coffee before bed.

"Isn't it odd?" she asked.

"Isn't what odd?"

"The weather, silly. Last year and the year before we had a heavy snowfall on Halloween and it was freezing cold. And three years ago, it rained and then froze so hard it didn't thaw again until April. I'm not complaining, mind you, but it's unusual to remain so warm this late in the season. We haven't had any rain this fall and only a few frosty nights. Here it is, November first, and we're still sitting outside with only a sweater to ward off the chill. It just seems strange."

Stretching to get the kinks out of her back and neck, she yawned and grabbed his hand as she went inside.

"Good-night. I'm going to bed. My back and neck ache from standing so long frosting all those cookies. I'll bet we had over a hundred treaters." Yawning again, she covered her mouth. "I saved a dozen or so cookies for your lunch. They're in the cookie jar if you want one."

In normal years, the first snow was expected either the last week of October or the following week. This year, 1948, the weather held. Days remained unseasonably warm even though nights grew frosty. As days shortened and the weather grew cooler, the sun shone brightly against cloudless skies. It was only natural, given all the cataclysmic events that had rocked the valley over the past few months, that residents eagerly swept gloom under the carpet. People were only too happy to shake off the burden of grief in anticipation of the coming holidays. Only Shortie continued to be haunted by visions of exploding mountains and the memory of a young man who loved and made life just a little bit brighter for those who knew him.

On Veteran's Day a parade was planned, complete with marching band and a display by the air base out of Spokane. All Vets were to dress in uniform and march in the parade to show support for those who served. Local papers covered the event with interest because it was the first Veteran's Parade held in the area.

Articles about the parade, unfortunately, coincided with other news filling the front page. Headlines drew attention to problems overseas, only this time from a place called Korea. Shortie read each article with avid interest. World War II hadn't been over long enough for people to forget the warning signs.

The day of the parade, Inja laid out his dress uniform while he shaved. There were few wrinkles and a good shaking got rid of most of them. Dressed, with his cap set at a jaunty angle, he turned sharply, giving a military salute.

"It still fits. All those pancakes haven't added a single pound to my middle," he bragged. Patting his flat stomach, he straightened his tie and pulled it snugly against his collar. It was only a parade, but he refused to appear sloppy in uniform. Pulling his shoulders back, he grinned at himself with pride in the bathroom mirror.

"How do I look, Inja? Do I look different than the last time I wore this uniform?"

"You look great," she told him. "In fact, you're even more handsome than the first time I laid eyes on you." For a moment she gazed at him dreamily, remembering. "Now, you'd better get going. It might take a while to get Blackie dressed. Bert's working at the bake sale and won't be there and I'm afraid he'll need all the help he can get."

Making his way painstakingly down the mountain, Shortie was careful not to scuff or mark his dress shoes. At the paved road, he rubbed each spit-shined toe against the back of a leg before crossing the street. Raising his hand to knock at Blackie's door, he was surprised to hear a deep voice raised in anger.

"What are you talking about, old man? I ain't fat, and if you say it again I'm going to wrap that scrawny neck of yours around my fist."

"Them britches is too tight. Now someone round here either shrunk 'em or you've put on 'bout thirty pounds of spuds and all 'round the middle."

Wheezy guffaws could be heard over Blackie's colorful description of Gabbie's mother. Wanting to ward off trouble before it began, Shortie opened the door and walked in. He blinked in surprise when he saw the stranger standing in the Clegg kitchen. It took him a moment to realize the stranger was Gabbie. The old man was clean, and his matted beard was neatly trimmed, holding no leftovers from last night's dinner. The characteristic wad of tobacco was missing from his lip, and he stood proudly erect, wearing a uniform that hadn't seen the light of day in years. It hung on the old man's body like a sheet over dry bones. Walking around him, Shortie stared in awe.

"I can hardly believe it's you, Gab."

"I'm a Vet," he said defensively, "and I'm gonna' be in the parade, too."

Doffing his cap, Shortie snapped to attention and gave a smart salute. "I don't know how old you were when you wore that uniform, but we'd be honored to include you in the ranks," he said formally.

The return salute was far from regulation, but heartfelt. Grinning widely, revealing his store- bought teeth, he pointed toward the bedroom.

"Buffalo butt's tryin' ta' git into his dress blues. Maybe you have a tater masher handy to help cram him in like a sausage." Hooting like a screech owl, he slapped his knee in merriment.

"You'll pay for that old man. You wait 'til I'm shed of this chamber of horrors...Gabbie, I'm going to knock you in the head. You tied my tie so tight, I can't breathe."

Shoving his hands in his pockets, Gabbie slouched into his usual stance and strolled nonchalantly to the door. "See ya at ta' parade if'n ya ever git yerself dressed," he teased.

Shortie followed Blackie's voice into the bedroom where he came to an abrupt halt. Placing a hand over his mouth, he stifled a chuckle before it left his throat. Irish was indeed stuffed into his uniform like a sausage. The pants stretched tightly around his middle with enough hanging over the belt to fill a second pair. Gaps around the buttons showed as they strained against the fabric. The jacket couldn't be buttoned and threatened to split down the middle if he dared breathe deeply. His tie was pulled against his Adam's apple like a noose; he was ready for hanging. He stood in front of Bert's mirror with his shoulders bunched and looking miserable. His face was bright red and he looked like a boil about ready to pop.

"Don't just stand there, get me out of this thing," he ordered. "If I move, it's gonna explode."

His tie was loosened easily enough, but the jacket was another matter. It was so tight the seams were beginning to split. With a great deal of jiggling, holding his breath and sucking in his stomach, he was finally out of the jacket and the pants. Grabbing a dark blue suit from the closet, he stormed, red-faced, into the bathroom.

He wasn't the only Vet who marched in the parade without full uniform. Several wore plain suits like his or wore the pants without the shirt or vice-versa. The size of Blackie's waist was certainly testimony of Bert's culinary skill.

Newspapers touted the parade a huge success. Gabbie was proud of the picture that showed him standing beside Shortie in a long line of marching Vets. People paid scant attention to the article, but read and reread news about the deteriorating relationship with Korea. The threat of another war was shelved for the time being, however, with the holidays just around the corner. Who could be worried about events overseas when Christmas was less than six weeks away?

After work, men continued to gather at Arden's, but chose to remain inside on cold days. Drawn to the welcome warmth of the little pot-bellied stove, they lingered over cups of hot coffee or hot chocolate, depending on preference. Some preferred a stronger beverage, which was fine, because a good profit was made from the sale of beer. Talk always turned to the weather. Even though days were cool to almost freezing, the skies remained clear.

"Weather's sure been off this year," Blackie commented one evening. "A man doesn't know whether to put on his long handles or dress in shirt sleeves. It seems odd, not getting any moisture this late in the season and still not a hint of snow."

"Ground's dry," offered a newcomer to the area. "I wanted to put up a fence and thought I'd have to wait till spring. Shoot, the ground's still soft enough to shovel and the soil's powder dry, so I went ahead and ordered the materials. I'm starting it this weekend." He gestured toward Shortie. "And with his help, it'll probably be finished over by Sunday afternoon."

"I 'member a winter just like this," Gabbie interjected with an air of self-importance. Ever since the parade, he'd teased Blackie unmercifully and strutted around like a peacock. Shortie noticed his appearance had changed radically since Veteran's Day, though, and not for the better. When no one paid him any attention, he continued his story whether they wanted to listen or not.

"Yes sir, it was a year just like this 'un. Long dry spring with little rain, hot summer, and a long dry fall. Didn't snow till March, and when it did, we were buried overnight under twelve feet of the white stuff. We lived like Eskee'moes, livin' in burrows under ta' snow. Muh' house was buried clean up to ta' chimbley. Ended up livin' in a cave with a she'bar and two cubs till it cleared off. Even the wolves come a beggin' fer food. Had ta' feed'em tablescraps jest to keep 'em alive." Nodding his head thoughtfully, he smoked a roll-your-own as he tipped back in the rocking chair.

"Is that true?" the newcomer innocently inquired.

"It's the gospel," Gabbie said as he rocked forward to face the man eye-to-eye.

"God help us," he gulped. "Do you think it will get that bad this year?" Gabbie shrugged noncommittally and closed his eyes.

"Don't listen to a word this old man ever tells you. He's shinin' you on," Blackie explained. "It'll snow, but I've yet to see twelve feet of it in one night. Two or three nights, maybe, but never in one." The man paled as Blackie cast a dark look in Gabbie's direction.

Shortie rolled his eyes skyward. He knew without a doubt the younger man believed Gabbie's every word, and Blackie had been suckered in again.

Rising early on Thanksgiving morning, Shortie started a fire in the cookstove and carried in several extra armloads of wood. Inja would be up early and want her morning coffee before she stuffed the thirty-pound turkey left cooling in the shed. They had decided to make it a real family celebration and invited everybody they knew. The dinner would be held at the Cleggs', where there would be more room. Bert would supply the potatoes, homemade rolls, relishes, hot vegetables, and yams. Inja was to bring the turkey, make the gravy, and bake two pumpkin pies. Ellen was bringing two pumpkin pies and two mincemeat. Evie would bring sweet breads for snacking and greens for a salad. Shortie needed to bake the pies before the turkey was put in the oven because Inja had never made a pie in her life. He'd baked pies for his brothers and sisters for years, and pumpkin was a snap. It didn't take him an hour to prepare three pies, two to take to Bert's and one to keep. Wiping off the counter, he wondered what to fix for breakfast. With a chuckle, he removed milk, sugar, chocolate and marshmallows from their places. Hot chocolate and oven toast would hit the spot.

While the turkey baked, filling the house with a heavenly aroma, he frequently went outside to peer over the side of the mountain to the road below.

"Come back inside and shut the door," Inja complained. "You're as bad as a little kid. They'll be here soon enough, so settle down. Remember, Evie has two kids to get ready, and from the sounds of it, a third is on the way.

"I know," he replied sheepishly. He was embarrassed to be caught acting like a child anxious for his mama's return. In actuality, it was the other way around. He was the second to the oldest of thirteen and when the old man left and his older brother took off to join the Navy, he was left to care for the others. He'd been like a father and had watched Evie grow from little girl to womanhood with a father's eye. He loved her and missed their long talks and her sisterly teasing. Knowing his worry wouldn't bring them any faster, he challenged Eddie to a game of checkers. They played until bright morning sunshine called them outside to enjoy the crisp, cool air.

Grabbing their jackets, Shortie hollered from the porch, "We're going to the tank. We'll be back shortly, just taking a walk to work up an appetite." They climbed the hill, hand-in-hand. At the tank, they drank fresh mountain spring water in huge gulps, letting it drip off their chins as they dipped their heads into the stream. The water was so cold it made their teeth ache and nipped their noses.

"That's one thing about this place I truly love. No place in the world has better tasting water and it's always nice and cold."

"Yup, I like it, too," Eddie agreed. Smiling happily, he enjoyed being with Shortie no matter what the occasion. Coming down the hill, they both yelled excitedly at the car parked in front of the steps. Evie stood on the porch waving.

Chapter 33

Running to meet her, Shortie greeted his sister with a hug and then swung her around to kiss her cheek before setting her firmly back on the ground.

"Rand," she screeched. "Stop that. Do you want me to have this baby right here on your porch?" She playfully cuffed his ear.

"Evie," he said with a sparkle in his eyes. "You are a sight for sore eyes. I've missed you."

"I've missed you too, brother. And I have so much to tell you. Lissa is pregnant again, and couldn't be happier. I heard from Frank the other day and he's doing well...." Taking his arm, she clasped it in her own as the two entered the house chattering animatedly. For the next few minutes, she filled him in on all the family gossip. He listened hungrily for every scrap of information. Inja didn't like going to visit his side of the family, so all the news he received was always secondhand. He promised himself a trip to visit each one of them come spring.

Shaking Lowell's hand in greeting, Shortie took the plump eighteen-month-old from his arms. "Who is this handsome fellow?" Tickling the child under the chin, he delighted in the baby's giggle that revealed several tiny teeth.

"This is Tommy, our latest, but number three will arrive soon. I expect the stork either late March or early April," Evie confided.

"Three children," he marveled. "It doesn't seem possible. Why, it was just the other day I tied ribbons in your pigtails and braided your hair."

"I'll have you know, I haven't wore pigtails or braids since I was a girl and that's been several years ago. Wake up big brother; time passes."

While waiting for the turkey to brown, the two families visited. The rise and fall of their voices could be heard out in the yard where Eddie showed Danny, Evie's oldest, where the cellar caved in and where Inja had fallen. The two boys were about the same age, but didn't look it. Danny was taller, heavier and already graduated to third grade. The two developed a close friendship that lasted through the years.

"Can you help me a minute?" Inja called from the kitchen. Following a delicious aroma, both men came to her side. The turkey was done and ready to be removed from the oven.

Lowell held the platter while Shortie lifted the huge bird from the roaster. Inja frowned when he tore a small strip of meat from the underside and popped it into his mouth. Closing his eyes, he savored the morsel and would have taken a second sampling except for the sharp rap across the knuckles from her wooden spoon. Instead, he made the gravy while she supervised.

They made two trips down the hill with the car. The first was to transport the women and children and the second to bring the food. Shortie carried the platter, loaded with bird, into Bert's kitchen. Lowell trailed behind with a huge bowl of gravy. Bert's house was filled with guests, and the volume of their combined voices filled every corner. The dog took refuge outside where it was cooler and quieter.

"It's about time you got here," Bert boomed. "I thought I'd have to send Blackie out to shoot down a raven or two if didn't show pretty soon." She held baby Tony on her lap, and as soon as Evie entered with her little one, she took him, too. Cuddling them both, she instructed Inja and Ellen to set the table while she got acquainted with her guests.

"Well, handsome," she addressed Evie's Tommy, "I've got to put you both down. Are you hungry?"

"Eat," he yelled.

"Well, I guess that answers the question," she laughed. Placing the child in his father's arms, she fed baby Anthony a bottle as she checked the gravy and inspected the turkey. Giving a nod of approval, she handed the baby to Blackie while she placed the final items on the table.

Children were allowed to eat at a small, makeshift table of their own while the adults seated themselves at an extended one in the dining room. When Pastor Adams stood to say the blessing, all mouths shut and heads bowed. His prayer lengthened from thanks for the food to a listing of several noteworthy blessings experienced throughout the valley. Blackie began to fidget and blow air through his nose like a bull ready to charge. When the "Amen" was said, Inja giggled at the frown of displeasure on his face.

"Amen," he thundered. "Let's eat. A man could starve to death around here."

Conversation tapered off as plates were filled and passed back and forth and appetites were sated. Evie took a last bite of potatoes and gravy and pushed her plate away with a groan.

"Am I ever full. If I eat another bite, I won't be able to get out of this chair." Ellen rose to pour coffee and Bert filled cups with warm, spiced cider for non-coffee drinkers. As they lingered over their drinks, she unknowingly dropped a bombshell.

"Inja, why didn't you call the other day when you were in town—or at least drop by to say hello? We could have had lunch or something."

Flustered, Inja dropped her eyes and took a quick sip of coffee. Without lifting her head, she scratched at a spot of dried gravy on the tablecloth.

"I haven't been to Spokane, Evie; wherever did you get such an idea?"

"Are you sure? It was just a couple weeks ago. You remember, don't you, Lowell? I was coming out of the doctor's office when you walked by," she explained. "You were talking to a tall, dark-haired man in a business suit. For heaven's sake, stop looking at me like that. I wasn't dreaming. I can even tell you what color dress you were wearing. It was a light blue sheath."

Glancing at Shortie, Inja kept her eyes glued to his. "I certainly don't want to argue about this, but I haven't been to Spokane since the last time we visited and for that matter, how would I get there? We don't own a car and I've never bought a blue sheath. You saw someone that resembled me, and, well, obviously you're mistaken."

"I could have sworn it was you." Grinning, Evie shrugged her shoulders. "I'd better have my glasses checked because whoever she was, she could have been your twin. She even had the same walk. But you're right and I must have made a mistake."

"I'm telling you for the last time," Inja snapped, "I was not in Spokane." Her sharp retort startled the baby, and he began to cry. Bert gazed at Inja in surprised silence.

"It wasn't me," she repeated.

Shortie studied her. "Evie must be seeing things as well as being pregnant, right, Inja?" he asked softly.

Pastor Adams cleared his throat and smiled candidly. "Please, this has been such a wonderful day. Let's not ruin our meal with suspicious doubt. If Inja says she wasn't in the city, then we must believe her." He smiled brightly, radiating good cheer. "Are you positive that who you saw was Inja? Is there the slightest possibility it was a mistaken identity?" He regarded Evie fondly as a sister in Christ.

Blushing furiously, she was embarrassed at being questioned in front of strangers. "If she says it wasn't her, then I suppose so."

Inja flashed a look of mute appeal at Shortie. Under the table she placed a hand on his leg, "It wasn't me—I swear it. You must believe me." Her voice dripped to a whisper for his ears only. Taking a huge swallow of cider, he nodded without speaking.

Pastor broke the tension in the room by throwing out an invitation to the boys. "Who's on for a game of checkers?" Both boys scrambled to be first.

"Old man," Bert teased Blackie, "I'm going to put the little guy down for a nap, and when I get back, I expect to find those two chairs empty so I can sweep the floor. So unless you plan on washing the dishes, you'd better find something to do."

"Okay, okay," he muttered. Standing, he stretched with arms over his head. "I'm going outside for a breath of fresh air. Maybe chop some wood to work up an appetite for pie."

"I'll join you," Shortie said. Snatching a roll off the platter Inja placed on the counter, he took a huge bite.

"If I ate like him I'd weight three hundred pounds in no time at all," she commented with a shake of her head.

Evie joined her at the door. "I know what you mean. As a young man he could eat and eat and never gain an ounce. All I have to do is smell food and my hips and backside get broader. Doesn't seem fair, does it?" They stood together for a moment with arms around each other's waists. Neither one wanted the other to have bad feelings.

Outside, the two men breathed in the cold, bracing air. It was refreshing after the confines of the house. "Feels good, don't it?" Blackie asked. "It's too hot in there for a man to be comfortable."

"Yeah," Shortie answered absently. Sitting on an outdoor bench near Bert's flower garden, he lapsed into thoughtful silence.

Motioning to the dog, Blackie scratched the animal's head, enjoying the companionable silence for a few moments.

"Can you hear them?"

"Hear what?" Shortie asked. Listening intently, a puzzled frown creased his face.

"Warning bells. Surely you've heard them before. Listen hard, because they're ringing all around you, trying to get your attention." As Blackie gazed off into the distance, his hand stilled from scratching the dog's ears. "Heed the warning, my friend. Things are not as they should be, and you need to keep your ears and eyes open," he pleaded.

"What do you mean, keep my ear and eyes open? I'm not totally blind, and I think I've heard enough for one day. You've got to understand, she's my wife and I vowed to love and cherish her until death. I can't break the vow I made to her and to God."

"It's funny you should mention God. You told me once to pray about something and I did. I must admit, He answered my prayer in a marvelous way. I'm still trying to understand why He would listen to me, a heathen, but He did." For a moment, a sheepish expression made the big man duck his head shyly. "You may not believe this, but I've been reading the Good Book, and doesn't it say somewhere that a God-fearing man shouldn't be linked with an unbeliever? Does Inja follow the same path you do or is she cutting out her own?"

"Evie was mistaken. I have to believe Inja or there's no hope for our marriage." Tears filled Shortie's eyes, and the pain etched on his face made Blackie ache for him.

"I hope you're right. Yes sir, I surely do." Keeping his eyes averted, he pretended to search for an errant burr or sticker embedded in the dog's silky coat.

When dusk brought evening shadows, everyone gathered their children to return home. It had been a wonderful Thanksgiving with plenty of food and good company. Evie stood on the porch with Shortie as Lowell packed the car for their return trip.

"Is everything okay with you? I mean, is everything okay between you and her?" Evie regarded him with concern.

"Everything's fine, little sister, except for one thing. Do you really believe it was Inja? Is there the slightest chance it was someone else?"

"There's always the possibility and I didn't have my glasses on. Maybe it was someone else just like she says." Her hand rested on his arm as she studied his expression. "You look so tired," she said softly, "please don't let this cause you grief."

"I don't understand all the sudden concern with my marriage." She knew better than to pursue the subject. The flared nostrils and stony expression displayed his true feelings.

"Please, I don't want us to part on an angry note, my brother. I'm worried about you and she must be too, because she called me twice this past month. She begged me to be here today and here I am. After all the things that have happened in your life over the past few months, it must be very hard for you. I was real sorry to hear about your friend. I know how fond you were of him. Putting all that aside, I love you, big brother, and don't ever forget it."

"I know, and I love you, too." Shivering, he pulled the collar of his jacket closer around his neck. Grasping the front of her coat, he buttoned it as far as it would stretch over her belly. "Stay warm, little sister. Hey, do you feel that? There's ice in that wind. Maybe we're finally going to get a change in the weather. It would be nice to get some snow cover before it freezes hard." As he gazed skyward, a dark cloud scudded across the face of the moon.

"It's time," she breathed. Taking her elbow, he walked her to the car. As brother and sister hugged in parting, she begged, "Open your eyes and ears. I don't want to raise a false alarm, but watch your back, okay?" He nodded in agreement and stood on the porch a long while after their car disappeared down the road.

Chapter 34

Late that night snow began to fall in light, feathery flakes, and within an hour increased to a downpour. The following morning children were delighted to find the ground covered with eight inches of new snow. Shortie groaned at the thought of carrying ice and completing deliveries on slick roads as he donned rubber-soled boots and heavy wool socks for the first time in two seasons. The day was cold, and a gray sky promised more to come.

It continued to snow intermittently for the next four days. Then the clouds disappeared and the sun came out and shone against the whiteness in dazzling brilliance. Children were ecstatic! The day was made for sledding and perfect for snowball fights and building snowmen. By evening almost every yard in the valley sported lopsided snow figures of various shapes and sizes. Nightfall brought back the clouds, and it snowed heavily until the wee hours of morning. When Shortie rose at his usual hour, he found a fresh layering of snow covered the path to the shed. Blowing on his fingers, he warmed them before hefting the axe to split kindling to freshen the fire. Winter had set in with a vengeance, and they couldn't seem to keep enough wood poked in the stove for adequate warmth. Inja wore more sweaters, and he dug out his long-johns. Eddie didn't mind the cold except at night. An extra blanket was all he required.

Christmas was only a few weeks away when Inja, Bert, and Ellen got together to bake every kind of Christmas goodie imaginable. Bert was especially excited; she had a child of her own to play Santa and buy for. The final adoption papers had been signed, and Anthony George Micheal was officially their son. Blackie was a proud papa and bragged daily about some new thing the child had done.

For a short time before the holidays, life seemed to move along peacefully enough, but lately a faint trace of tobacco smoke lingered in the house when Shortie returned home. He became quieter and isolated himself from social activities. Bert had quit smoking, so he was back where he'd started. Who did his wife entertain while he was at work?

"It's time to plan the sledding party," Ellen announced one afternoon.

"When should we have it—right before or after Christmas?"

"What about the night kids get out of school for the holidays? It's a Friday, so no one would have to be up early the next morning," Bert suggested.

"That's a good idea; remember last year's party? Tony and Maria must have crashed at least fifty times before they finally made it to the bottom of the hill. They looked like walking snowmen by the time the party was over." Ellen laughed in fond memory.

"Don't mention Tony around my husband," Inja warned. "He's become so moody, he about bites my head off every time he speaks to me. I think he blames himself for the whole affair, pardon the pun."

"Gee, what would make a guy like Shortie so cranky?" Bert regarded Inja with a suspicious eye. Sometimes she enjoyed making the younger woman squirm by nailing her with a look from her squinty eye. She knew Inja wasn't the victim in this situation, but lacked the evidence it.

"We'll have a bonfire, hot chocolate, coffee, marshmallows for roasting, and doughnuts for dunking. It'll be fun," Inja said as she refilled their coffee cups, keeping herself away from Bert's scrutiny. "It's easy to organize, and we can let everyone know by posting a sign in the store window."

What with plans for Christmas and the holiday season, the night of the sledding party was soon upon them. Shortie hurried home from work, and with Blackie's help, the two dug a fire pit in the snow and started the fire. Gabbie refused to be left out of such an auspicious occasion and supervised their efforts. He blew out the flame several times before they finally got the paper to catch without his help. The fire was soon snapping and popping, sending sparks and flame into the air. It drew the attention of every child within a two-mile radius.

"Don't get too close to the fire," Shortie instructed one little boy. "Eddie, don't throw any more wood on there. Hey, little girl, watch the hem of your dress. Eddie, please tell your friends to stay away from the fire pit. Don't burn yourself."

"Give it up, my friend. If they get singed once or twice, they'll learn to stay back. If you keep this up, you'll be a nervous wreck before the party even begins." Blackie wasn't tactful as he faced the children with a monstrous glare. "The first one to step any closer is going to wear my belt across the seat of their pants, so back off." They not only stepped back, but scattered and fled. With a satisfied nod, he gave Shortie a told-you-so look. "Well, that takes care of that. I'm going home for dinner and I advise you to do the same. The party won't start for a couple of hours, and there's plenty of time to grab something to eat."

"I think I'll stay and watch the fire, make sure we have a good bed of coals."

"Suit yourself." Blackie headed home, swinging his lunchbox and whistling a Christmas tune. Shortie chuckled at the difference in the man since he'd become a father. He laughed easily now and hadn't threatened anyone, except Gabbie, in over a month.

Dark closed off the valley early in winter, and Shortie wasn't alone for long. Eddie brought him a plate of stew, and Bert sent over a thick roast beef sandwich. He wolfed down both dinners and seated himself comfortably on a log. Children, with their parents, soon filled the area, pulling sleds, toboggans, and inner tubes behind them. It didn't take but a minute for sleds to be pulled to the top of the hill. The first runs were slow, but as the snow compacted and the night air became freezing, sledders zoomed down the hill with excited screeches.

Shortie stayed by the fire sipping hot chocolate until Blackie challenged him to a race. His sour expression brightened, and he laughed uproariously as he raced downhill, taking curves at breakneck speed. He didn't have to be tempted again, but grabbed a sled every time one was available.

"Want to go for a ride?" he challenged Inja with a devilish grin.

"Not if you're going to break both our necks getting there." She glanced apprehensively to the top of the hill. "Do we have to start from up there?"

"Of course, that's half the fun," he said as he grabbed her hand, pulling her along. Once at the top, he seated himself so she sat in front of him, but he could still steer with his feet.

"Are you ready? Hold on and lean when I do," he instructed. "Hey, Irish, give us a little push, would ya?"

"Wait," she shrieked, "don't go too ffffaaaasssttt."

Screaming all the way down the hill, she drew quite an audience by the time they came to an abrupt stop at the bottom. "Oh my," she said in surprise. He laughed when she jumped up and demanded he take her again. They climbed the hill and raced down until they were wet clear up to their hind ends. By mutual agreement, they relinquished the sled to Blackie until they dried out. Warming their backsides by the fire, they enjoyed a cup of hot chocolate and a doughnut.

"Hey, woman," Blackie called Bert. "You going sledding or not?" He stood next to the sled, holding the rope out to her. Peering at him in the dark, she decided he looked innocent enough.

"I won't go with you unless you promise a nice, safe ride. Remember, I'm a new mother," she joked.

He eyed the top of the flexible flyer and then studied the size of Bert's hips. "I don't know," he said as he stroked his chin. "You've put on a few pounds over the past couple of years, and my stomach muscle has grown a bit as well. I don't think there'll be room enough for the both of us." He patted his belly and rolled his eyes, giving Eddie a wink.

"Why you rotten...." she sputtered, "are you calling me fat? I'll have you know I haven't gained a pound in over ten years. If anyone around here needs to lose a few pounds, look in the mirror, buster." She shook her fist, daring him to step just a few feet closer.

"Darlin'," he said as he put his arm around her, "you ain't fat and them dimples around my middle are just love handles. Now, do you want to give it a try?" He planted a noisy smooch on her cheek and placed the rope in her hand. "I'll even help pull it up the hill."

At the top, Bert turned around to follow the route down with her squinty eye. "I ain't rode one of these in over fifteen years, but if you can do it, so can I." Grabbing the rope, she sat astraddle the sled with both feet planted firmly on either side. The rope dropped to the ground when she tucked her skirt in around her legs and pulled on her gloves.

"Anyone want to ride along?" she bellowed, "there's plenty of room." Looking around, she was disappointed to find not one single volunteer. Even some of the children stepped away and shook their heads. "Well, old man," she ordered Gabbie, "give me a starting push, but not too hard."

Gabbie didn't maneuver well in the snow and stepped carefully in the deep drifts. He was moving as fast as he dared when he found himself lifted in the air with arms and legs flailing.

"You ain't had a ride yet, old man, and it's time you did." Blackie plunked him down on the sled where he scrambled to gain his balance. The next thing he knew the rope was thrown and the sled kicked off throwing him back against Bert. His head hit her ample bosom, cutting off his air for a time between two pillows. His feet flew up and his hands gripped the sides of the sled so hard, he felt his fingernails bite wood.

"Steer this thing, old man, steer," she screeched.

"I cain't, I cain't see."

"Put your feet out and guide it then."

"I cain't, they don't reach,"

"Grab the rope, do something, you worthless bag of bones." Bert was slightly hysterical as they raced down the hill, gaining momentum as they went. She gripped him so hard, he thought his ribs would crack. He wasn't about to let loose of the sled and take a chance of falling off. Somehow she got hold of the rope and handed it to him. Having nothing else, he clenched it between his teeth, closed his eyes, and prayed for mercy.

The ride seemed to go on forever as they careened around curves on one runner and then slammed back on course. Blackie was laughing so hard he couldn't have stopped their reckless ride if he had wanted to. Shortie tried to slow them down by throwing a shovelful of ash under the runners of the sled. The sled only swerved crazily as the runners sped over the hot coals, sending out a magnificent shower of sparks. Some of the children rolled some giant snowballs at the bottom of the hill, and they hit one of the frozen rounds of ice head on. Bert rolled off, landing painfully on one hip. On impact, the rope flew from Gabbie's mouth, sending his store-bought teeth sailing into the air. Light from the bonfire illuminated them against the night sky before they disappeared, buried in one of the many snow banks.

"No," Gabbie moaned as he felt along the ground. "I've lost muh teef. He'p me find muh' teef," he begged.

Blackie went ballistic. His face contorted as his crazy guffaws echoed off the hillsides.

Shortie fought to maintain control, but couldn't help the twitching at the corners of his mouth as he helped Bert to her feet. Holding her backside, she limped home. "You'd better not darken my doorstep tonight, Blackie, or so help me, you'll wear one of my cast iron skillets for a hat."

Her echoing words sobered the big man immediately. Touching a bald spot on his head, he remembered a similar warning he had ignored. "Can I sleep on your couch?" he asked Inja. He didn't dare show his face around home until morning.

Gabbie lamented the loss of his teeth for several weeks. Even though he hadn't eaten a meal with his teeth since he'd gotten them, he used every opportunity to remind Blackie of his loss. Guilt persuaded the big guy to go out in search of the lost teeth. He found them when he cleaned out the doghouse. He was shaking out the dog's bedding when something hard fell out and clattered to the floor. They were chewed on some around the edges, but intact. Gabbie accepted them gratefully with heartfelt thanks to the dog. He ignored Blackie and refused to speak to him for days.

The weather remained agreeable for several weeks after the holidays. Then one evening in late January, clouds moved in and the sky darkened.

Sometime between midnight and morning, it snowed heavily, and then the clouds cleared away. Morning dawned with blue skies and blinding sunshine. It became almost routine as winter slid from January to February. First there was a thaw, followed by a heavy freeze. Snow crusted over and roads would be icy, and then another heavy snow covered the ice, making travel precarious.

The first warning was when the school closed because the bus couldn't make the hill. Children were happy about their unexpected vacation, but some residents in the valley were nervous. Heavy snow clung to the hillsides in layers, looking like they could be peeled off in thick slabs like an onion.

"I want off this mountain," Inja begged. "Look at all the snow on the hill. What if it started to fall? We'd never get out in time." She paced the house nervously. Jumpy and irritable, she snapped at Eddie and rarely spoke to Shortie, but would look at him guardedly when she thought he wasn't looking. Every time the phone rang, she about jumped out of her skin and ran to answer it as if to stifle the insistent ring before it drove her crazy. It was time to move his family before something tragic occurred.

"I'll call Irish and see if I can borrow his truck to get you and Eddie out of here. Pack the few things you'll need and be ready to go in an hour. I'm sure you can stay with the Chadwicks until the weather breaks."

Her nervousness was contagious and he had to dial the number twice before finally getting through. Blackie answered and told him he'd already moved Bert and the baby to the Chadwicks'. He planned to stay at the house only through the night and then he was leaving, too. Gabbie and his daughter had left by train the day before, and Arden wouldn't open the store until the danger was over. He promised the use of his truck and would help move Inja and Eddie within the hour.

When he hung up, he was surprised to find her in the front room, staring at the blank screen of the television set.

"Can I take it with me?"

"You mean take the TV? You've got to be joking or crazy or both. There's no way we can load that thing, and Blackie's taking a chance as it is to drive up here." Turning her to face him, he could see the fear in her eyes. "Take only what you need. We'll come back for everything else later, when the weather breaks." He smoothed her hair and stroked her back, trying to ease her anxiety. "Now get your stuff packed and I'll see to Eddie." He was surprised she headed for the bathroom, where she threw towels, washrags, makeup, shampoo and the floor rug into a bag. She seemed determined to leave nothing behind.

When Blackie honked, he was quite a distance down the road, but had come as far as he could. Slipping and sliding down the hill, Shortie threw two suitcases into the back of the truck and helped Inja in. Eddie grabbed him around the legs and sobbed brokenheartedly.

"We can't leave without you. Please come with us; what if we never see you again?" His tearstained face looked into Shortie's with fear in his eyes.

"Don't you worry. I'll join you as soon as I check in at the plant. Besides, I've got to find Old Joe and make sure he's okay. You take care of your sister now, and I'll see you in the morning if not before," he said as he placed the boy safely on the front seat between Inja and Blackie.

Blackie gripped his arm. "Stay safe and don't stick around too long. Start down the hill as soon as you can and I'll pick you up when I come back for my dog."

Shortie nodded and waved them off as Blackie backed the truck carefully down the road. Hurrying to the house, he headed for the bedroom, where he threw the closet doors wide, searching for the cat. He was shocked to find Inja's side completely empty. She'd left nothing except a mismatched pair of stockings.

Dropping Inja and Eddie off, Blackie checked on Bert and the baby, then headed back to the valley. He met Shortie coming down the road.

"Did you see my dog anywhere?"

"I haven't seen a sign of anyone's dog or cat. Even Old Joe is missing. It's eerie, and listen—have you ever heard quiet like this?"

Blackie gunned the engine and sped down the hill. Both men breathed a sigh of relief when they left the valley and entered the city limits of town.

In the wee hours of morning, Spex, Blackie's dog, left the old shed for his usual early morning trek up the mountainside. Following the path made by hundreds of foraging animals over the years, he maneuvered quickly. He'd made countless trips up and down the mountain and followed the same path of deer, elk, and even bear in their season. He was hunting and kept his head to the ground and his tail bushed. The odor he followed was strange and hid the familiar scents from his sensitive nose.

He advanced up the trail without his usual snuffling in the snow. Stopping abruptly, he raised his great head skyward, sensing something was different. His nose quivered, putting him on the alert. The early morning dark was the same, but the air had a frosty stillness to it that had never been there before. Slowing his pace, he stopped frequently to cautiously sniff the air. He'd met a bear on the trail once, but this scent was different. Bear smell was strong and hung in the air for hours after the bear had gone. This scent was subtle, almost not there at all, but an ominous presence just the same.

Silence weighed heavily, an unseen threat to the animal, which caused his fur to stand on end and his heart to thump wildly in his chest. Stopping in mid-stride, he growled menacingly at something he neither saw nor smelled.

Some primal instinct warned him to go no further. Lowering his raised forepaw to the ground, he fought back the need to run. Slowly, he turned and gingerly retraced his steps down the mountain. That's when he felt it! A movement, a shifting of the earth beneath his paws that was so slight he wouldn't have noticed it if he had been running. Instinctively, he knew his life was in imminent peril. When his paws hit the first road, he leaped forward and took off, a dark streak breaking through the morning dawn. He didn't slow until the lights of town beckoned.

Men at the dairy gathered around a radio, listening to the weather forecast. Blackie and Art, unable to get to work, listened too, with sinking hearts. They faced an uncertain future.

They heard it at the same time. Starting as a low rumble, thunder sounded in the distance. Heads snapped up when the thunder intensified, louder, until an ear-shattering roar shook the town. Like a massive freight train, the roar filled the air with its sound until it reverberated inside of them. Shouting to be heard, some men ran for cover while others ran to cars or trucks and headed to the valley. It was for certain: a series of snowslides had hit the valley, but how many, they wouldn't know until they got there.

They managed to get as far as the school. The road ahead was blocked by snow with no way to get around it. Parking the truck at the school, they grabbed shovels from the back. Before they could go any farther, the road had to be cleared, and until a bulldozer was brought in, hand shoveling would have to do. The snow was wet, heavy and filled with ice. It froze to the shovel blade, making the work even more tedious. When a path was finally cleared wide enough for the truck to get through, the roar of another slide thundered in their ears.

"Busch, it's on your side of the mountain. Oh my God, I think it took your house." Blackie's face turned ashen when a third rumble sounded from below them.

"Forget the shoveling, Irish. We'd better make tracks out of here or we'll be the next ones to go." Shortie hurried Art along in front of him and motioned to Blackie over the roar of the slide. By the time they reached the pickup, sweat ran down their faces and they were soaked from the inside out. Throwing their shovels in the back, they tore off down the hill, sliding sideways most of the way.

It took two days to clear the upper road using all the manpower and snow removal equipment that could be spared. The valley wasn't the only area with avalanche conditions. Burke Canyon, Mullan, and Wallace had spot slides in several areas until bulldozers were able to clear them away. They were lucky there were no fatalities.

Shortie was relieved when they were given the go ahead to return home. Even though the danger was over, he'd already made up his mind to move. The Cleggs, who lived on the opposite side of the valley, were safe. They prepared to go home, and everything was loaded with the exception of Inja.

"Where is she? I've looked everywhere and she's nowhere to be found. Eddie, did you see Inja leave?"

"No, I ain't seen her," he shrugged. "Maybe she went uptown with Mrs. Chadwick."

"She didn't go with me," Irene Chadwick declared. "I asked her to, but she refused to step foot out of the house. Said she had to wait for somebody. Now who do you suppose she was waiting for?"

"I don't know." Shortie rubbed the back of his neck, feeling a prickle of warning. She'd been missing for over two hours and nobody had seen her. Where could she be?

"I've got to get Bert and the kid home. Do you want to wait or pick her up on the return trip?" Patience wasn't one of his virtues, and he was tired of waiting.

Raking a hand through his hair, Shortie rested a worried gaze on Eddie. The boy reflected what he felt and followed his every move with an apprehensive expression.

"Is Inja gone? Will she come back?" he asked in a voice that quavered with the threat of tears.

"She must have gone visiting without telling anyone. She's bound to be back soon and will wonder where we went. I want you to stay here while I go check on the place. Tell her we'll be back in a couple of hours. Can you do that for me?"

Eddie nodded his head and accepted Bert's reassuring hug. Settling himself on the couch, he resigned himself to wait for his sister. Shortie waved as they pulled out of the driveway and headed for home.

As soon as the door slammed behind them, Shortie dropped the "everything's okay" façade. His fingers drummed nervously on the door and when they drove through town, he craned his neck trying to spot her. He expected the worst, but wasn't prepared for the sight that met their eyes as they parked the truck.

"What on earth...." Bert gasped.

Shortie climbed out of the truck and ran, stumbling to a pile of rubble at the base of the mountain. There in the snow was a picture frame that had held their wedding photograph. Over a ways farther was a leg from the kitchen table. His eyes followed a path of debris along the hillside to where the first road had met the second. The house and everything in it was gone, buried under ten feet of snow. He circled the area several times, his face glazed with shock.

"It's gone, all gone," he repeated over and over. He dug in the snow like a madman looking for anything salvageable. There was nothing to find.

"Come on man, it isn't safe here. See that overhang, it could come down at any time. Look, I know how you must feel...." Blackie tugged on his arm, trying to get his attention. He came to his feet, ready to comply, until a long black car drove slowly down the road. Inja, the only passenger, gazed at him through the window. He saw her tears as she waved good-bye. Bill Anderson, the driver, reached out and pulled her to him in a comforting embrace. The television set that had once graced his front room was in the back.

For a moment, Shortie watched them pass, his face devoid of all expression until it hit him all at once. He dropped to his knees and moaned, "No, not this, my God in heaven, don't take her, too."

It's a terrible thing to see a strong man break, but he had reached his limit. Heartbroken sobs wracked his body as he kneeled in the snow. Blackie stood helplessly by, not knowing what to do to help his friend. Tears filled his eyes as he watched the face of the man he admired most contort in a silent scream of agony.

In the midst of Shortie's grief, he heard a familiar voice speak to his heart. *"You are not alone. I will be with you always to carry you when you fall."*

"Why Lord, why did You take it all away? I loved her so much. This is pain I cannot possibly endure."

"I will be with you, to strengthen you and prepare you for the future. You must be strong—think of the child that needs you."

A picture of Eddie rose so vividly in his mind, he expected to see the child standing at his side. For a moment he felt the boy's pain and doubled over from the shock of it. He had prayed for a son, and the Lord had provided. No matter what the future held, he would always have the love of this child. The boy needed him more than ever to get through the trauma of being abandoned. Removing a handkerchief from a hind pocket, he blew his nose, firmed his shoulders and set off down the hill to start picking up the pieces. With the Lord's help, he would build a new life for himself and his son.

Epilogue

The winter of 1949 was not soon forgotten by locals and was compared to other winters for many years to come. Shortie never forgot and carried the memory of the little house on the mountainside close to his heart. He learned a lot there, not only about love, but about life.

Inja contacted him through an attorney when she filed for a divorce, claiming irreconcilable differences. He was advised not to contest the terms, but to agree to everything. She didn't ask much for herself, and surprisingly signed over full custody of Eddie. Her main request was that Eddie be taken care of and provided a good home. Occasionally, she wanted to visit the boy, but only when Shortie would be at work. He couldn't figure out why she refused to see him until he got her letter. She had become Mrs. Bill Anderson and had all the money to play with she could possibly want. But, as life will teach, marriage is a lonely place when based on anything other than love. She begged his forgiveness and told him she still loved him. As the days sped by, turning into weeks and then months, his grief faded to a dull ache that he carried with him for years. In the future when he looked back on their life together, he realized how selfish she had been. She took and seldom gave while he gave and seldom expected anything from her. This was a mistake because their relationship remained shallow and never developed into anything lasting. He also failed to recognize her needs and fears and filled his time with work instead of making time for her. His heart broke all over again when he discovered her unfaithfulness included more than one. She had been with one other.

He and Eddie were kept busy. The first thing they had to do was find a house. He bought a huge barn of a place two doors down from the Cleggs. The old woodstove was discovered buried in the snow several feet away from the path of the slide, and with the help of his neighbors, he dug it out and carried it into the kitchen of his new house. The shiny chrome fenders were never found and neither was the water reservoir, but otherwise, it was intact. After it was hooked up to a new stovepipe, the stove warmed the house just as it had before.

Everyday, he read the newspaper headlines with growing concern. The problems between North and South Korea were escalating, and the possibility of another war seemed likely. He thought about visiting the nearest recruiting office to reenlist, but Eddie needed him more. At first, he thought the child would be terribly broken up by the disappearance of his sister, but he accepted the news stoically. He cried, got it out of his system, and seemed happier than he'd ever been before. He looked forward to spending the summer with Aunt Evie and Uncle Lowell.

Old Joe showed up one day looking scrawny, but otherwise healthy. He looked around the place and poked his nose into corners of unused rooms. The cat must have decided the house was satisfactory because he found a place behind the stove, curled up and went to sleep. Blackie's dog had returned long ago, so the cat's return was a pleasant surprise.

Fall was right around the corner when newspapers told about the withdrawal of U.S. forces from South Korea. The Secretary of State outlined a U.S. "defensive perimeter" in the Far East that excluded Korea. The little country was left to the mercy of the North Koreans. Unification with communistic North Korea was being forced upon them. Shortie thought about the plight of the people in South Korea and decided he could enlist for a short stint if his knowledge and expertise in munitions would be needed. He didn't get the chance to do more than think about it, however, because he received an invitation he couldn't refuse. The U.S. Army sent him notice to report before the end of the month. He fooled them, though; he went down the next day and enlisted in the Air Force. Maintaining his former rank, he was assigned to immediate active duty.

Placing his cap on the seat, Shortie placed an arm around the child sleeping beside him. Eddie had been so excited when they boarded the train and had kept his face glued to the window for over an hour. He finally slept with his head burrowed in his lap. Sharpening the crease in his dress blues, he remembered a similar ride that seemed a long time ago. This time he paid little attention to the passing scenery. There was too much to occupy his mind.

Eddie would be fine at Evie's while he was away, and Blackie and Bert would care for the cat and watch over the house, but what about himself? Would he be sent overseas? If something happened, would Inja allow Evie to adopt the boy? Smiling to himself, he placed his worries into the hands of the One who could handle them. Even if his future was precarious, he was confident the Lord would hold him safely in His hand. He couldn't help but wonder, though, how soon would he return and if he could give Eddie all that he needed. Only God could provide an answer, and for the time being, *He* wasn't talking. Shortie's heart was filled with a reassurance that he could look to tomorrow with hope.

> *The Lord himself goes before you and will be with you; he will never leave you nor forsake you. Do not be afraid; do not be discouraged.*

> *Deuteronomy 31:8*